Echoes of the Timeless

Catia Batalha

Echoes of the Timeless

Second Edition

CB DHARMA PRESS

A CIP catalogue record for this book is available from the National Library of
New Zealand.

ISBN 978-1-0670930-0-6

This is a work of fiction. Names, characters, businesses, places, events and
incidents are either the products of the author's imagination or used in a fictitious
manner. Any resemblance to actual persons, living or dead, or actual events may
be coincidental.

More resources on
www.catiabatalha.org

First Edition published in 2023

CB Dharma Press
Waiheke Island
Auckland, New Zealand

About the Author

Catia is a psychotherapist, spiritual teacher, author, and mystic, devoted to guiding souls on their journey of awakening, healing, and self-discovery. Moved by a deep reverence for the hidden wisdom that flows through all traditions, she has spent much of her life immersed in the holistic philosophies of the East and the psychological sciences of the West.

She holds the knowing that within each being reside the seeds of unconditional love and radiant wholeness. Her work is an offering to those longing to ignite their inner light, return to the essence of who they are, and embody the highest possibilities of their being.

Drawing from ancient and timeless streams of wisdom, such as Yoga, Tantra, Buddhism, Shamanism, Gnosticism, Indigenous teachings, and other esoteric lineages, Catia weaves a tapestry of remembrance and insight, inviting others into a more compassionate, harmonious, and soul-aligned way of living.

May your echoes guide you Home.

Chapter 1 – Echoes from Another Life

In the deepest part of Sofia's subconscious, there was a hidden memory of a perfectly harmonious civilisation where Spirit and Nature were one. In this distant world, beings lived in a sacred rhythm with existence. It was a time when separation had not yet crept into consciousness, and unity was not an ideal but a lived experience. The veil between the visible and the invisible was thin, and all species, human and non-human alike, coexisted in respectful alliance, each recognising the value, wisdom and contribution of the other.

Society thrived not through dominance or accumulation but through deep cooperation. The needs of the collective and the fulfilment of the individual were not in conflict. In fact, they nourished one another. People were deeply connected to their inner callings, and from that inner clarity emerged creative expressions that benefited all. Each person was seen and celebrated as a unique constellation of gifts, sensitivities and preferences. Rather than being compared or moulded into sameness, they were lovingly guided to discover the roles in which their essence could flourish. They were not defined by productivity, but by authenticity.

Work was not a burden but an inspired offering. Projects were chosen for their beauty, meaning and the joy they brought. Communities gathered to co-create art, medicine, music, stories and technologies that enhanced life's wonder and harmony. These were not mere tools of utility but expressions of gratitude and reverence for existence.

Humans lived with open hearts, moving through their days with kindness and generosity. Their relationships were sacred explorations. They cherished the many layers of union (physical, energetic, emotional, mental, and spiritual) not as possessive bonds, but as mirrors in which the divine could reflect itself. Love was free and abundant, not bound by fear or control.

Freedom was not the right to do as one wished, but the graceful ability to be in full presence with one's nature, and to act in ways that served life. Joy arose not from indulgence but from belonging. Beauty flourished not as an ornament, but as an expression of truth.

Prosperity in this world was not measured in currency or conquest. It was understood as a flow of energy: creative, natural, and interspecies. All beings offered their abundance willingly. Birds shared songs that healed. Trees gave fruit and insight. Rivers offered their flow as teaching. Reciprocity was not enforced by law but guided by the heart's intelligence.

Life was not merely about surviving or achieving. It was a dance between the finite and the infinite. People were deeply present with the changing circumstances of their earthly lives, yet simultaneously rooted in their immortal spirit. They remembered who they truly were: eternal sparks of the Great Mystery. They consulted this cosmic intelligence, often gathering in quiet communion to ask for guidance, healing or vision. It was not a distant deity they called upon, but a living presence within and around all things.

They knew Spirit as Father: guiding, protecting and uplifting. They knew Nature as Mother: nurturing, holding and recharging. The Earth was not a resource, but a living being to be revered. Her animals, plants, winds and waters were kin. Her cycles were the rhythms by which they lived. Ceremonies, songs and sacred stories were woven into everyday life to honour her presence.

These humans also walked in remembrance of their ancestors, not as burdens from the past but as luminous mentors. The wisdom passed down was not static tradition, but living essence, evolving with each generation. Through this reverence, they continued the ancestral task of shaping a civilisation that supported the flourishing of all species.

It was a society where magic, science and philosophy were not divided but interwoven: multiple faces of the same quest for truth. They understood the subtle laws of energy and matter, the alchemy of mind and heart, the spiral logic of dreams and the sacred geometry of life itself.

And so, in this golden civilisation, all beings – whether feathered or scaled, human or elemental, visible or hidden – lived happy and free. Spirit smiled through every pair of eyes, and Nature sang through every breeze.

When the inhabitants of this world died, their memories were erased so they could start a fresh new journey in the next life. However, for some beings, their essence was so powerful that it found ways to prevail, in the form of echoes that secretly reverberated through their subconscious, so they would never fully forget who they were and where they came from.

Sofia was one of the beings who could sense these echoes. *Were they dreams? Utopian desires? Recollections of a past life?* There was no way of knowing… But as life progressed, they started to become harder and harder to grasp.

Chapter 2 – The Present Life

One of Sofia's earliest memories was of her first day of school. She was extremely excited to get to know other children and connect with them. She imagined everyone learning new activities, helping others, sharing materials, bonding over lived experiences and discovering the world together. Her fellow students' successes would be her successes, and from anyone's failures, they would all learn and support one another. If anyone were lonely, the others would be there to keep them company; if one of the kids did not have a pencil or a book, they could borrow from someone who did; if they had trouble understanding a lesson, others more knowledgeable on that topic would offer to study together; and whenever anyone needed comfort, their classmates would provide a warm smile and loving hug. Sofia felt ecstatic about entering that new world she had fantasised about for such a long time as a lonely child.

Until that day arrived, Sofia could not have imagined that children could be competitive; that there would be quests for power over others; that they could be selfish, inconsiderate, or greedy; that the happiness of the collective did not matter to most individuals. She could not have conceived that some people would be happy to have too many clothes while others did not have enough, or enjoy an abundance of food while others starved. She could not have anticipated that some people could lie and manipulate others to get what they wanted or push them down so they could come out on top. And in her wildest dreams, she could not have predicted that people could reject each other for being different, dim themselves in order to fit in, or be forced to do what was expected rather than encouraged to discover who they wanted to be.

No, Sofia had not been prepared for any of that... So, most of her earliest memories involved feeling absolutely crushed and heartbroken by how people treated one another. She saw people ruling over others rather than lifting them up, being mean to each other to gain popularity, and thinking only of themselves instead of considering how others might feel. More shockingly, all of that individualistic behaviour was supported by their educational system, which not only encouraged competitiveness but also only taught disciplines like mathematics and science while failing to impart sound moral values and cultivate interpersonal skills. Sofia simply did not have a framework to understand how her teachers believed that adding and subtracting numbers was more important than being kind to their peers. She soon realised that school was not going to be an exciting exploration of what it means to be a human being, but rather a pre-defined journey that others had already laid out according to their questionable priorities. Of course, that approach bred individualistic, goal-oriented children rather than kind, community-focused, value-oriented human beings. She felt lost, disconnected and lonely beyond what any words of any universes could describe. Deep down, Sofia felt as if there must be more to life. But, having retained no conscious memories of a previous existence, she started to doubt her echoes and her inner knowing of a better way to live. What remained was an innate feeling that she was missing something big, some secret key that would make it all OK. However, adults made it very clear that any different way to live was just her fantasy and that this was what *real life was like*.

Psychologists say that children learn how to be in the world in the first seven years of life, following the examples of their parents, caregivers and society. Sofia grew up in a proud household and absorbed many helpful beliefs from her surroundings in those early stages. Namely, "I am a valid being with the right to exist", "I am worthy of wealth and abundance", "I am powerful enough to do anything I set my mind to", and "The world is full of worthwhile adventures". Nevertheless, pride often comes with a shadow side, so she also inherited some belief systems and coping strategies that led her on a path of conflict and loneliness for the decades to come, such as: "I'm always right, therefore, if there is a difference of opinions, others must be wrong", "If I am suffering, the world is responsible for that", "I am entitled to control reality according to my will," and "I'm pleased to support others as long as they agree with me; otherwise, I'm allowed to punish or ostracise them". Acknowledging different perspectives, taking responsibility for her feelings and fully accepting others were not concepts she was familiar with. So, when she felt scared or humiliated at school, she drew on her coping mechanisms, which involved acting as if she were better than everyone else and attempting to control others. Deep down, she was only hoping to prove she was valid so that she could make friends, be loved and not feel so painfully alone. However, her arrogant approach did not bring her the connections she longed for. So, she made extra efforts to be better than everyone else – surely, she would be accepted if she were *the best*. But people liked her even less. At home, she had learned that vulnerability was weakness, so the more anxious and hurt she felt, the more she showed strength and confidence and the more she felt disconnected from herself and others.

As years passed, Sofia lost herself further in these patterns. Eventually, she came to believe that she was simply shameful and unacceptable. At that point, she had completely given up on the idea of a world where people would connect and operate as one. The utopian society she had fantasised about when she was younger had caused too much grief, to the degree that it was threatening her health – she suffered from an unexplainable heart condition on and off. Sofia had a half-sister and a half-brother who visited every summer; she was especially connected to the sister, who was exceptionally kind and loving, and to some extent, unconsciously reminded her of the reality where she came from. When her siblings arrived, Sofia recalled that feeling of connectedness, kindness and acceptance, which was all she wanted. But when they left, Sofia would feel desperate, lonely and empty. She would have such strong panic attacks that her breath would stop and she would take a peek into death. Death seemed peaceful when compared to living. It became a source of comfort and relief, a dear friend who could take the loneliness and misery away.

Perhaps as a result of her close connection with death, when Sofia was twelve years old, she decided to move on from life. She was simply unwilling to carry on with her immense suffering and was much happier to end things. Sofia would not be the type of person who threatens to kill herself to get attention; in fact, she would hide it from everyone so there would be no interference in her plan. One day, she set a date for her last day on Earth – she gave herself one more week to live. The relief she felt when she made that decision was as if the weight of the world had been lifted off her shoulders. She could feel enthusiasm and appreciation for life again now that the end was near, and that each experience was the last.

The Universe, however, had different plans, and to this day, she cannot explain what followed. Her parents had organised for one of her classmates to spend the weekend at their place – the same weekend she had planned for her death. *How unlucky! How inconvenient!* Plus, how unlikely, since that had never happened before. Nevertheless, upon reflection, she decided to put off her plans for one week; after all, she had waited so many years – another week seemed like an acceptable sacrifice.

Some people might say that there are benevolent beings, entities and ancestors who look after human beings and intervene in crucial moments of their lives. Sofia had no other explanation for how that weekend took place when it did and how it saved her life. Having nothing to lose, she decided to be completely herself with her friend – her authentic self, not the strong, arrogant *persona* she had developed. Yet, to her surprise, she was fully accepted and celebrated in her messiness and vulnerability, and most importantly, she was not alone. Through that blessed friend and occasion, Sofia regained a sense of connection, meaning and joy in life. She had gained something to live for: friends. Apart from her immediate family, that was the very first bond she had managed to establish. It was possible, after all, to feel connected in life. Gradually, she made a few more friends who meant the world to her. That changed everything and made life worth living. Death would remain a dear but distant friend to Sofia: at the back of her mind as a relieving possibility in times of despair – a symbol that she would never *really* be out of options.

Sofia was unaware of it while growing up, but the series of painful events that characterised her youth could be seen as masterfully choreographed to lead her to the major psychological death and consequent rebirth that she would experience down the line. In her times of agony and despair, she naturally saw her circumstances as random, chaotic and destructive. She could never have predicted that they were, in fact, the necessary pieces of a puzzle from which, like a phoenix, her true self would rise from the flames.

Chapter 3 – The Journey So Far

To fully understand the significance of love and emotional connection for Sofia, we must go back to the beginning of her life.

Sofia was born of true love, between an educated, dedicated woman with a firm sense of direction and unyielding views on how life should be lived, and a strong, affectionate man who had come from an economically disadvantaged family yet was proud to have broken the cycle of poverty and created a wealthy life for himself and his children.

Sofia's mum was dedicated, attentive to their practical environment and committed to Sofia's physical and intellectual growth. She would study with Sofia when the subjects seemed complicated or tedious; pass by Sofia's favourite bakery to get the croissant she liked and see the happiness on her face when she received it; look after her when she was sick better than any doctor or nurse and always know what was needed at home, ensuring that nothing was missing. Unfortunately, her mum's focus on acts of service and gifts did not match the ways in which Sofia understood and expressed love (a concept Gary Chapman coined as *love languages*). That meant that while Sofia appreciated such qualities, sadly, at the time she did not recognise them as love, which left her feeling unloved.

Sofia's dad was sweet, affectionate and warm; he was little Sofia's prince charming and greatest source of adventure and excitement. He would drive the tractor on their farm and sit her on his lap while she ecstatically pretended to be the one doing the driving; hang her up in trees and throw her daringly into the ocean, showing her how to have fun in nature; tell her stories about animals to keep her engaged while she was eating her food and hold her in his strong arms, as if nothing else in the world mattered. Her dad's *love languages* involved intimacy and quality time, which matched Sofia's. That meant that she fully understood his love.

Overall, this could have been a balanced household, with physical, intellectual and emotional needs met (some from Mum; some from Dad), except for one fact: Her dad's pursuit of wealth kept him away for extended periods of time, sometimes weeks in a row. So, little Sofia would lose her dad, the one who embodied love in the few ways her young heart could recognise, suddenly and without notice, for reasons that a baby or toddler could not possibly comprehend. Feeling powerless and hopeless, she eventually concluded that love could simply be taken away from her and, therefore, could not be trusted. Sofia was heartbroken. Sometimes she would cry heavily for reasons that no one around her – including herself – could understand: the abandonment was too unbearable for her little psyche to process. If anyone had asked her what she wanted, it would not have been the most luxurious mattress or the finest food… All the money in the world could not begin to make up for the ongoing loss of her dad and the love that he represented in her life.

It was not until much later in life that she learned to admire his brave life quest to transcend poverty and find a wealthier life, and honour him for succeeding and sharing his abundance. Without him fulfilling his life quest, she might not have had the economic freedom to follow her *own*: to find what truly mattered to the human heart and soul.

So, while Sofia grew up having all her material needs met, emotionally, her story was one of disconnection and devastating loss… The loss of the utopian civilisation where she was from, of the father who was intermittently absent due to work trips, the mother who did not speak her love languages, the friends with whom she failed to connect, the half-siblings who came to visit once a year and then left, and in many ways, the loss of herself. Sofia would not realise until decades later that from those trials and heartbreak grew her devotion to unconditional love, and from the depth of her suffering, her heart gained an equal amount of room for empathy for those in pain.

As Sofia grew older, her upbringing became increasingly rigid and more and more was expected of her. Her parents taught her to be the best, to study harder and *be more successful* than everyone else, while not engaging in

15

social events or deep personal connections. All the while, in Sofia's heart, all that mattered was to *be loved and happy*. However, those values were not acknowledged or considered a priority in her household. Her mother valued education, and her father, financial wealth. While other kids were having fun moulding playdough, Sofia was being taught educational games and made to study during weekends and holidays, to the degree that she was asked to skip the first year of school because she already knew how to read and write. As soon as she reached pre-adolescence, she had performance-based financial incentives instead of an allowance that allowed her to explore the world in her own way. That meant that if she had poor grades, she would have no money. In short, she was encouraged to value her career rather than her happiness. Perhaps that could have stuck, but the deep emotional suffering Sofia felt in spite of her scholastic success ignited her resolution to prioritise and pursue love and happiness rather than financial wealth or social status. Those became *her* measures of *success*.

Whether it was due to her family's prioritisation of a financially stable career, the conservative Catholic background that underlaid her culture, or the fear of her deviating from the predictable path that had been carved out for her, Sofia was made to attend very stern schools and had her freedom highly restricted (when compared to her peers or other people of her age). Her parents no doubt believed they were doing what was best for her; however, they imposed their proud and rigid view on what "was best" rather than stimulating an environment where they could figure it out together based on their shared values (which, from Sofia's end, would have definitely included love and happiness). Consequently, by the time she reached her teenage years, she had gone through a wide range of restrictive situations, such as being forbidden from sleeping over at her best friend's house due to her not being a *good influence* on Sofia, being obligated to spend New Year's Eve at some posh adult party instead of in a cosy home gathering with all her closest friends, being forced to perform actions that went fundamentally against her values, or getting spanked with a belt so she would learn how disrespectful it was to send a little paper message to her female classmate asking if she wanted to have lunch together. As situations like those started to accrue, Sofia began to feel oppressed, caged, controlled, desperate, and really, REALLY angry. That imprinted the value of *freedom* into her soul. Hating her life, she renegaded the Catholic God that her cultural upbringing had taught her. As she saw it, either that Being was an all-mighty figure who allowed all that suffering, or He did not exist. Either way, it did not seem like a God worth having faith in.

Loathing the physical world around her, Sofia took refuge in two other worlds: imagination and spiritism. In the former, she would lie in bed with her eyes closed for hours, daydreaming about entire universes where she was loved and free, people were kind and accepting, and there was justice. In the latter, she discovered that she had a natural ability to sense the presence of spirits. She read more about the topic, explored it to some degree, and even had a mystical experience where she met with her *spirit guide* (a protective entity that is said to look after a person). She was generally unsure if the experiences she had gone through were real or not. Regardless, after some scarier and more intense ones, she became frightened of exploring that world on her own and gradually shut down those capabilities.

Other people might have coped with their despair by being compliant with their environment, but the fire in Sofia's soul burned too bright. Though her mind had forgotten, the echoes in her subconscious still remembered what it was like to be free. While she would have been willing to give up her life, she was not willing to do so with her freedom. So, Sofia started to live two separate lives. She split herself into the *good little girl* who studied, spoke in an educated manner and went to bed early, and the *rebel*, who snuck out late at night, guzzled all the alcohol she was given and embarked on crazy adventures. Unfortunately, one of the many issues with that approach was that the *rebel*'s crazy adventures were completely unsupervised and unsupported, as she had no access to adults who could help her make sense of the world or alert her of potential dangers without shutting her down. That was how Rico came to happen in her life.

Sofia had just turned fourteen when she met Rico, who was four years older. At the time, she was ill-equipped to see how possessive and

17

controlling he was; all she saw was someone who passionately loved and wanted her. She finally had the love of a man *permanently* in her life (as opposed to in the form of a Dad who could take it away when she least expected). As far as she saw it, Rico loved her more than anything. She was determined to keep him in her life at all costs, which was one of the reasons why she ignored the many warning bells. Other reasons involved the absence of a frame of reference, the lack of adult supervision, the deep-rooted belief that if there was a difference of perspectives, then only one perspective could be right (therefore his), and the conviction that if someone else was unhappy with Sofia, she was to blame and had to fix it.

Sofia could not afford to lose his love. As such, she buried any negative thoughts or feelings about him in order to maintain his image as her *perfect* prince charming. She translated everything he did into expressions of love. When he forbade her from being friends with the classmates he considered *bad influences* on her, she thought that was natural because she had learned to accept control from her parents. When he forced her to dress in conservative clothes so she would not be attractive to others, Sofia thought it was normal, as she had learned that people condition their loved ones for their own protection. Throughout the countless times he coerced her into having sex with him against her will, Sofia took his reasoning on board, believing that there was something wrong with *her* if she did not feel like having sex, that *she* was to blame for his desire due to allegedly "being so sexy", that *she* was responsible for pleasing him to keep him from physical pain, and that *she* needed to appease his insecurities by proving to him that she was sexually interested. When he got increasingly insecure and jealous if a few days passed without them having sexual intercourse, there was no one to explain to her that it was *his* problem as opposed to hers, that she was not doing anything wrong and that it was *his* job to work on himself. In fact, she had no concept of personal development or accountability for one's feelings at all. Instead, Sofia figured that she was responsible for his feelings and that it was easier and less disruptive for her to have sex with him to keep him satisfied and soothe his insecurities. That way, he would not control or pressure her for a few days, granting her a sense of much-needed freedom.

18

That was merely the tip of the iceberg of what turned out to be a four-year relationship. During that time, Sofia's group of friends made many attempts to convince her that his behaviours were inappropriate. Still, instead of believing them, she allowed Rico to convince her that they were just jealous and against their relationship and, as such, should not be in her life. One by one, Sofia lost the dear friends that literally meant the world to her and made her life worthwhile, until she was left completely alone – making it all the more vital not to lose Rico's love. With her friends gone and her parents against any romantic interactions, there was no one to protect Sofia or advise her on what to expect of herself, her partner or her relationship.

While Sofia's mind was determined to sacrifice her sexuality to please Rico, her body decided that was not an acceptable price. It started to develop unexplainable physical symptoms that prevented her from having sex with him. Without any knowledge of psychosomatic conditions (psychological conditions that express physically through the body), Sofia was simply – and secretly – grateful for those restrictions. Sadly, Rico was not ready to settle for that, so when she set some boundaries around sex in conventional ways, he started coercing her into doing so in increasingly awkward and uncomfortable ways. When she developed even more prohibitive symptoms that required stronger boundaries, he suggested even more questionable ways. One day, being forced to masturbate him in a smelly old stairwell of a creepy abandoned building for the nth time, Sofia was left with absolutely no choice but to face the facts: she was being sexually abused, had been manipulated into having no friends, and his *love* was not real love; it was a pleasure-driven obsession that he was ready to protect at all costs.

That relationship left scars for decades to come, but from it, Sofia learned what love was *not*. That was, in itself, a crucial lesson.

In her late teens, grieving the loss of her friends, abuse from her boyfriend and profound anger towards her oppressive school and home environments, Sofia brought herself to a single session with a psychotherapist – a nice lady who saw her and empathised with her pain and hopelessness. While there were no obvious solutions to be found, Sofia felt acknowledged, accepted and relieved. The most significant part of that session happened towards the end, when the therapist said something that Sofia never forgot: "You can't make your family share the same values as you, but you can create your own family with *your* values". That was the moment when Sofia's dream to have children was born. Starting her own family could end her suffering and disconnection, creating a home with her values and people who were more aligned with her, having the love she always longed for.

Some people know what they want to *do* in life from a very young age. Though for Sofia, all she knew was how she wanted to *feel*: happy, loved, free. That made it challenging to fit into the life her parents wanted for her, as they had completely different measures of success. However, she did her best to meet their world and chose a culturally acceptable professional career. She first thought of occupations in the realm of helping people, which was what she knew she liked. Though for some reason, she undertook an aptitude test, which claimed that she was gifted at essentially everything except psychology and medicine – the exact careers she was vaguely interested in. At that stage, Sofia felt so discouraged and disempowered that she believed it, so on the day of signing up for university she chose a course more or less at random, one that did not feel like a huge sacrifice and met her parent's financial expectations: she chose IT Software Development and Management.

Pursuing that society-approved lifestyle was a painful contrast to the passionate life force that lay deep in Sofia's soul. The underlying feeling she experienced has no known name, so let's call it *the emptiness*. The *emptiness* is an inner state of meaninglessness, purposelessness, lostness, unfulfillment, apathy, joylessness and lack of aliveness and excitement. It led her to turn to alcohol, which was the only thing she had found that could bring moments of aliveness and connection, or at the very least, escape and relief. In that context, she met Silvio. Silvio was a cool, fashionable, muscular guy; slightly dark-skinned, good-looking, with short brown hair, brown eyes and average height. He was fun, energetic and passionate. They both enjoyed partying and fell very much in love and were supportive of each other.

Right after Sofia finished university at age twenty, her parents very generously rewarded her with the financial means to start her own small IT company. She worked diligently, performed a range of distinct roles (from IT developer to manager, marketing engineer, accountant and cleaner), and made enough money to support herself financially. Nevertheless, the more Sofia ticked the boxes from her societal and familial expectations, the more she realised they were not fixing or even making a dent in the *emptiness,* as she had hoped. She still had one major card up her sleeve though: having children – but Silvio was not yet ready.

The life of alcohol started to expand, with more festivals, heavier drinking and more friends from the party world. Sofia was in her early twenties when she went with Silvio to a festival where she drank non-stop for four days straight – not an unusual occasion for them. However, that time, after staying up all night, they drove back to the South of Portugal where they lived. On their way to Faro they stopped at a petrol station, half asleep, half pumped on coffee and adrenaline. Sofia went to the toilet, and as she looked in the mirror, she felt like her heart had stopped… The image that the mirror reflected back was so distant from who she truly felt herself to be that she did not even recognise the lifeless figure staring back at her. To escape that disturbing reflection, Sofia decided to quit her job as soon as possible and move to Lisbon. She had to believe that she could do better than just passing through life; she had to find out if she could actually *feel alive* – even if she did not know how.

Over the following years in Lisbon, Sofia and Silvio went through many experiences, challenges and adventures together. In her mid-twenties, they bought a beautiful house in an affluent neighbourhood. Life was comfortable and stable. Sofia buried her need for meaning, belonging and wonder somewhere deep in her psyche and instead used TV shows to get a sense of excitement, alcohol to feel more alive, gourmet food to satisfy her body (since she had no soul-nourishing food), and yearly tropical island holidays to rest from the exhaustion of her twelve-hour work days in a job that did not mean much to her. Professionally, Sofia worked for a renown multinational IT company. They valued and commended her for her excellence with technology, people and processes – essentially, all the major aspects of her job. There should have been no problem, yet the ruthless *emptiness* persisted. Her professional life was financially prosperous but unfulfilling, her friends connected mainly under the influence of alcohol, and her relationship with her parents was distant and guarded. Yet by their standards, she was *successful* – apparently by everyone's standards except her own.

In Sofia's darkest moments, she glorified and idealised a single hope based on what the psychotherapist had proposed all those years ago: one day she would start her own family and they would all be happy, loved and free. That possibility finally opened up after nearly a decade of being with Silvio, when Sofia was twenty-seven. They planned everything to perfection, chose the best season to get pregnant so that the baby would be born in warm weather, studied the best techniques to get pregnant and followed them strictly. Three months beforehand, Sofia stopped taking the pill; they bought ovulation tests and a digital thermometer in case those failed, made digital graphs of her cycle, consulted books about pregnancy, installed an app to track the evolution of the fetus, researched the best brand of folic acid to take and the most hydrating lotion for her belly, and picked the best obstetrician. They were fully ready to have a baby and fulfil Sofia's lifelong dream.

Sofia knew that she was pregnant long before a pregnancy test confirmed it. She could feel the soul of that little being in her belly; it flooded her with absolute unconditional love in a way she had never felt before. Her heart opened, she experienced consistent and unshakable joy, life suddenly felt hopeful, and she felt connected, fulfilled and excited about the world. Every moment felt meaningful, every movie felt touching and every step felt like walking on clouds of wonder. The *emptiness* was gone. She felt endless patience and compassion; nothing could bring her down.

The first ultrasound revealed a little dot; the second, a slightly bigger shape. After the first eight weeks, which they had been told were the riskiest period, the doctors said they were essentially out of the woods. Sofia felt an almost supernatural connection to that baby to an extent that she had never thought possible. She discovered the depth that a connection between two beings could reach, as if their souls were one and they were so intimately connected that nothing could tear them apart. She and Silvio turned the small room in their house into a nursery, as it was the one with the furthest window from the ground, so the baby could not reach it. The room had central heating so the little one would always be warm enough. They decided to paint one wall in a light green tone to go well with the white and blue IKEA furniture they liked, and the mattress was the safest and most comfortable that money could buy. Everything was perfect.

One day, Sofia started feeling impatient, slightly annoyed, less joyful, empty. She was too terrified to assign meaning to those feelings, though she knew somewhere deep in her psyche that was how she felt *before* the pregnancy. A few days later, she went to the doctor for a routine ultrasound. Silvio did not even accompany her as there was no significant reason for him to be there, plus he had to work. Sofia laid down for the ultrasound as usual and the lady doctor moved the scanning device in multiple directions, but she was not able to notice much movement inside. *Was that taking longer than expected, or was it just Sofia's impression?* She found it strange that she could not hear the baby's heart… In fact, there was no sound at all; everything looked still. Terror struck her like a punch in the gut. The doctor sat her down and sighed. She said that she was really sorry, but the baby was no longer alive. Sofia experienced a sudden burst of rage and screamed at the doctor, barking about how incompetent she was and how irresponsible it was to make such unfounded claims. She demanded to be seen by another doctor. The doctor teared up in empathy and looked at her in sorrow and grief. Choosing not to respond to Sofia's aggressive claims, the doctor decided that the best course of action would be to agree to refer her.

In a state of absolute terror, Sofia brought herself to see the other doctor. That one had more monitors and fancier scanning devices; Sofia thought for sure it was better equipped to show her baby. *Why did she even go to that other doctor?* However, after the exams, when there was only silence and stillness again, it was as if Sofia's own heart had stopped too. As if the world had imploded onto itself and the dream that took her a lifetime to build had crumbled, and with it, all that she was. As if life was completely and utterly meaningless, and the whole universe had been shattered to pieces, ravaging everything that ever was and leaving nothing but sheer destruction behind. Tears were convulsively rolling down her face and her body was shaking uncontrollably as she stared at the lifeless shape in the high-definition monitors. Absolute agony was burning her from the inside out; every part of her being was hollering inaudible screams. She went home and sobbed until she passed out from exhaustion. Life, as Sofia knew it, had come to an end. And nothing, not even death, could console her.

Sadly, the horror was far from over. The baby did not exit Sofia's body spontaneously, so she was instructed to induce a miscarriage. Many people are unaware that a miscarriage is similar to being in labour – painful contractions expel the fetus and the placenta out of the body. For three days, Sofia bled out thick, dense pieces of blood and tissue, portions of her dead child, the dearest soul she had ever known, the one she had longed for all her life and adored most in the entire universe. That was followed by another ten days of heavy bleeding to empty out the content of the womb. With each mass of blood that left her body, it was as if a piece of her soul left too – until she was reduced to nothing.

When Sofia was told that the baby had died, she knew that she would never again see his little heart beating, his body growing, she would never get to hold him in her arms, sing to him, see him smile, hear him say 'Mummy' or celebrate his first steps… That was excruciatingly painful. But having to see her baby come out in pieces like that completely broke her. She bled all her dreams, hopes and beliefs away… Nothing was left of her but a distant memory of a planned and predictable existence with a vague sense of direction and drive, and shattered pieces of a fantasy of a happy family with a sweet baby in her arms. After that, everything became totally and utterly empty. That marked the beginning of Sofia's rebirth.

Sofia could not have known at the time that the emptiness created by the death of her unborn baby – who she called Alex – would generate a vortex from which she could turn her life completely inside out and from which new life could be born – not in another baby but within Sofia's own self, which now had the space to emerge.

Within a few weeks, Sofia moved out of her house, left her relationship with Silvio and spiralled into a self-destructive phase involving many regrettable decisions that caused suffering to herself and others. Nevertheless, she was determined to turn her external life into the wreckage that her inner life already was. Consciously or unconsciously, she wanted everything she owned to die since the only thing that mattered to her had died too. Silvio tried to be supportive, but really, he never stood a chance. He was part of the dream that needed to die too.

Chapter 4 – The Mystery Card

When all the pieces of Sofia's life had turned to dust, the slate was clean. One night, just as she was about to fall asleep, she gazed at the new moon through the open window and felt a slight breeze. At that moment, a crow landed on her window sill. It chirped, and for a second, it seemed as if it was talking to her. As it retook flight, her eyes closed and she fell into a deep sleep. That night she had the strangest most vivid dream. She dreamt of an enchanted forest where she was walking under the faint light of the stars and the new moon. Suddenly, a crow appeared; she followed it all the way to a hidden cave. The entrance to the cave was covered in vines, but as she touched them, they opened to reveal a door. As she entered, there was a bonfire in the middle of the cave; the crow had disappeared and in its place a wizard had risen. He said, "The doors of the universe are about to open. Are you ready to enter?" Sofia pondered and nodded affirmatively. He asked, "Are you prepared for everything you think you know to be destroyed?" To which she instinctively answered, "Everything already has." Then he looked her straight in the eyes and said, "Sofia, if you are indeed ready, you must meet me tomorrow night here in the forest. Listen to the signs; *this is not a dream*." Then the crow chirped at the door of the cave, calling for her to exit through the same path, and as they reached the entrance of the forest, she looked back and saw a sign that said *Serra de Sintra* (Sintra Mountain). Then the crow looked at her and said, with a sense of urgency, "Wake up!"

Sofia woke up. Her heart was racing as if the dream had been real; she looked around to ensure she was still in her room and everything was in its rightful place. The wizard's words resounded loudly in her head, "This is not a dream." The clock showed 09:09 a.m. She could not shake the feeling that the dream seemed so lifelike. She forced herself to dismiss it, made breakfast and turned on the TV. The first image that came up was of the Sintra mountain – the exact one from her dream. A Buddhist event was taking place there that day, in a place called Quinta da Regaleira. The wizard's words resurfaced in Sofia's head: *"Listen to the signs."* She had officially lost the plot, she concluded, after hypothesising that dreams could interact with reality to point her in a specific direction. Then again, it did not matter if the situation seemed insane, she had nothing to live for and a small part of her that believed in magic wanted to go there to see if something special would happen. Sintra was not too far from where she lived, so it seemed doable. She was unwilling to miss work though, so she planned to leave just after work and catch the evening part of the event. She got off work on time, but there was an accident on the highway and she was stuck in traffic for over an hour. By the time she arrived in Sintra, the event had already started and they did not let her in. A feeling of rage and disappointment took over her. How naive of her to think there could be anything mystical to life, how useless it had been to drive all the way there for nothing, and how stupid she was, hoping for something meaningful to happen. That feeling was replaced by convulsive tears as she sat alone by a little fountain under two ancient-looking trees. The faint sound of the wind momentarily comforted her; she dipped her hands in the fresh water, appreciating that sensation and the beauty of the place. At that moment, a young man arrived, paused for a second, and sat beside her. He said, "I need to speak with you about something very important, perhaps even life-changing. Are you ready to listen?"

She looked at him in doubt and said, "You must have mistaken me for someone else; I don't believe we've met."

He replied, "You are here for a reason, as am I. A journey awaits you, one for which your soul has been preparing you for many years. Only you can choose whether to embark on it or not." Sofia felt astonished but intrigued. His words resonated at a level that she could not explain, and yet, logically, they made no sense at all. "What journey could you possibly be talking about?" she asked.

He replied, "You may have figured out by now that life is not only what it appears to be. Big pieces are missing; ordinary things seem meaningless, shallow… As if life was meant for something more than studying, having a job, raising a family and dying. The whole thing feels somehow unfulfilling and unexciting. People are walking around on auto-pilot, surviving rather than living. Yet there is no one to explain what living really feels like or what it entails." Sofia was speechless. She could not have expressed that better herself. It was as if she had been fully seen for the first time in a while. By that perfect stranger. *How could he know so much about her perspectives?* Her brain was so overwhelmed that she could not process what to say to him. He smiled, with the kindest smile and brightest eyes she had ever seen and said, "I have a gift for you, it's big. It will be demanding. Eye-opening. Mind-blowing. I won't promise it will be easy… but I can promise it will be worth it." He paused and took out a shiny business card from his wallet. "I will leave you with this card. There is a course this weekend, go to it, then you'll understand more. You won't have to pay for anything during the entire process, don't worry. After that everything will change… if you're ready." Sofia was still at a loss for words; that whole situation was so far from her reality that she did not even know what questions to ask. *Could she still be dreaming?* He got up and said, "Saturday, nine a.m., be at that address if it feels right for you. Wow, I feel so excited about your journey; it will be like nothing you've ever experienced before. I hope we meet again one day and you can tell me all about it. Blessings sister; it has been beautiful to meet you. Namaste." He joined his hands in front of his chest, bowing slightly, and left.

Sofia put the card in her purse and went home, still dazzled and confused. *"Blessings sister; it has been beautiful to meet you"? Who was that guy? A foolish hippie? Cult leader? LSD wanderer? Outstanding human being offering her a once-in-a-lifetime opportunity that she was about to turn down out of fear?* Demoralised, she mentally placed that whole day in the crazy basket. As she got home, she fell immediately asleep.

She went to work the next day, but faced with the possibility of genuine excitement, work seemed extra meaningless (even if the previous day had been just a crazy experience). *Was it even worth attending the weekend course the young man had mentioned?* She did not even know his name! *Was that some kind of scheme? How could that be, though, if he said she would never be asked for money? What else could he want then?*

As the week progressed, it was as if life had gone completely flat. No meaning in anything, no pleasure, everything seemed totally pointless. *Surely, the course would be a crazy thing and there was no point in going, right?* She just had to keep living one day after another, and who knows maybe one day she would find some vague sense of happiness again, or not.

On Friday, she woke up, reached for the alarm clock and knocked down her purse in the process. The shiny business card that the man had given her fell off and she realised she had never even read it. The front of the card had a single sentence: "Be prepared to change everything or nothing at all." On the back, there was the address. She looked at the clock; it was 09:09 a.m. *How was it possible that she kept repeatedly seeing the same time?* "OK," she said. "I surrender, you win. I will go to your crazy course; hopefully, I'll get out of there with both kidneys intact and preferably not brainwashed."

Sofia arrived at the address on Saturday morning; the place looked like a Yoga school. That reassured her a little, somehow, she had a sense that Yogis were peaceful, honourable, non-kidney-stealing people. She entered the room quietly and sat down to listen to the teacher. As he started speaking, something extraordinary occurred. Sofia felt like she already knew everything he was teaching, even though she did not recall ever having learned it. He was talking about chakras (the centres of energy of human beings), psychology, philosophies about life and death, consciousness, ego and more. It all seemed so familiar that she could finish his sentences in her head. Some people may have called that an awakening, others a remembrance... One thing was for sure: After one morning of being there, she knew that her life was about to change forever. Though at that point, she had no clue how much life could *actually* change.

The teacher, a Swami from a classical Yoga tradition, introduced the Yoga path as a journey of awakening the soul, turning unconsciousness into consciousness, and realising someone's true nature as a holistic, spiritual being having a human experience. A process of harmonising the layers of one's being (physical, energetic, emotional, mental, spiritual), discovering the secrets of life and the universe, and realising their wholeness and divine essence.

Sofia knew in the deepest parts of herself that she wanted – needed – to experience that; there were no words for her gratitude and relief hearing that such a path existed. She now knew that this holistic wisdom and connection to the universal mysteries were the elements she had been missing her entire life, and that the emptiness and meaninglessness she had always experienced were a direct result of their absence. The despair she had always felt, as if nothing mattered and there had to be more to life, had finally come to an end. The *emptiness* had vanished. The door to the mysteries had been opened, and for probably the first time in her life, Sofia felt truly alive.

The Swami started by explaining the Law of *Karma*, or in other words, action and consequence – if a person puts an energy out into the world, that energy eventually circles back to them. That happens not in a linear but in a causal way. Not necessarily in the same form, by the same person, or even in the same lifetime, but it will come back. He elaborated that our actions are either driven by consciousness (our higher self) or unconsciousness (our ego). When they are driven by the latter, they often cause suffering, which then comes back to us so that we can learn the respective lesson. Not as payback – even if it does maintain some form of justice in the universe – but so we can truly understand the consequences of our actions and become more conscious. That is how we evolve both as individuals and as a species. He explained that *karma* is one of two ways that human beings learn, the other being *dharma*, meaning the spiritual teachings and wisdom gained throughout life. The more *dharma* we integrate, the more conscious we will become and the less *karma* we will generate, as our actions are less likely to cause suffering.

The Swami proceeded to say that this connects to the Law of Resonance (in some traditions, there is a variation of this known as the law of attraction). It is based on the fact that everything is made of energy – a fact that scientists have long proven. Energy vibrates at a particular frequency, which will resonate with elements (objects, people) of similar frequencies. That is why a specific tone of acute screaming can break glass, for example. What that means for humans is that we attract what we are. If someone is loving and kind, that is the type of energy they will be vibrating and consequently attracting from others. Naturally, if someone is vibrating fear, anger, selfishness or greed, that is what they will attract. Our beings yearn to awaken, become conscious and whole, and reach their full potential, so through these laws, they call to themselves the exact circumstances they need in order to do so. For example, if someone is afraid, through the laws of resonance and *karma*, they will attract situations in which their fear can be played out so that they learn trust, self-empowerment, or self-confidence.

Sofia was both fascinated and crushed by this information. In the deepest part of herself, she knew that to be true but the implications for her life were overwhelming. *Could it be possible?* That would mean that it was her own soul that called into her life all the circumstances she had gone through; that it was *karma* from her own past actions that attracted all the people who hurt, oppressed and abandoned her; that she needed all those experiences to transcend her ego and progress on her path; that she was ultimately responsible for her own suffering; that every painful situation in her life had not been there randomly or to tear her down, but to build her up; that she would continue to call in those types of experiences until she changed herself and became more conscious. On the other hand, Sofia found that knowledge empowering. It meant that she had the ability to change her life completely, that she could influence what she attracted by learning her lessons and changing herself, that she was not powerless to affect the reality that surrounded her, that there was a divine intelligence behind all that happened in her past and a point to it, that there was a path to follow and she was not lost.

The Swami continued. There is a teaching in Gnosticism (another esoteric tradition) that describes two paths in life. The horizontal path, which most people are aware of and focused on, involves what one does in the material world, such as going to school, having a job, buying a house, having projects, etc. These things lose their significance in the moment of death. The second path is the vertical path, the path of consciousness. It ranges from complete unconsciousness, disconnection from Spirit and unawareness of the mysteries of the Universe, to wholeness, wisdom and spiritual enlightenment. In theory, not only do we take this awakened consciousness with us after we die, but we also choose the specifics of our next lifetime (such as family, culture and environment) based on what will be most likely to offer the learnings we still need. He claimed that the goal of a Yogi was to ascend through the vertical path, awaken their consciousness and attain self-realisation. Buddhists would add that once that happens, one is free from the *wheel of samsara* (cycles of life and death) and no longer bound to reincarnate. Until that day, Sofia thought Yoga was about becoming healthier and fitter, perhaps more peaceful at best. *How could these teachings not be available in mainstream Western society? How can people be focused on what to wear and what others are saying when there are so many universal truths to discover, ruling all our lives? Isn't that like constantly playing a game you don't know the rules to?* Sofia's mind was blown, her spirit felt nourished and her heart felt humbled but alive and full of excitement. That was what she had been missing all along, no wonder she felt utterly empty without it.

At that point, only two hours of the course had passed and it had already changed her life. The Swami mentioned that one could study Yoga for many decades – Sofia simply did not have the tools to envisage how much life could be changed in that amount of time.

Unmoved by the life-shattering realisations inside Sofia, the Swami carried on. He proceeded to talk about the Law of Correspondence, which claims that everything that exists in the macrocosm (the universe in all its physical and subtle aspects) can be experienced in our microcosm (our being and its internal dimensions). That is relevant because the elevated qualities

Yogis seek, such as unconditional love, compassion and peace are frequencies that exist out there in the universe, which means we can also experience them inside ourselves. Take radio frequencies, for example, we know they are all around us, yet we cannot see, hear or feel them. However, as soon as we turn on a radio, it translates those frequencies into vibrations that the human ears can recognise (sound), and we can therefore hear them. Similarly, the subtler frequencies – such as unconditional love – are also all around us; we just need the proper *devices* to tune into them. Those devices are the *chakras* (energy points in the human body). There are seven main chakras, subdivided into tens of thousands of sub-chakras, connected through hundreds of thousands of *nadis* (energetic meridians between chakras). Eastern medical traditions such as acupuncture are also known to base their treatments on this type of network.

Each chakra is a channel that allows us to tune into a particular vibration. The chakras that are most active in us determine the way we see the world. More often than not, we are not seeing the world as it is; we are seeing it through the lense of our chakras, which, if imbalanced, generate a distortion of the truth that hinders our potential – for example, feeling as if we were powerless to follow our dreams, and as such, not even trying. This phenomenon also carries a self-fulfilling quality – it confirms and reinforces the reality we believe in. However, if our chakras are balanced, we have clearer views of the truth and unrestricted access to our full potential. For example, if our third chakra is balanced, we can draw on courage, determination and discipline, whereas if it is imbalanced, we may experience anger, pride or selfishness. Chakras are more complex and multidimensional than that, but essentially by balancing and activating them, we can tune into their subtle frequencies and have their highest attributes manifest in our lives. That is also the real potential of Yoga poses (called *asanas*, in Sanskrit, the ancient language of Hinduism), which is to balance the chakras we need in order to harmonise our being.

That information alone would probably have taken Sofia months to process. Yet the Swami ruthlessly continued, as if determined to reset her entire existence. He explained that for all those reasons, the reality we experience outside of us is a reflection of our internal reality. It shows us what we attract based on our internal resonance, feelings and beliefs. If we resonate with elevated, subtle states of being, we are pretty much living in heaven. If we experience suffering and are tormented by ego and unconsciousness, we are living in hell. Sofia realised then that the religious stories she had learned were actually true, but they were metaphors for states of consciousness that we experience inside of ourselves, rather than some fire-lit or harp-sounding places where we go after death. That also meant that we have the power to create heaven on Earth – or hell.

If all that were true, Sofia knew that she had no choice but to take full responsibility for her life, her states of being, her actions and her past, and be accountable for everything that happened from that moment onwards. She could no longer blame others for her suffering. She picked up the new journal she had bought and wrote: *I am fully responsible for how I feel. I could live in prison for decades, yet my spirit could still be free. I could be surrounded by violence and still feel peace. I could face the dark night of the soul and still shine sovereignly in the light of my being.* She had no idea how to actually do that, but for the first time it *felt* possible. Nothing she had heard in her entire life had resonated with her more than that.

How could life be vastly more complex than Sofia thought, and every single grain of wisdom just lead to countless more questions? She desperately needed answers. Could reality really be entirely different from what she had always thought? She posed that question to the Swami. He confidently replied that it was quite possible. He argued that the reality we perceive is typically a product of our mind. Though it may seem objective, it is entirely subjective. For example, when we look at a tree we think: "This is a tree", which seems like an objective thought. However, there is really nothing objective about seeing the tree. The process starts when our eyes capture the tree. Then, signals travel from our eyes to the brain. Finally, our brain compares those signals against its own concept of a tree and concludes: "This is a tree". So, the process of seeing a tree is entirely mental. *Does the tree even exist outside of our mind?* That is more of a philosophical question. Either way, our thoughts and belief systems determine how we see the world; therefore, if they change, we can experience a radically different world.

Life felt different to Sofia from that moment onwards. It was no longer a random series of mostly unfortunate events but a journey towards her higher self and holistic potential. Granted, most of the elements of that journey were still unknown to her, which was definitely unsettling, but for the first time in a long time, she felt some faint trust in life and the path she was on. With that feeling, an old memory emerged. Of being a little girl and feeling like she was part of a vast intelligence of the Universe that was present everywhere. Of feeling as though she could control the waves of the ocean or hear the thoughts of the animals and the wishes of the wind. The feeling of magic had returned. She suspected that her new life revelations would be similar to discovering that it was actually Mum and Dad who put the Christmas presents under the tree: Once we see reality for what it is, we can never really believe in Santa Claus – or our old belief systems – again.

The Sofia that finished the Yoga course on Sunday evening might as well have come out of there with a new name, as she felt so fundamentally different from before she arrived.

At the end of the course, one of the school volunteers gave an envelope to each person in the room. The Swami explained that it was an invitation to embark on a one-year mystical journey of self-discovery. He shared that Yoga formed the core foundation of this odyssey, enriched by key teachings and experiences from specific esoteric, Shamanic and indigenous traditions to create a truly transformational experience. Nothing would have to be paid and they would have no responsibilities but to learn about life and the Universe. The journey was starting on the next new moon. Should they accept it, they must be at the school on that specific date, ready to go away for the whole year. Either way, the school wished them an excellent rest of life and thanked them for their time together. With that, the Swami and the volunteers placed their hands together in front of their heart in prayer position, bowed, and saw the students off with a Namaste. Sofia was left speechless.

Chapter 5 – The Leap of Faith

Sofia felt overwhelmed for several days, trying to process all she had learned and experienced. Work seemed more meaningless than ever, to the point where it started to feel unbearable to be there. *But how could she just leave her life for a year – were they insane?* She would have no job when she got back! At the same time, for the very first time, she started to remember who she really was, the universe finally made sense and she felt excited about life. *How could she give that up? Also, how could they pay for her expenses for a year, and why would they?* She felt perplexed; the possibility of leaving everything behind seemed like an enormous leap of faith.

They say that teachers can offer knowledge but wisdom can only come from within. After that crazy course Sofia needed to integrate all the knowledge she received, to turn it into wisdom. She had to process every single event in her life to reassess how she was attracting it, if it came from ego or consciousness, and how it aligned with her higher self… *What even was her higher self?*

Who is she? Where does she come from? Where is she going? Why is she here? Sofia began to realise how little she knew about the things that really mattered in life. Until Alex so tragically passed away, she thought she had all the answers and everything seemed evident and predictable, even if it felt superficial and lifeless. *How could everything come crumbling down in such a way? Could reality be entirely different than she had imagined? Was it possible that there was a whole mystical world out there that she had never tapped into, underlying everything that exists, of which most people live their entire lives completely unaware?*

Sofia left her house and went to a place where the Tejo River meets the Atlantic. She always felt at home with the ocean. As she felt its fresh breeze on her skin, smelled the salt and humidity brought in by the gentle waves, and listened to the sound of seagulls circling the air her mind was quiet. Suddenly, everything was as clear as the sun shining above her. *Why was she worried about losing a job in which she was not even happy? Had she such little faith in life that she thought she would never again find another way to support herself, should she lose that?* Sofia imagined herself on her deathbed, revisiting that very moment and the two completely different lives that could have resulted from it. *What would she have chosen?* The decision was between a predictable but shallow existence that meant nothing to her and a journey through the mysteries of the universe and the fabric of life itself. Which, she realised, was no choice at all.

She turned in her notice for her job and apartment, let people know she would be away for a while, ignored her parents' shocked and disapproving reactions, and started packing up everything she owned.

Sofia was thankful that the new moon had finally arrived and with it the excitement of exploring more of the vast and exciting unknown. As she ate her last breakfast, she turned on the TV perhaps for the last time in a while. It was showing an entertaining documentary about New Zealand, claiming that they had more sheep than people. Sofia laughed to herself, not really believing it but feeling happy for that to have been her last memory of TV for some time. She closed her big backpack, locked everything behind her and made her way to the Yoga school, ready to be away for a year.

The Swami was there to greet the students with a smile. He said, "Welcome to the journey of your life. My name is Ananda. Let's go, we wouldn't want to be late to the airport, would we?" Sofia was surprised. "Airport? Where are we going?" Ananda had a cheeky smile when he replied, "To the end of the world."

There were twenty-one people in that group including Ananda and two of the school volunteers, Ron and Devimar. As they arrived at the airport, the students were given tickets that said, "Auckland, New Zealand."

As they sat in the boarding area, Ananda gathered the students and said that they would be taken through an experiential journey of the chakras, awakening consciousness, understanding the psychology of the human being, becoming aware of the ego, studying Yoga philosophy and learning the deeper truths about the universe. *Wow*, Sofia thought to herself. That literally sounded more interesting than anything she had ever heard in her entire life. Excitement was back and so was hope. This could be the biggest mistake of her life. Or her most incredible adventure.

Chapter 6 – Muladhara Chakra

From Auckland airport the Yoga group was taken to the North Shore, where hidden amongst the beautiful green New Zealand native bush was an *ashram* – a type of Yoga community, which in this case was comprised of a big house with shared rooms and facilities, including a big studio, where classes were held. Some of the students felt slightly fearful or concerned, being far away from home, having dived into the unknown with an uncertain and unpredictable future ahead. Not Sofia, though. She felt an almost ecstatic sense of freedom which she had never experienced before, as if someone had released her from heavy, lifelong chains. Having nothing but what was in her backpack was refreshing; having moved away from the habits and expectations of a standard society life felt liberating; belonging to something bigger than herself that nourished and contained her felt absolutely precious. Sofia was savouring each moment, and her deepest wish was for each second of this experience to last as long as possible… Her only fear was that this might end.

The group sat down for their first class. Ananda shared that there were seven modules to come, focusing on the seven main chakras, each lasting for seven weeks and taking place in a different country.

Someone in the class asked, "Why the different countries, why could they not just learn things in the same place?"

The Swami explained, "We do not notice the biases of our culture until we see them through the lens of another culture."

Most of the students were Portuguese and had lived their whole lives in a monocultural country, so at the time they could not have appreciated how fundamentally different other cultures and value systems could be. Though they soon would. Ananda continued, "Also, the energy of certain places is completely different from others. If you drink the water or eat the food from

New Zealand, you will receive different nutrients that will change the chemical composition of your body. By breathing the air and taking in the properties of the biosphere in its nature, your blood will be oxygenated with different particles. Different emotional connections and experiences with people here will lead to distinctive hormones. Exposure to new thoughts and belief systems will bring new brain synapses. New circumstances and learnings will allow your spirit to manifest differently, which will affect your creativity and life force. Essentially, these different experiences are designed to awaken different aspects of who you are and bring consciousness to the parts that are dormant, in other words, to your *shadow*."

Ashram life required setting aside time for daily tasks, such as cooking, cleaning, shopping and taking the rubbish out. Additionally, the students had two hours of mandatory *Yoga sadhana* each day – the practice of Yoga postures and exercises. That was the extent of their responsibilities. The school indeed paid for all their food and accommodation.

The course structure consisted of one day of class per week, every Monday. The class was about Yoga, and the rest of the week was about embodying and integrating the Yoga values and principles into daily life. Yoga was not at all seen as something you do on a mat but as a way of living based on awakening through every circumstance in life. They said that in some traditions, monks would go up to mountains and meditate for twenty years, aiming to reach enlightenment but that was not their approach in Yoga. The class was encouraged to use every situation in life to discover more about themselves and apply the values of their higher self. So, during the rest of the week, the students were prompted to deepen the concepts that had been learned, meditate, journal, explore the land, experience the culture and the locals, and follow their intuition and the Universe's synchronicities to experience what was needed. Someone asked what a synchronicity was and why it was important. Ananda clarified that synchronicities are a type of coincidences rooted in the cosmic intelligence of the Universe. They could be improbable occurrences or events that inexplicably happen multiple times in a row (sometimes under different circumstances). Essentially, they are a way for the cosmos to support people or show them that they are on the right path, meaning aligned with their higher self and the expansion of their consciousness. Sofia reflected: *That explained the times the clock kept showing her 09:09!*

The New Zealand journey was about Muladhara, the first chakra, also called the root chakra. The Swami explained that it was located in the perineum area and related to the Earth element, the sense of smell and the ability for grounding and stability. People with a strongly activated Muladhara are sometimes described as *steady as a rock*, not prone to frequent changes. In the infrequent times that they accept something new into their lives, they are incredibly stable, reliable, patient, consistent and unlikely to quit, which often makes them prosper. People with a balanced Muladhara tend to experience a strong sense of safety and security in life; they know they have the right to exist and trust that the world is a safe place. Primal survival instincts are related to this chakra; at this level, people experience an objective, terrestrial consciousness, pragmatic awareness and connection to the environment. This is the chakra that relates the most to people's raw physical existence, governing body instincts, impulses and instinctual drives. People balanced at this level tend to be strong, vital and healthy, with appropriate body weight and healthy sexual levels (from a virility and procreation aspect, not necessarily the desire, enjoyment and connection aspects, which relate more to Swadhisthana, the second chakra). He claimed that if people started awakening this chakra, they would develop these qualities and could even experience its extra-sensory phenomena: a super acute sense of smell. That seemed slightly far-fetched to Sofia, but she had an open mind and was keen to explore and see for herself. *If those energies were indeed related to the first chakra, hers must be pretty dormant,* she thought, as they were not very prominent in her – especially the sense of smell, which for her was almost non-existent.

On their first weekend, the students were explained that New Zealand was a bi-cultural country, with English and Māori cultures. As such, Ananda argued that to really experience the country they had to meet Māori – the indigenous people of New Zealand (or Aotearoa, as it is named in Māori). So, they were taken to a *marae*, a communal place where Māori *iwi* (tribes), *hapū* (sub-tribes) and *whānau* (families) meet, gather, celebrate, mourn and practise spirituality and connection with their ancestors. Most students had never met indigenous people and felt excited and curious; some were slightly anxious.

The students were received through a *pōwhiri*, a Māori ceremony where the tribe welcomes new people. As they arrived, a lady performed a mighty calling that they understood as a signal to come forward and they were guided to sit on the benches facing the *iwi*. An elder from the *iwi* rose and spoke words in Māori that the group could not understand, but they clearly felt his power (something Māori call *mana*, a natural authority, strength and confidence). His speech did not feel like a warm, soft embrace but rather an expression of sovereignty and spiritual force from someone with the influence to welcome or ban foreigners from their community. The man's body was covered in tattoos, in fact, many other people from the tribe had tattoos too, some even on the face, chin and lips. Sofia would not have known at the time that those tattoos (called *tā moko*) were often known to tell the person's story and were closely tied to gender roles, ancestral heritage and spiritual significance. After the man spoke, his *iwi* got up and sang a song that the class later came to know as "Te aroha."

When they sat down, Ananda got up and said that his country was Portugal, his mountain was Serra de Sintra, and his river was the Tejo; then he stated the name of his grandparents and parents and, finally, his own name. Ananda explained that they were a group of Yogis who came in peace and sought to become more conscious and awaken their holistic potential as human beings. He added that they would humbly like to ask for the tribe's blessing as the people of the land, and also offer their service for anything that might be necessary. He offered the contents of a little bag as a small token of gratitude for their welcome and said that his group honours and respects each person in the *iwi*. As he sat down, another person of the *iwi* stood up, also with *mana* and resoluteness, though his speech was softer.

That person spoke a few words in Māori, which were indiscernible to the group, but based on Ananda's introduction, Sofia could pick up that he was also naming his country, perhaps his mountain and river, ancestors and finally, his name. Sofia could not take her eyes off his long dark green necklace, which seemed to emanate its own mysterious life force. She noticed that several other people from the *iwi* also had similar stone necklaces but in different shapes and sizes. After that brief introduction, he addressed the group in English. His message was about the unique significance of *whenua* – the land – for Māori. That is such that Māori would call themselves *tangata whenua,* literally translated as people of the land. He said, "With gratitude we receive from the land, but as a way of reciprocity we also give back. The cells in our body exist by eating, drinking and breathing from the land, so we only exist here because the land exists and when we die, we go back to the land. So, we, the people, are the land's guardians, never its owners." When Sofia realised how arrogant it was to believe that people owned the land, she was struck by great grief. She recognised her self-importance and all the damage she had done to the land, all the while treating it with no gratitude and taking from it in excess with no reciprocity. Sofia felt so ashamed that she could have buried herself there and then. Instead, she did her best to contain her tears but concluded she deserved that suffering. She discretely placed one hand on the land and said, "I'm so sorry…" Before her tears could hit the ground, she saw a Tui approaching (a native bird with a distinctive white tuft on his throat), landing on a wooden pole, observing them.

Oblivious to her pain, the man continued. He stated he would also like to speak to the significance of *whānau* – family. He said that Māori see individuals in the context of the collective. "People serve their family and community, which in turn serves them. A healthy, well-functioning community is one where people look after each other, children learn from a variety of adults, elders provide their wisdom, and people of working age provide their *mahi*, their work. The community must empower and encourage each person to find their individual identity, as well as their place in the collective. When people discover and apply their skills, qualities and roles, they create a balanced and fulfilling home for the community members. The individual improves the community and the community improves the individual. It is believed that when the *mana* of one individual is uplifted, it uplifts the *mana* of the whole collective. That means that one person's success is the success of the entire community. Hence, people need to treat each other with dignity, respect and equality, and to support, uplift and protect one another." To finish his speech, the man warmly welcomed the group to their *marae*, their *iwi* and the land of Aotearoa, and wished it would be a cooperative, mutual and honourable relationship. He said that from that moment onwards, they were welcome to the *marae* any time, whether they simply wanted to visit or find some maintenance tasks they could help with.

Sofia was left to wonder what a community like that would look like. All she had ever known in this life was individualistic, self-centred competitiveness, with each man for themselves – a me-first mentality, albeit a mentality that always felt wrong to her and which she never understood. Sofia was taken back to her childhood days when she expected that people would act collaboratively in school or that at least teachers would encourage it. Somehow, that communal way had always come naturally to her, which was why she could never identify with the Western society that was presented to her. Why would people benefit themselves to the detriment of the collective – don't they see that it diminishes the collective and therefore makes *everyone* less happy? It seemed obvious to her. Yet without having been introduced to that collective mentality until now, Sofia wondered how she could have known it intuitively since such a young age.

After the man spoke, the *iwi* rose and sang again, after which they lined themselves up in a row. The same man explained that the *hongi* – the ritual they were about to perform – was a sacred practice in Māori tradition, where two people press their noses together, connect their foreheads and breathe the same air as a symbol of unity. Given that so much violence has tainted Māori history, that was a way for both *iwi* to show that they had come in peace, seeing as that was such a vulnerable practice. It is said that while people are sharing the *ha* (the breath of life) and their foreheads are united,

44

both people's ancestors meet each other. Ancestry is essential to Māori, who claim to be able to trace their lineage back to the beginning of times and draw on the spiritual strength of those who have come before them. After that explanation, one by one, starting with Ananda and ending with Ron and Devimar, the class was to perform a *hongi* with each person of the *iwi*.

Sofia was very sensitive to energies and felt very scared as she was about to perform her first *hongi*; it seemed way too intimate and vulnerable. Yet when she witnessed first-hand how spiritual and profound her first one was, she appreciated and embraced the following ones. Sofia fell into a deep state of peace as a result of the *hongi* process. She had also been very impressed, even if painfully touched by the *pōwhiri*, given the realisations she had about land and community. That powerful experience also confronted her with the shallowness of the rituals of her own (Western) society. Instead of a deep, tear-provoking ceremony to welcome strangers, they would shake hands and, at best, say, "Hello, welcome." No wonder she could not find meaning in anything; it was as if Westerners had managed to surgically strip away Spirit from daily existence. She felt overwhelmed again. As grateful as she was for the Māori ritual, the meal offered afterwards and the small sharing circle sitting on mattresses at the end, she was relieved to return to the *ashram* where she could take time for herself.

Sofia had been in the school for a week and it already felt like a month. She felt as if she had learned and changed more during that time than in the rest of her entire life. Sofia was also starting to realise that time was relative and people's sense of time was subjective. She suspected that that year was going to feel like ten years or a lifetime.

Sofia was in the same room in the ashram as a gender-fluid person from her class who immediately felt like a soul sister. Her name (she responded to *she/her* as well as *they/them* pronouns) was Anney. Anney was a force of nature, a wild soul; she had long purple hair on half of her head, the rest shaved, brown eyes, relatively short, energetic, raw, always looking as if she had arrived from the forest or was ready to go back into it. Sometimes she would stop everything and run into the woods, saying that the spirits of the forest were calling her. She would come back hours later with mud all over her body and flowers and branches in her hair, happy to have served the forest however she could. She never wore shoes and hardly any clothes either, weather permitting. She also spoke to animals and trees alike, probably more so than humans. Anney and Sofia would sometimes walk through the beautiful New Zealand forest and Anney would eat random leaves and berries. She felt as though she was part of the forest, which contrasted heavily with Sofia, who felt totally disconnected from nature.

The second week had arrived. In class, Ananda explained the symptoms of an imbalanced Muladhara chakra. "The primary ego associated with an imbalanced Muladhara is fear. The most extreme symptoms include existential terror of annihilation, fear of being emotionally, mentally and physically wounded or attacked, persecutory anxieties and projections. Essentially, the world feels like a scary place. On the more extreme end of the spectrum, some common psychological conditions can be associated with this chakra, such as hypochondria, paranoia, eating disorders, schizophrenia and obsessive-compulsive tendencies. At the milder end of the spectrum, people can still experience a state of alertness, stress, anxiety, restlessness and preoccupation. That is often compensated by an excessive concern with self-preservation and individual comfort, which leads to strong attachments, self-centred behaviours, incapacity to share, greed, financial and material insecurity, materialism, hoarding or a tendency to accumulate material possessions. The impulse to satisfy these primordial needs may result in raw forms of aggressiveness and attack.

"Other symptoms can include a lack of grounding, such as a disconnection from home, primary relationships, societal norms and nature. People can find themselves in a jungle state of mind, with frequent fight-flight-freeze responses.

"Since this chakra is the primary energy source that our body draws from, its imbalances can lead to inertia, chronic fatigue and a tendency towards laziness. Imbalances of the Earth element can result in a tendency towards rigidity, incapacity for change and lack of patience and perseverance."

Sofia thought to herself that the qualities of that chakra must not be very active in her, but she also did not really experience most of its imbalances. Ananda explained that it might mean that her Muladhara was probably not very active but also not very imbalanced.

Each week, the class studied Muladhara more in-depth and explored it within themselves. They also practised some meditations, specific exercises, and of course, the postures for that chakra, which seemed to be around the elongation or compression of the sacral area. They only ever taught one posture per week, because each one is considered to attune the person to a specific state of consciousness (by opening up and shutting down particular channels in the body), so they want the students to experience it fully.

The following week, Ananda brought up the topic of awareness of one's surroundings. That skill came more naturally to some people than others; some felt intrinsically connected with the physical aspects of reality, whereas others, like Sofia, tended to connect with the emotional, energetic or spiritual ones. For the latter group, when the Swami unexpectedly asked them to close their eyes and describe the room around them, they had very little to say. They could only vaguely recall colours or shapes and often failed to register objects, dimensions or directions. Sofia realised that if someone asked her to describe a person she had recently met, she would not even be able to tell the length of their hair, or if they had a beard, glasses, or what type of clothes they wore. Indeed, she was not grounded in the physical world. Reflecting on that, Sofia realised that she was constantly in her mind. Whether she was thinking about the past, planning the future or questioning the present, she was rarely ever smelling the rain, listening to the dogs or touching the leaves. In other words, she was hardly ever *present*. How much happiness did she experience, being only in the mind? Not much, as the vast majority of what the mind does is to regurgitate information it already knows. Aliveness and excitement happen when people are consciously there to experience them, which is only possible in the here and now. That was just the tip of the

47

iceberg on the topic, yet it marked the beginning of Sofia's journey into presence, which she would continue to deepen as her learning journey progressed.

A week later, they talked about the topic of the body. Sofia started paying attention to her body and grasped how disconnected she felt from it. Determined to change that, she wrote in her journal: *The body is the temple for our soul to experience human life; the vehicle through which we can explore human existence. Hence, it deserves care, consideration, respect, protection and gratitude.*

Through the pursuit of self-care, Sofia began to attract circumstances that resonated with the topic. One evening she attended a women's circle, where they performed a meditation to connect with their womb. She realised that she did not even know exactly where her womb was or what was its size, shape or colour; even trying to visualise it creatively just led to a blank screen in her mind. Sofia was shocked. The womb, the alleged home of the sacred feminine, the woman's source of power and creativity, the core place from where she is said to manifest her essence in the world... and she felt absolutely nothing. Sitting there with the other women who looked so peaceful in meditation, Sofia cried. She cried for the decades that she had been disconnected from her womb, ignored her intuition, oppressed her creativity and forced herself to use her body to please men... She cried for all the symptoms that her womb tried to give her; painful menstruations, endometriosis, sexual disorders... She cried for the neglect she had shown towards herself. Through her tears, she finally visualised her womb. By entering through an invisible door, she saw herself inside the womb. She had imagined it would feel warm, red, soft and welcoming. Instead, it was charcoal black, dry, hard and terrifying. Sofia was crestfallen, realising how her womb had stored all the trauma and neglect she had experienced in the past. All the times she had been inappropriately touched by men, coerced into having sex, or forced against her will were there, imprinted into her womb. Her betrayal of herself – the self-abandonment, the lack of boundaries. All the times when she let men touch her against her will. All

48

the times when she made excuses for them or fooled herself to keep their "love". All the times when she gave herself up so she could meet their expectations. Seeing those memories stored in her womb, Sofia was horrified. She *needed* to make things right, but she was unsure if she had the wisdom or the courage to do so, as her subservient patterns ran deep. One thing was for sure, though: that experience started a journey of reconnection with her sacred feminine.

The following week, they talked about food. Ananda explained, "Our bodies are different every time of every day, influenced by circadian cycles, astrological cycles, seasonal cycles, moon cycles, environmental cycles, life cycles, psychological cycles, menstrual cycles, the climate, food that was consumed, amount of water drunk and countless other variables. We cannot simply say *spinach is good for you*. Our body holds its wisdom about what it needs, how much, and when – the key thing we need to learn is *to listen*. Western culture strongly wants us to believe that doctors have the ultimate wisdom about our bodies and what is best for us, yet the facts tell a different story. Scientists say there are about thirty-seven trillion cells in the human body; each of them knows precisely what to do. Among many other complex functions, they empower dozens of organs, which have ingenious roles such as filtering our blood, supplying oxygen, maintaining body temperature, producing hormones and digesting food. All of that is happening every single moment, under our partial or complete unawareness. Scientists made some progress in understanding some of these phenomena, but still to a minimal degree – otherwise, we would have the cure for cancer, the ability to clone organs and the knowledge to create a new life artificially. So, who is the authority regarding the knowledge of our body, if not the body itself? It may be sick sometimes; however, not only is it like that for a reason – meaning to help rather than hinder us – but it also holds the keys to being healthy. It may be confused or intoxicated, probably because we didn't listen in the first place, but once detoxed, it has the possibility to tell us exactly what it needs. So, instead of disempowering our bodies by eating or doing what we are told is *best for us*, or demanding how our body should behave, feel or look, we could start consulting and collaborating with it to hear what it has to say. We can shift the paradigm and recognise that our body is wise instead of stupid (after all, it can direct thirty-seven trillion cells at the same time, without ever taking a break), that its symptoms have good reasons (which are there for us to decipher), that the solution is somewhere inside us, that the body is capable, and that it just needs our support and ability to listen. Instead of hiding its symptoms with medication or being upset at it for not complying with our society-conditioned beliefs, we can work to understand what it needs us to change, add or remove. Instead of criticising its pains or illnesses, we can question what they are trying to say about our imbalanced emotions or toxic environments. Instead of taking other people's word about what we should eat, we can go to the supermarket and feel what the body is drawn to. Instead of being suspicious of the body, as if it were dumb and useless, we can trust that it's a wise teacher. Instead of trying to live up to society's expectations of what our body should do when it's menstruating or sick, we can show more respect for this vessel which so brilliantly allows us to experience human life. If we develop these skills, we may work harmoniously with our body as allies."

Listening to the Swami, Sofia noted a question in her journal: *How do we manage to justify our profound mistrust in our body when it is constantly doing things that all our thousands of scientific minds put together haven't even come close to figuring out?*

Ananda proceeded to say, "We are what we eat." It means that, quite literally, the food we eat turns into the cells in our body. He mentioned five types of food that allegedly poison our bodies – sugar, alcohol, drugs, coffee and meat (or other dead animals). At the time, Sofia thought that she would be comfortable giving up sugar, drugs and coffee, but she was not so sure about alcohol and she was even more hesitant about meat. Chicken was her favourite thing to eat! Yet the Swami claimed that we ingest the meat that has been imprinted with the caged ways in which the animals lived and the terror of their death, plus we get the *karma* of harming other beings – killing has a dense vibration that keeps us in the lower chakras. Even the Dalai Lama said that the consistent consumption of meat reduces the human ability for compassion. While all these arguments made logical sense to Sofia, she thought she was probably many years away from having the motivation to become a vegetarian. Sofia said to herself, half-jokingly, that she would leave food for her last ego, just before enlightenment. That said, she did feel quite healthy with the vegetarian diet at the *ashram* and noticed that she had been eating a lot less over the last few weeks. Some people claimed to be eating more, though. Ananda justified that by saying that Muladhara balances one's body, allowing them to tune into how much they need to eat, which can be more or less than what they were eating before. Food is an enormous part of the culture in Portugal; people eat three to five times a day, often quite significant portions of food. That was also a big contrast to New Zealand, where food seemed to be a necessity and took as little head space as possible. The students also learned about intermittent fasting, in which a person would abstain from food for sixteen hours a day, for example, eating only one meal at ten in the morning and then another at five in the afternoon. Trying that was a powerful cleanse for Sofia. Between the intermittent fasting and the vegetarian diet they offered at the *ashram*, for the first time in her life she did not feel ongoingly constipated.

One day, Sofia came across a local workshop about growing food. The woman leading it explained that she established a reciprocal relationship with plants, talking to them as beings, watering them, asking them what they need and requesting permission when she would like to pick something. She said she was not yet able to be fully self-sufficient, but she tried to eat as much as possible from her garden, as it gave her the appropriate products for the season. The lady also said that she noticed trends, like when she was craving meat it was because her vitamin B12 was down, in which case she would supplement with superfoods. "I had to learn the language of my body," she declared. She discovered that her body tends to be attracted to fresh vegetables and fruits since they have more vitality than processed ones. She loved foraging local healing herbs, as they possess the right anti-parasitical, antimicrobial, antifungal and antiviral properties to deal with the threats of the land. She made it sound as though plants were there to help the beings of the land adapt and thrive in it. "So that one day when it's the plants' turn to eat humans, they get to eat healthy ones!" she joked. Lastly, she talked about hemp, spirulina, ashwagandha, amaranth, maca, moringa, baobab and other superfoods that Sofia had never heard about. That all felt very insightful and inspiring for Sofia; she fantasised about one day doing a big detox, after which her body would be much purer and capable of letting her know what it needed.

On the sixth week, Ananda talked about relaxation. He argued that our bodies are typically in a constant state of tension. The mental agitation generated by our many egos influences and contaminates our physical, energetic and mental aspects, moving us away from our natural state of calmness and health. "An anxious mind cannot exist in a relaxed body," he claimed. He went on to explain how our nervous system works. Namely, our state of mind, emotions and even our breath contribute directly to the activation of either the sympathetic system (responsible for the contraction of our organs) or the parasympathetic system (responsible for relaxation). When we are exposed to a stressful situation, the sympathetic system is activated and there is an immediate stimulation of the adrenal medulla (a part of the adrenal glands on top of the liver). The adrenal medulla produces adrenalin, which is generated quickly but is also very fast to leave the system after the period of agitation. That is useful if we are in a dangerous situation and it does not impact us long term, as our body breaks it down quickly after it stops being produced. However, when our system is under stress for extended periods of time, the adrenal cortex (another part of the adrenal glands) starts to become active and produces cortisol. Cortisol, unlike adrenaline, does not leave the system quickly; instead, it tends to linger around long after exposure. It also results in a range of serious, long-term physical and psychological health issues, which explains, for example, why it is not easy to jump out of depression, as it takes a long time for the hormones to leave the body.

Fortunately, Ananda argued that human beings have a great tool to regulate the nervous system, which is the breath. Humans are holistic beings, with several *koshas* (bodies) that interconnect and influence each other (he said that topic would be covered in depth in another class). Those koshas are influenced and united by the breath. Some ancient traditions would go as far as saying that it is the breath that bonds our spirit to our body, which is why if we stop breathing for long enough, the spirit leaves the body and we die.

The breath is especially related to our energetic body, as the *prana* (the subtle energy of life) is received from nature around us through the act of breathing. There is a direct connection between the mind, the nervous system and the way we breathe. By slowing down the breath, we relax the body and mind and engage our parasympathetic system. How do we do that? By performing abdominal breathing (pulling the air into the belly in the inhalation and using the abdomen to push it out in the exhalation) rather than shallow breathing with the top of our lungs, which is how most people tend to breathe. Most of the class realised they had not been breathing properly their entire lives – or relaxing fully, for that matter.

Sofia found New Zealand incredible regarding the relaxation topic. Employees seemed to have a harmonious work-life balance (compared to Portugal), people were expected to follow their passions professionally (as opposed to trying to fit into what the market needs), bosses were expected to be supportive and understanding, work conditions were not stressful in most places, happiness was prioritised, outdoor activities were highly encouraged, family time was valued. Because it was a multicultural society, people were very accepting and considerate of each other and encouraged to be themselves instead of judging others for being different. Being a small country, people still knew and looked out for each other and the streets were mostly safe… It was a wonderful place to feel relaxed.

On the seventh and last week of the Muladhara module, the topic was nature. Sofia was afraid that theme would come, as it would highlight her disconnection from it, especially having Anney around to mirror that. Ananda explained that, as the Māori elders said, human beings exist as part of the whole. He elaborated: "Our biological cycles, when harmonious, should be aligned with the seasons, circadian rhythms, moon cycles, ecological surroundings and astrological influences… The Earth is constantly growing the exact types of vegetables that its humans and animals need for well-being in each season. The sun, ocean, trees, fresh air and fertile land can nourish people in profound ways and bring them into alignment." Sofia had lived in cities for almost two decades; she was constantly indoors, with asphalt under her feet, a roof over her head and air conditioning acclimatising her air; she had become oblivious to the hours of the sun and the cycles of the moon… Having become aware of that now, she felt like a violin player who could not see or hear her orchestra; regardless of how well she played, she was always disharmonious within her environment. It seemed like every week opened up a huge dimension of life that Sofia had overlooked. *How big could that Pandora's Box of life be?* Every day that went by, more questions were added and fewer answers became clear. She started to grasp the depth of Socrates' quote: "One thing I know is that I know nothing. This is the source of my wisdom." At least now she knew that she knew nothing – and that, in itself, was a glimpse of comforting wisdom. She decided to start walking barefoot like Anney and seeking ways to be more aligned with nature.

As their time in New Zealand was coming to an end, Sofia's heart was filled with gratitude for that land and the experiences she had been offered. She wanted to give back somehow. So, she went to the *marae*, where she had been on the first week, to provide her services and help with anything they needed. As she arrived, she noticed that one of her classmates, Paulo, was there. He had the same idea! Paulo was a very tall yet otherwise typically Portuguese-looking man; short brown hair, brown eyes, fit, more glamorous than most. He emanated peace, kindness and trustworthiness. That felt reassuring to Sofia and his calming presence brought her a much-appreciated sense of safety and support. Sofia was not very skilled at fixing things, so she helped with simple tasks such as cutting the grass, tidying up the common spaces, weeding the garden, serving food… Conversely, Paulo was a gifted handyman; he fixed electrical problems, built furniture, worked on the wireless network and did various other impressive tasks. Nevertheless, what fascinated Sofia the most was his humility. He seemed to not need acknowledgement and was simply happy to help from his internal place of abundance. Paulo was just as content wiping the floors as he was fixing appliances because it was not about what he wanted to do… it was about how he could be of service.

Sleeping in the *marae* was special. Sofia had a sense that spirits or ancestors were guarding the place. Even having suppressed some of the spiritism skills she practised during adolescence, she could still feel their presence very strongly there. It also felt like the mountain was alive and the earth was actively holding them. As if the wind was kindly offering oxygen and freshness and the sun was consciously pushing vitamin D through their skin. As Sofia drank the water, she felt as if she was becoming part of the river. At that moment, she had taken a first glimpse at feeling like a part of nature, which felt magical. Memories arose of when she was a child, climbing trees, talking to animals and communicating with the intelligence behind them all.

Another interesting phenomenon happened. While chatting with some of the *iwi* in one of the common spaces, Sofia noticed a strong smell of orange, which no one else seemed to be aware of. After some detective work, she found Paulo eating an orange in a faraway building – the *whare kai* (kitchen hall). *Ha, super-smell,* she thought. *Maybe Yogis know what they're talking about after all.*

As Sofia was about to meet Paulo to leave the *marae* and return to the *ashram*, the Māori elder she had met in the *pōwhiri* fair-welled her with a *hongi*. He thanked her for coming, opened her hand, and in it placed a necklace with the green stone she had seen the *iwi* wearing. He said, "This is *pounamu* (New Zealand greenstone). This piece is a symbol of *mana*, courage, strength and determination. This land acknowledges its connection to you. May your soul always lead the way and the ancestors accompany you. Note that you will not be the owner of this piece, as it is not our place

55

to own the land or its elements. But if you so accept, you shall be its keeper."
He finished by saying with a smile, "Aotearoa will call you back one day. I
hope you answer the call." They took a moment to honour such a beautiful
gift. She expressed her gratitude as best as she could, and left feeling very
touched. She looked at Paulo's phone as he turned on the GPS to lead the
way. The time was 09:09 p.m.

Such an intense journey that had been for Sofia; she had only learned
the first chakra and it had already completely changed how she saw the world
in multiple ways. She could not conceive what the world would look like to
her in a year. Now she understood the message on the school's business card
given to her in the beginning: "Be prepared to change everything or nothing
at all."

As she waited for her fellow students and teachers to leave Aotearoa
New Zealand (or the *Godzone* as some of the locals called it, short for God's
own country), with the *pounamu* on her neck and her bare feet on the ground,
Sofia breathed in the air while feeling how that land had become a part of
her. Ananda placed tickets in everyone's hands and Sofia was excited to find
out where they were going next. She had asked him before, but the Swami
had not revealed anything. There seemed to be an element of mystery in the
school, she did not understand why, but it interfered with her need for
control. Sofia realised she wanted the future to be predictable in order to feel
safe. Though who was the *she* who needed that, her ego or her higher self?
Surely her higher self did not need to know the future to feel safe… Her
thoughts were interrupted by Anney grabbing her with the intense
excitement that only she could express: "Yaaaaay, I've always wanted to go
to Jamaica!" Sofia looked down at her ticket and indeed, it read "Kingston,
Jamaica."

Chapter 7 – Swadhisthana Chakra

As soon as Sofia took one step out of the aeroplane, she was struck by a wave of the most tranquil, pleasant energy she had ever felt. It was as if the whole country was saying: "Come in, chill, enjoy." She could not have imagined that one land could feel so different from another. She wondered if all lands felt that different and she had not been sensitive or aware enough to notice it before, or if Jamaica had a very distinctive energy. Looking outside, she could see a clear, warm, turquoise ocean calling her in. However, it would have to wait until some practical things were taken care of.

The group was taken to a small community; some people would have called it a camp, with tiny huts for sleeping and medium-sized huts for shared spaces: a kitchen, toilets and a venue for classes and workshops. The accommodation was quite simple, which did not bother Sofia, but some people in the course struggled with sharing small rooms, sand everywhere, minimal toilets and cold water. *Was it their spirit reacting against those things?* No, only their ego. Circumstances are neutral; the suffering is in people's responses. The fact that some people enjoy it and others do not proves that the response is entirely subjective and, therefore, changeable. So, to react against something concrete and unchangeable is absurd. *If we can't change what it is, at least we can change our reaction, then we can be at peace with it,* Sofia concluded in her mind.

The group gathered for the first class of Swadhisthana, the second chakra. Ananda explained that Swadhisthana is located in the pelvic area and corresponds to the element of Water. It relates to the sense of taste and the qualities of fluidity, sociability and sensuality. People actively balanced at this level usually find it easy to be sociable, friendly, enjoyable, and soft.

57

They tend to interact pleasantly with others, blending into social environments like a fish in the water.

He described that unlike Muladhara, which was focused on individual survival, Swadhisthana expands one's horizons to social networks and values the pursuit of connection, enjoyment and pleasurable things. Free from Muladhara chakra's burden of survival, a person can discover that life is full of sensations, which can produce intense pleasure and displeasure. This duality is at the core of Swadhisthana chakra: pursuing what feels good and avoiding what does not.

Ananda claimed that it is common for people at this level to be interested in fashion, social arrangements, social roles, fame and politics.

The Swami also said that sexuality, erotic sensations and sexual instincts are at the core of this chakra. An intense desire to merge with the world through the senses is present; the person can explore the capacity for movement and bodily expression, seek pleasure and explore sensuality and sexual connections.

Swadhisthana-awakened people have a high adaptability to change and no issues with changing course. They are as graceful emotionally as they are physically in how they move and interact with the world.

Creativity is one of their key features; they tend to be interesting, easy going, approachable and imaginative, sometimes to the point of daydreaming.

Lastly, Ananda stated that this chakra is responsible for healing and regeneration.

Wow, that sounded like an interesting journey, Sofia thought. *How different from the first one!*

Ananda mentioned that because the conditions of the camp they were living in were very humble, people were most welcome to volunteer to help the locals if they felt called to. Sofia was keen to volunteer, as she felt good about contributing, but surprisingly she found herself wondering if Paulo would also volunteer here, perhaps hoping they could share that experience. In the few moments she shared with him, multiple situations had intrigued and impressed her, which could have easily gone unnoticed given his humble nature.

During the day, the group was encouraged to explore surfing – something Sofia had always been drawn to! That whole experience felt like a dream to her. *What if it was indeed a dream?* The thought of waking up and discovering that life was meaningless again terrified her. She took a deep breath and grounded herself in the present moment: that land was really there, she was also there, all of it was real; there was nothing to fear. Looking at that bright blue ocean, feeling the sun and the warm water, riding the waves (or attempting to), enjoying the sweet breeze and the warm nights… Sofia wished those days would never end. That school, that journey; she was part of something greater – finally, she had found meaning and was no longer lost and alone.

Somehow, the days were pretty busy with the two-hour Yoga *sadhana*, the shared tasks, learning and surfing. Yet at the end of the day, there was a time when everything was quiet, during which people read or journalled. Sofia figured that would be a suitable time for volunteering. She spoke with one of the people from the camp and they told her they needed help building a big hut for events. That involved picking up materials from nature, cutting, constructing, disposing of unused materials and whatever other tasks emerged. Now that Sofia felt more connected with her body, she could not ignore the subtle tingling feelings of excitement in her belly as she imagined whether Paulo was there. As she arrived, a surge of energy in her chest and stomach hit her when she saw that he was actually there. He seemed happy to see her too and walked to her straight away, filling her in on the specifics of where they were at with the work and what still needed to be done. He seemed knowledgeable and reliable, which inspired trust in Sofia. They got to work and there was a beautiful energy between them that did not even seem to require words. They were together in spirit, serving the community for the greater good.

Night after night, they worked on that project. Sometimes other volunteers came, other times not. Yet even when they did, Sofia and Paulo always felt like the space holders, orienting others and staying a bit longer towards the end. Sometimes they would just exchange a few words about topics that had come up during that time or share small stories about their lives. Other times they would have a long conversation about life and the universe.

The week went by, which for Sofia felt again like a whole month. In class, they spoke about the symptoms of an imbalanced Swadhisthana. Ananda said, "Frustration is typically the ego at the core of this chakra. A vicious cycle is created by seeking new and more exciting objects of pleasure while becoming bored of the current ones. Consequently, the person leaves activities, things or people one after another without ever being fully satisfied; as such, their desires are never truly fulfilled. Such accumulation of frustrations can cause mood swings and lead to psychological outbursts or martyrdom.

"In relationships, the intense desire and passion that often happen at a Swadhisthana level can result in strong feelings of unhealthy attachment, jealousy, envy, co-dependence and fear. One can become possessive, controlling and manipulative and experience suspicion or obsessions. Because of these psychological characteristics, if the other chakras are not harmoniously balanced and activated, the person can become overly emotional, dysregulated, and experience overwhelming states of agitation, confusion or forgetfulness.

"Social skills are often impaired when this chakra is unbalanced. Hence, social anxiety can be high and craving social validation can become so dominant that the person develops a chameleonic personality, losing themselves to please others. That leads to resentment and a continuous struggle to establish harmony between the inner and outer worlds. In other words, they lack the agency to stand by their ideas, emotions and principles regardless of others. Their conflict avoidance, combined with excessive concern about self-image and people's opinions, often leads to people-pleasing. The absence of the Water element can cause a lack of fluidity,

60

softness and flexibility. That also manifests at a physical level, namely a rigidity in the body and movement.

"A wide range of sexual disturbances is related to the malfunctioning of this chakra, deriving from either overexposure or lack of access to the senses. These can be influenced by a range of factors, such as the person's traumas, developmental history, religious upbringing, cultural beliefs and familial influences. A common example is how those with a religious upbringing can associate sexuality with deep feelings of shame and guilt, which then keep unbalancing Swadhisthana.

"This chakra is often driven by pleasure, so unless the person has the willpower to stand by stronger values and principles (characteristics of Manipura, the third chakra), it is common for people to find themselves caught up in addictions, irresponsible behaviours and unconsciousness."

Sofia felt very scared of Swadhisthana chakra, as she suspected she had a lot of sexual traumas buried deep inside and did not know the consequences of bringing them to the surface.

Jamaica was particularly good at Swadhisthana, Sofia reflected. They were fluid, easy going, adaptable, sociable, fun and pleasant; their whole approach and *motto* was "Jamaica, no problem". That way of being resonated with Sofia. She realised what a contrast that was to Portugal, where things were structured, conditioned and controlled. In the mindset of Jamaica, there seemed to be far more space for freedom and creativity, though there was also uncertainty. The Portuguese mentality was more monotonous but predictable and efficient; if someone played into the system, they could easily get things done. Neither of these ways of being and living was right or wrong; they were simply distinct and different people would resonate more with one or the other.

That night Sofia went to volunteer but Paulo was absent. She was surprised to realise the contrast to how excited and supported she felt when he *was* there. She felt like she could achieve anything if he were present. Moreover, she noticed that volunteering was no longer only about helping the community… The most magical part of it was connecting with Paulo.

That was a scary thought, as it brought up her insecurities and fears of rejection. Plus, she was not even sure of the nature of her attraction to him; maybe he was just a fascinating person. She decided that she should just breathe, definitely not panic, and let things be whatever they needed to be. Besides, she had just gotten out of a ten-year relationship not that long ago, where she lost a son and wrecked her life. Surely it was not a suitable time to start a new relationship; she was just beginning to learn how to live and should keep things light – Sofia reassured herself.

The following night, Sofia's firm determination to keep it light did not stop the burst of excitement she felt in her chest when he saw Paulo again at the hut. He explained that he had wanted to be there the previous night but felt exhausted and slightly ill. Having rested for a day, he was feeling refreshed and keen to get back to work. At the end of the night, it came up in conversation that he had a girlfriend back in Portugal, who he had been with for three years. Sofia stopped breathing for a moment but, at the same time, felt genuinely relieved because that made things clear and straightforward, taking away the ambiguity. She decided she would make the most of him as a friend.

Night after night, Sofia and Paulo's conversations got longer and longer, deeper and deeper. One day at lunchtime, just as she was about to enter the communal area, he *kidnapped* her and said with the biggest smile, "Today we eat somewhere new." Surprised, she followed him into the woods, wondering where on Earth he would lead her. He stopped by a tree with a large trunk and pointed upwards: "This way." She looked up and noticed it seemed like a simple enough trunk to climb; it was big and solid, with multiple support places and inclined enough. As she climbed higher, she noticed a man-made structure at the top, where some wooden planks had been built into a flat space. She reached the ledge and saw what it unravelled: A quaint picnic mat covering the floor under a very impressive plate of spicy grilled cheese-filled mushrooms, delicious-looking sautéed vegetables and rice. There were also two coconuts with straws and some wonderfully comfortable cushions. As they sat down and enjoyed that wonderful banquet, little birds came and looked at them from a distance. Paulo placed some pieces of rice on his hand and reached out to them. The bravest one hopped closer and closer and, to Sofia's surprise, came and ate directly from his hand. When the others saw it was safe, they came too. Seeing how surprised she was, Paulo said, "You can try it!" Which she did, and the birds ate out of her hand too. To Sofia, that felt no less magical than if forest fairies had joined them. From that high place, with the world at their feet, Sofia felt like there was nowhere in the universe she would rather be and nothing she would rather be doing.

The following week, the Yoga class talked about duality, craving and aversion. Ananda explained that human beings have six receptors that are continuously receiving sensations: the sense of smell, eyesight, touch, hearing, taste and thoughts. These instantly transmit their sensations to the mind, whose natural tendency is to react – either with craving or aversion. On one hand, when the mind receives what it deems a *pleasant* sensation, it desires to retain it and craves more. If it gets it, it is happy and if not, it is unhappy. That duality generates attachment. Our attachment to things causes suffering because our peace of mind and emotional balance become dependent on external factors. We then feel compelled to control reality so that we get what we crave. However, even if we eventually get it, it will probably not give us the satisfaction we had hoped for because it was the logical result of our hard work, as opposed to a magical gift from the universe. On the other hand, when the mind receives an *unpleasant* sensation, it wants it to disappear; we feel aversion and reject the object of that sensation. If the sensation remains, we start to experience discomfort, restlessness or heavier emotions. Our peace becomes dependent on that sensation ending, again making us dependent on external factors to be at peace.

Sofia started noticing that the craving-aversion pattern was deeply ingrained in her life. She could literally think of anything in life and immediately tell if she was attracted or repelled by it, whether she liked or disliked it, whether she wanted it or not. Constantly pulled by pleasure and repelled by displeasure. That was the Swadhisthana pattern. Most people she knew were also doing that. *Was there even a different way to exist?*

The teacher proceeded to explain that the solution for that pattern was to replace our *reaction* pattern with *observation*. Instead of reacting (with craving or aversion), we observe the sensation as it is without trying to judge or change it. Each sensation, pleasant or unpleasant, has the same characteristics: It comes into existence, exists, and then ceases to exist. Everything is impermanent. Because we have not fully comprehended the reality of impermanence within ourselves, we tend to think of sensations as permanent when, in fact, they are not. They come, stay for some time and then go away – each and every one of them. When we change our psychological structure because of a sensation (whether pleasant or unpleasant), it strengthens our reaction pattern, leading to more suffering. When we observe from a detached place, we resonate with a place of consciousness and serenity. In Yoga, we aim to reach that state of equanimity, in other words, a peaceful state of mind that cannot be disturbed by external circumstances. In the pleasure-driven Swadhisthana state of consciousness, most people tend to become attached (to their partners, possessions, status, or the objects of their desire) and lose their equanimity. Yet attachment comes from the ego, whereas it is possible to relate to things and beings in a loving yet non-attached way. Ananda said they would study this in depth when they reached Anahata, the heart chakra. Though everyone in the class was already wondering… *Could love indeed exist without attachment? What would that look like?*

As the class debated the theme of relationships, the students started to enter a very enthusiastic, chatty mood, with lots of talking and giggling. At some point, the Swami stopped them, amused by what he was seeing and asked the class to notice their inner state. He said that every single time he taught Swadhisthana, that bubbly state occurred. Swadhisthana energy is the same energy we use for talking, so people become chatty and giggly. That was when Sofia realised that in the classes, Ananda was not merely sharing knowledge… He was also giving an energetic initiation to the state, chakra or posture that was being discussed. That made it extra important not to miss a single class.

Towards the end, they did the asana part of the class and the Swami taught the new Yoga posture for the week. Asanas for Swadhisthana typically consisted of hip stretches and pelvic compression or elongation.

As homework, Ananda encouraged the class to reflect on their relationships (to people, objects, animals) under the light of non-attachment.

Ron, the other volunteer, who was much younger than Ananda, was now also teaching some of the classes. One day, he and Sofia happened to be having lunch together and the topic of sexuality came up. She shared with him that she did not feel like she had sexual energy and was wondering if she was asexual. He looked at her for what felt like a long time, perplexed. Sofia wondered if he did not know that the term asexual refers to people who do not have sexual feelings or desires. Just as she was about to clarify that, he shared that her statement did not match his perception of her at all. He perceived her as a very sensual being with a prominent sexual energy. Sofia was vastly more shocked by what he said than if he had told her he did not know what asexuality was. *Was that how people perceived her?* If that were the case, it would appear that she could not feel her sensuality yet somehow still emanated it. In other words, it was unconscious! That would explain why men had flirted with her all her life. Perhaps they believed she was interested. *Wow, everything does come from within; maybe I was attracting them!* she reflected. That meant that she did indeed have sexual energy but was disconnected from it. When she shared that with Ron, he said, "Sexual trauma creates a door between the person's sexual self and their mind. Their psyche keeps that door locked to protect them from further trauma. With love, patience and consciousness, one day they can open the door again, when it feels safe, and reclaim their sexuality."

"Great," she mumbled sarcastically. "Because I didn't have enough things to work on."

Another interesting thing that Ron mentioned was that when we have an active Swadhisthana, we radiate a pleasant energy that causes other people to be drawn to us. He said that while he was practising Swadhisthana, random people would approach him on the street, old friends would call him wanting to connect, and similar strange phenomena. Sofia found that fascinating and got the sense that he was also excited about their conversation – maybe even excited about *her*.

The following week, they approached the topic of sensuality, one of the core aspects of Swadhisthana. The teacher explained that sexual energy, erotic energy, vital energy, social energy and creative energy were based on the same life force. When someone's sexual energy is awake, they live in a state that feels like being in love with everything in the world – a state of ecstasy, pleasure, connection, delight and elation with all beings. Their current mission was to awaken that energy.

In the sequence of what they were learning, the class was offered to join biodanza, a holistically-oriented dance class. The teacher was a beautiful, friendly, lovely Argentinian woman, Agnes, whose smile made the world shinier. At the beginning of the class, she circulated *mate* (a South American herbal tea offered in a traditional wooden cup) around the students' circle while introducing what they were about to do. She described biodanza as a personal development system originally created by a Chilean psychologist, Rolando Toro. It uses music, movement and feelings to deepen self-awareness, holistic healing, and reconnection of body, emotions, mind and soul. She explained that in the class, they would be having a few *vivencias* (experiences); some were individual, some in pairs, and some in groups. These were designed to work on each person's relationship with themselves, others and the universe. The experiences are delivered in a particular flow to stimulate specific aspects of their being: vitality, sexuality, creativity, affectivity and transcendence. The only indications Agnes gave the group were to refrain from using the spoken word or wearing socks.

At first, Sofia felt very resistant to the class. She did not know how to dance; it all seemed scary, awkward and embarrassing. Nevertheless, bravery ran through her veins and she was determined to heal, plus she was not one to shy away from a challenge. Besides, Sofia felt slightly more at

66

ease when Agnes gave that inspiring introduction, so open and welcoming. She could not have anticipated the deep journey within her own body that biodanza would send her on.

The class was powerful. It began with a circle, people holding hands, walking, simple things that allowed her to relax. Then it became more stimulating; the music intensified and Sofia had some experiences of release. When it slowed down again, the experiences became deeper and at some stage, people leaned on each other and allowed their bodies to lay down and rest on the floor. After that brief period of rest, the pace slowly picked up again; they were meant to dance with one person, then move on to another and so on. Sofia felt her heart accelerate dramatically at that stage as she saw Paulo right by her side. She felt divided between excitement and the impulse to run for the hills. In the end, she chose not to run. Their eyes met, their arms embraced, their rhythms aligned and their energies synchronised. She noticed the kindness of his expression, the firmness of his touch, the brightness of his being, the vulnerability of that moment. The teacher gave the queue to exchange partners, but their eyes could not part and their bodies refused to let go. Instead, their arms squeezed tighter, their hearts came closer, she placed her head on his chest… Time stopped around them and the world disappeared. There was nothing else, no one else; it was as if the universe had dissipated and the only thing left standing were those beings, that moment. There was no place where she ended and he began, or he ended and she began. They ceased to be two people moving and became one organism being moved. They danced through that song and the remaining ones until long after the music had ended. By the time they were ready to part, everyone else had left. They gently stepped back from each other. Sofia placed one hand on her heart and another on her womb and closed her eyes for a moment to integrate the experience. She could still feel Paulo's energy as intensely as when their bodies were together. They gazed into each other's eyes one last time, after which they made their way to their respective rooms.

Sofia was in a state of ecstatic trance. On top of which, that dance had completely burst her platonic bubble. Until then, she had managed to convince herself that what they had was only a friendship and she had no romantic feelings for Paulo – but that ship had now sailed; in fact, it was happily cruising on the other side of the world. She was both exhilarated and crushed. That experience; the oneness, expansion, love with no boundaries, spaceless, timeless… *How could that even exist?* She had no idea how to process what she had just experienced. Her mind bounced between *"He can never find out I feel this way; I can't destroy a three-year relationship; we need to distance ourselves!"* and *"I have to be honest; integrity is non-negotiable."* She could hardly sleep that night. Regardless, she had no more solutions that morning than the previous night.

Sofia decided to go for a walk on the beach but as she was on her way, Paulo found her. He said that what he had felt the night before was undeniable, so he called his girlfriend to break up with her after that. Sofia could not believe that he might have felt the same way, and especially that he had already acted on that. Without the shackles of the past, their bodies could no longer tolerate the present distance. They embraced each other and kissed passionately, surrendering all their troubles and concerns to the ecstasy and grace of that moment. They explored their newly found intimacy by hanging out and making out for the rest of the day. In the evening, they picked a spot on the beach under a palm tree to admire the moon while hearing the group at a distance, singing songs with the locals, playing guitar and drumming around a bonfire.

The following week, the Yoga class was about creativity. They learned that the left side of the brain commands the right side of the body, which relates to the *yang*, masculine, solar, emissive energies, and the functions of language, technical skills, logic and reasoning. The right side of the brain rules the left side of the body, which corresponds to the *yin*, feminine, lunar, receptive energies, and controls the functions of abstract meaning, intuition, emotion, imagination and creativity. They learned that Western society predominantly uses the *yang* side, which unbalances the system as people have become too logical and lost their natural intuitive and creative capabilities. As homework that week, the students were asked to draw, sing and create art of all kinds, in addition to working on the previous aspects of Swadhisthana.

On Sofia's way back to her hut after class, a stranger greeted her and told her all about their life. Interestingly, a remarkably similar encounter had happened just before class, which made it twice in one day. She smiled and remembered Ron's teachings about Swadhisthana: *Random people are approaching me!*

Just as Sofia was about to reach her hut, Paulo approached her. He asked if she wanted to go out for tea in a little place he had discovered. They went for a walk and there was already so much love between them that it did not matter what they did or talked about – one could almost feel it in the air. The place was pleasant and joyful; he said it reminded him of a place he used to go to when he was younger. Like most Portuguese people, Sofia was a strong coffee drinker and had seldom had tea in her entire life. Yet drinking it now with Paulo, she discovered how wonderful, tasty and uplifting it could be. It was a beautiful experience, which they would come to repeat many times in the future. On their way home, they went to the grocery shop and bought some treats. They listened to music, philosophised about life, laughed, cuddled and eventually slept next to each other. Before they fell asleep, Sofia felt relieved that he did not pressure her to have sex. She still carried the sexual trauma from her first boyfriend – the belief that she was responsible for pleasing him, so if he was in the mood she needed to satisfy him. She noticed how her trauma made her dread engaging sexually with men, which was a big challenge in a relationship, as men tend to expect sex. She knew that once she gained more intimacy with Paulo, she would feel pressured to have sex with him (whether he actually pressured her or not). Intellectually, Sofia was aware that she should probably not do anything she did not feel like doing, but after so many years of coercion, she had taken on the role of the coercer towards herself: she no longer needed men to pressure her – she did it to herself. She knew that she should change that; start to honour and respect herself... but did she feel entitled to do so, *and would she be strong enough to do it when the time came?* Avoiding that thought, she was relieved that that phase had not arrived yet.

The next morning, Paulo woke up still holding Sofia in his arms and said, "Good morning, *ya habibi*." Apparently, it was Arabic for "my love." They cuddled and enjoyed each other all day. Speaking Arabic was one of countless impressive and unusual skills that Sofia came to learn about Paulo in the months to come.

Agnes had grown fond of that group and decided to offer weekly biodanza classes until they parted ways. During the next class, Sofia discovered how ashamed of her body she felt. She noticed herself dancing in socially acceptable ways rather than allowing her body to express itself however it wanted. Instead of exploring her own creativity through movement, she would look to others to check what was appropriate, as if they had access to some hidden information that allowed them to know what was acceptable while she did not. If others accidentally looked at her, she would feel terribly embarrassed. There she was, diminishing her body and her wisdom again. Witnessing that, she decided it was more important for her to be encouraging and supportive of herself than to face the consequences of potentially moving in shameful ways.

On the sixth week of Swadhisthana, they spoke about sexuality. Tantra was one of the backbones of their Yoga school, so they had a lot to say about the topic. Though Tantra was known in the Western world primarily for its sexual component, the school taught the holistic Tantric philosophies about everything in life and the Universe. The teacher talked about love-making, describing it as the ultimate act of union between two people. He explained that when a man is fully polarised in his masculine (and also balanced in his feminine), and a woman fully polarised in her feminine (with a balanced masculine), the two lovers can connect through their words, their touch, their kiss, their energy... Their love grows and multiplies; they immerse themselves in one another, expand and rejoice... Their energy grows until it becomes ecstatic; they involve each other in a dance of *yin* and *yang*... They tease, laugh, cry, surrender... They start to dissolve in one another; the feelings intensify, they grow closer and closer... Until they cannot possibly grow any closer, they are one energetically and psychologically, at which point the physical manifestation has to catch up... They penetrate and receive each other's bodies, minds, hearts and souls; the two consciousnesses awaken and unify, their beings merge fully into one. From a Tantric perspective, that is the potential and largely part of the point of love-making.

Ananda mentioned that, sadly, that is not how Western people typically tend to see sexual intercourse. From their pleasure-seeking Swadhisthana level, they make it goal-oriented, aimed at reaching orgasm and satisfying their personal desire. Tantrics, on the other hand, do not see orgasm as a goal; the love-making act is about enjoying the senses (which is why it is called sensuality), being present and aware, loving each other and awakening themselves. Both lovers enjoy and delight in each other without aiming to reach a particular place, so there is no pressure or expectations. If there are orgasms, they should not involve ejaculation. Especially for men, for whom these two processes happen almost simultaneously. Orgasm and ejaculation are actually two separate processes, the Swami explained, that should be separated so that the man does not lose his vitality and level of consciousness by ejaculating his life force out of his body. He claimed a regular man would typically take a whole week to recover physically, energetically, emotionally and mentally from a single ejaculation. The Swami gave examples of people from the school who had practised sexual continence for years and then started ejaculating again for procreation purposes; they claimed to feel noticeably dumber, slower and more aggressive in comparison. He added that the longer men practice sexual continence, the more powerful, expansive, longer, whole-bodied orgasms they have. After he said that, there was silence in the room. It did not feel like any of those students had thought of sex that way or experienced merging transcendentally with another human being, let alone separating orgasm from ejaculation. Even Sofia, who felt so many blockages around sex, found the thought of that kind of physical union intriguing and exciting. Adding a spiritual dimension to love-making could definitely make it more appealing – she pondered. She was unsure what to think about the gender-binary view of the situation, of sex being seen as something between a man and a woman. *What about other gender identifications and sexual orientations?* She wondered what Anney might be thinking and feeling. Since the topic was already confusing enough, she decided to let that be for the time being.

Sofia and Paulo kept on seeing each other, now with a more romantic ethos, continuing to impress each other on a daily basis. One day he would 'kidnap' her to see a local theatre, another day, she would recite romantic self-written poetry to him on the beach. They always had exciting stories to share about their lives and philosophical questions to explore. Gradually, the relationship became more physically intimate, which was further out of Sofia's comfort zone. She could sometimes feel his sexual energy but internally she felt a subtle aversion – she did not feel ready for that; it felt scary. However, instead of pressuring or betraying herself, she chose to communicate her fears and took a leap of faith sexually. On the other hand, Paulo was comfortable sexually but opening up emotionally felt vulnerable and scary, triggering old avoidance mechanisms... Yet he chose to observe those fears instead of following them, and to communicate them with Sofia, taking his own leap of faith. Sofia was far from knowing everything about Paulo, but what she did instinctively know was that he was honest and transparent, with no agendas, hidden intentions, lies or manipulation. He was who he was – the kindest, most caring, patient and supportive person Sofia had ever met.

Sofia told Paulo that maybe she should push herself to make love; otherwise, who knows how long it would take her to feel ready. He instantly replied, "Absolutely not. *Primum non nocere.*" He paused, gauging whether or not she knew what that meant. "It's Latin for *First, do no harm.* I would rather have no sex than have you do it if you don't feel like it." Sofia had to stop to integrate what he was saying – she could not believe a man would say that. *Was he trying to be nice, or manipulate her, or was that truly genuine? And would he feel differently if that meant not ever having sex?* If only her first boyfriend had said that to her. She was aware that it was her responsibility to set boundaries and say 'no', but if men had the wisdom to support women in doing so, it would be so much easier. They can work collaboratively to ensure that the sexual relationship is always based on love and consent. So simple, right? Where was that piece of wisdom fifteen years ago? She was once again mind-blown. In hearing his refusal to push her into something she was not ready for, something inside her relaxed. She felt more open and available to her own sexuality and to him. Though in the back of her mind, there was still the matter of the pressure she might put on herself.

Since Tantra removed the pressure of orgasm-seeking, Sofia could be present with her body and attuned to what she wanted, explore what felt right and stop when she no longer felt comfortable. She no longer had to pressure herself towards a particular goal. With that, she felt safer and they started having more sensual interactions.

The sensual opening was another Pandora's Box for Sofia. The first thing she discovered was that when she was meant to feel excited, her womb area made sounds, which meant that her body was probably excited but she simply could not feel it in her mind or emotions. That corroborated the theory that the trauma had created a disconnection between her body and mind. Rico was happily living his life with no clue how much he had damaged Sofia's. *Why does he get to live freely while I carry out this life sentence? How is that fair?* Sofia asked herself. Feelings of anger started to arise – the rage she had suppressed all those years to keep receiving his love and remain in the relationship. She had thought his actions were *normal*. At least now, she did not believe that any more. Yet she was suffering the consequences of her past beliefs; when she was intimate with Paulo, sometimes she would get sudden flashbacks of Rico's body which would feel repulsive, scary and, of course, extremely off-putting. With all the patience in the world, Paulo would accept her and be prepared to offer any support he could. Regardless, that was bigger than Paulo. That was PTSD.

Sofia's love for Paulo was different than she had ever experienced. With the focus on non-attachment, she was mindful of not outsourcing her love to him but instead radiating that energy and life force from within herself and only then sharing it with him from that place. That made her bigger and more expansive, closer to herself and overflowing with light. It also completely changed the way she saw relationships.

The last week of the Swadhisthana module had arrived; Sofia was happy to hear that the theme for that week was healing. Ron, who was teaching the class, said that this chakra is connected to our natural healing abilities. He explained that we have five bodies, or *koshas* as they are called in Yoga. The physical body (*annamaya kosha*) is our densest aspect and consists of a complex combination of cells, tissues, organs and systems. He said that pain and physical illnesses usually manifest at this level, though they typically start at the other levels. The physical body can store memories for numerous years, preventing one from overcoming past situations. He claimed that Yoga *asanas* could help remove that. Then, there is the energetic body (*pranamaya kosha*), also called the bio-energetic aura. This body is made of the subtle energy of life, called *prana* or *chi*. It contains the life force in our body and strongly correlates with the breath and subtle anatomy (chakras and *nadis*). It nourishes the physical structure with the energy and information necessary for its harmonious development. Illnesses can be detected at this level well before they manifest at a physical level. Next is the inferior mental body (*manomaya kosha*), the astral or emotional body. Thoughts and emotions are processed at this level. The following is the superior mental body (*vijnanamaya kosha*), the higher intellect, capable of discriminating, evaluating and deciding. It does not refer to everyday thinking but to superior mental activity, which takes place in abstract cognitive processes, intuitions and meditative conditions. It enables the person to establish a direct connection with inner vision and deeper truths, reaching a profound understanding. Lastly, there is the bliss body (*anandamaya kosha*), the subtlest of the five bodies, comprised of peace, overwhelming happiness, ecstasy and pure love, naturally residing in our higher self. Experiences regarding this elevated level appear in deep states of communion with the ultimate reality. It is the last veil that covers the divine essence of any human being.

Ron continued, "Our *koshas* are holistically connected and affect each other (positively as well as negatively). Traumas, psychological imbalances and environmental issues can express through the body as ailments or diseases. The body part where we have the symptoms is usually symbolic and directly related to the imbalance; for example, a heart attack can represent a broken heart, shoulder pain can represent too much responsibility on one's shoulders, and pain in the neck can represent a metaphorical pain in the neck. We call that psychosomatic illness, meaning that it originates from psychological reasons. Don't get me wrong, that does not mean the pain is made up; it is definitely real." He explained that the body gives us symptoms that point directly towards the issues we need to deal with. Someone asked, "Are all pains psychological? What about injuries caused by accidents? Surely, they are just coincidences, not manifestations of our psyche, right?" Ron smiled, as he had asked the same question when he was studying. He replied, "It's not that simple. First of all, our external world is interlinked with our internal reality. We are part of a cosmic consciousness that also wants us to awaken, so yes, things can happen because our being is pulling the strings through our external circumstances. Moreover, there is another element to that. Say you have a motorbike accident and you hurt your lower back. Why did you hurt the lower back and not your upper back, shoulder or neck? We have specific places in our body that are especially fragile or prone to get hurt – precisely because of those imbalances in our psyche. So, when there is some kind of accident, those parts are more at risk than the others. One last but crucial point: Yoga says that life starts by giving you a little nudge. If you don't listen, it gives you a shake. If you still don't listen, it slaps you in the face. If you keep on ignoring it, it will throw you under a bus. So, if you've had a serious accident, you've probably ignored the nudge, the shake and the slap in the face."

Sofia was reminded of Alex, her unborn son. She was sure that he was her bus. *How many warnings had she had before that and did not listen?* Maybe that mirror in the petrol station was one, and she could think of a few others in her life. She also thought of her endometriosis (a three-centimetre cyst currently attached to her right ovary that gave her excruciating pain

75

during menstruation). She asked, "What are the psychosomatic reasons for endometriosis?" He told her to see him after class since they no longer had time to approach such a complex topic. *Or was he using that opportunity to connect personally with her?* Sofia asked herself, noticing that she could not distinguish between her fears about men and a potential intuition.

After class, Ron and Sofia headed to the cafe to discuss the topic. He told her, "I suppose we can start by acknowledging that endometriosis is a disease exclusively in the female organs; hence it is related to the connection with the feminine. What I've learned about endometriosis in particular is that it has to do with an imbalance between the feminine and masculine, usually linked to rejection of or anger against the masculine, which is perceived as abusive, oppressive and forceful... Let's consider that the primal nature of the sacred feminine is to welcome – to bring in (based on the anatomy of our sexual organs, where the predominant direction of the male is outwards and the female inwards). Endometriosis is essentially the womb expelling its cells instead of holding them in, or in other words, inverting its natural flow. Part of it relates to the woman's relationship with the feminine: rejecting her soft aspects, as vulnerability is perceived as a risk (they need to be strong, otherwise may be abused). In other words, the feminine does not feel safe (in the psyche or the womb). The other part relates to their relationship with the masculine: Either rejecting it (kicking it out emotionally, as well as symbolically through the womb, because of the perception that it's abusive, often specifically sexually); or being too much in the masculine (to be strong, or because of the current masculine-driven lifestyle). That changes the woman's energy flow to outwards, which goes against her primary nature and symbolically changes the direction of the womb."

Sofia was stunned by that explanation. That was her exact story! *Was that what her body had been telling her all along?* She could see how her body was a wise ally (as opposed to a dumb, incompetent, fragile, uncooperative vessel), showing her symptoms so she could release the pain and the trauma. She also realised how harsh she had been on her body. Grieving for how inconsiderately she had always treated her body and

76

feeling the urgency to heal, she pleaded, "I'm so sorry body..." She asked Ron, "So, what is the solution?"

"Well, you might have to figure that out for yourself, but here are some educated guesses: Love, a tremendous amount of it. Self-love. Love for others. Forgiveness. Healing your perception of the masculine, which may have been internalised as abusive or oppressive. Healing the masculine aspects in yourself. Identifying the primary (underlying) emotions that you've gone through and letting them go. Letting all the *stories* go. Letting everything go. Tuning into your needs, wants and especially the things you don't want. Setting boundaries. Trusting yourself to uphold those boundaries. Connecting with the feminine parts of you. Finding strength in your vulnerability. Releasing intergenerational trauma and collective unconscious beliefs that you may be carrying. Possibly a lot more; just hold that question in mind and trust that the universe will give you answers, and your body too," he replied.

Sofia joked sarcastically again: "Just that?"

Ron said there was a special gift for the class that week for those who chose to accept it. He went outside for a minute and came back with a woman. She sat beside him and announced, "Hello beautiful people; my name is Jade. I will be offering a one-week course on tantric massage starting today, for whoever feels called. The interested students will be learning, receiving and practising tantric massage. This practice is for improving sexual health, healing sexual trauma, increasing libido and intensifying pleasure. Students will be naked and highly likely to experience orgasms. We will create a compassionate, respectful, healing and safe environment for everyone. As a training practitioner, you will perform healing sexual touch on others, and as a client, you will receive it. There will be no sex in this course. Classes are every day this week from three to six p.m."

When Sofia thought she could no longer be shocked by the course, they would throw in something like that. Yet it sounded like the perfect tool for what she was trying to heal. *Was she ready for that, though?* She was probably too disconnected from her body to be able to answer that question.

Nevertheless, as her classmate Elixir (she called him 'the yes man') would say: "Life is offering me this, so it must be for me." His mantra was to say yes to life. Elixir was a tall, wild, hippie-looking man with brown hair and eyes, wearing donated clothes or just a sarong, with a smile on his face and an aura that radiated positivity, joy and excitement. Sofia spoke with Paulo and asked him how he felt about joining the course. He said it was not something he had been thinking about but if she wanted to do it, it could be an interesting exploration together. Sofia was unsure about seeing him give and receive orgasms to another person; she had never been through anything like that and did not know how she would feel. Somehow though, Sofia felt that it would be OK because she and Paulo were a team; they trusted each other and were very much in love. They were strong together. So, they decided to try it.

That brought up a conversation about the nature of their relationship. In the school, there was a lot of discussion about polyamorous relationships – relationships where people are free to love and make love to more than one person. Tantrics often saw monogamy as a contract between two people based on fear and control, where people compensate for their insecurities and lack of self-love by keeping the other person from being with other people they could be attracted to. From a Tantric perspective, not only was that restrictive of their freedom but also based on made-up culturally-biased ideas, such as that there is something wrong about loving two people at the same time or that once someone is in a relationship, they stop being attracted to other people. Conversely, Tantrics would argue that attraction is something that happens at a soul level when one soul recognises that the other has qualities that can awaken another; therefore, by exploring one's attractions, one would be likely to awaken more and faster. On the other hand, fear and jealousy are egoic traits, so we should not feed them or let them rule our lives. If we want our life to be ruled by love, we must put love at the forefront and not restrict each other's ability to love. In principle, both Sofia and Paulo wanted to live that way, but they had no idea how they would react if one of them fell in love with someone else. "What if we do this and end up consumed by fear, jealousy and despair?" Sofia asked him.

Paulo replied with a story about a boy and his grandfather, where the boy asked, "Grandfather, I have two wolves inside me; one is scared, angry and violent, and the other is peaceful, protective and wise. Which one will win in the end?"

The grandfather replied, "Whichever one you feed." Both Sofia and Paulo knew which wolf they wanted to feed. So, they agreed to try polyamory, even though neither of them was actively seeking other partners. But if one day it happened, they would cross that bridge when they came to it.

Most students joined the tantra massage course, a fact that Jade was happy about. She started by explaining that they would be learning three types of massage. "The *sensitive massage*, which involves soft touch over the whole body and is designed to awaken its bio-energy, expand and circulate the sexual energy of the entire body, and open up the possibility of whole-body orgasms. The other two are the *yoni* and the *lingam* massages, which consist of specific healing techniques performed directly on the sexual organs with a firm touch. If you haven't heard these terms before, *yoni* means vagina and *lingam* means penis in Sanskrit," said Jade.

On the first day, the class learned the *sensitive massage*; half of the students received it, and the following day those same students offered it. It was interesting for Sofia and Paulo to see each other touching other people naked, yet somehow it felt entirely natural, healing, even clinical. It was as if there was nothing sexual about it.

On the third day, they all learned the *yoni* and *lingam* massage techniques. On days four and five, the students practised offering and receiving *yoni* or *lingam* massage with a person of the same gender. On days six and seven, they did the same with someone of a different gender. Sofia wondered what Anney might have done, as she did not identify with either gender. However, as Anney had chosen not to attend the Tantra massage course, that was not an issue.

It felt like a very respectful and clinical environment. The students were there to heal and to receive healing; there was utter respect for the vulnerability of the practice – that was the nature of the energy. It was undoubtedly an interesting new experience for Sofia, which somehow did not even feel too challenging. Still, if she were to be honest with herself, she did not feel like she experienced noticeable healing as a result, either. Other people said they had, though; plus a small minority felt triggered, insecure, ashamed and, in one case, abused. They knew they had their own processing to do, with Jade's support if needed. In the end, Sofia's takeaway was learning that sexual energy is a powerful energy that can stir up a lot but potentially also heal deeply.

When that process was over, Sofia and Paulo exchanged sensitive, *yoni* and *lingam* massages between them. That felt safe to both of them and it was interesting to share experiences. Regardless, since neither of them experienced perceptible healing from it, it was not something they decided to continue practising. As Ron kept saying, "There are countless techniques in Yoga; try them all and keep the ones that work for you." Perhaps that was just not their practice.

By the time the class was ready to leave Jamaica, a few things had changed. The new hut that Paulo and Sofia had so diligently worked on was ready and beautiful; the locals had given them two "Jamaica, no problem" tea cups (one yellow and one orange, which they treasured for years to come); Agnes decided to join the group for the next journey and offer more biodanza classes; and most people surfed better than when they arrived. It had been another paradigm-shifting journey, which all the students were very grateful for. Sofia, for one, was unquestionably going to miss the clear warm ocean and white sands.

Ananda arrived with the new plane tickets. In the previous weeks, Sofia had tried once again to find out the following country, but it was in vain as the Swami was not keen to feed her ego. That information was irrelevant (if not detrimental) to their spiritual growth; therefore, it was not given. When Sofia finally received her ticket, she instantly recognised the "LIS" next to her name. Lisbon, Portugal. Now that she had more awareness, she felt hesitant to go to the country where she had spent all her life and developed her egoic patterns. She was afraid of what she might discover about herself and others. With that thought, she was overtaken by a gloomy mood.

Chapter 8 – Manipura Chakra

The class was staying in the *ashram* in Lisbon, which was small and in the middle of the city. Despite the city's historical beauty, the most sensitive students could feel a barrier of dense, chaotic, anxious energy there, especially since the group had been away from cities for over three months. The scarcity of nature, the cemented ground, buildings everywhere, crowds, cars beeping, impatience and pollution were quite difficult for some, including Sofia, who found herself avoidant.

In the Yoga class, they started discussing the third chakra. The teacher said, "Manipura chakra is located in the belly and connected to the element of Fire, the sense of eyesight and the qualities of power, activity, drive and transformation. While the previous chakras had a strong focus on the physical and interpersonal levels, Manipura offers a new level of individual freedom, enabling a keen sense of self-agency and a well-defined personality. People with a healthy activation of this chakra tend to have a strong, often magnetic and extroverted personality, with a good sense of self-worth, self-esteem, and a grounded self-confidence that cannot be shaken by external elements. That allows the person to rise above other people's opinions, social norms, the pursuit of enjoyment and the pull of bodily instincts and be their higher self, which conveys a sense of autonomy and independence.

"This chakra allows the person to be deeply connected to their values and ideals, drawing a sense of honour and pride and reclaiming the right to act without shame or inhibitions, based on living by their principles and knowing their intrinsic value. Their clear and firm attitudes are revealing of willpower, assertiveness, diligence and a strong sense of responsibility that moves things forward.

"People with a harmonious Manipura typically have the capacity to change their circumstances by drawing on their innate resourcefulness, passion and spontaneity.

"They experience an inherent dynamism, which allows for personal growth and self-improvement. Their mind is engaged, versatile and prepared to make decisions, reach conclusions and adapt, which, allied to their motivation, leads to success and mastery at work and in life.

"At this level, people can be influential, often in positions of leadership and authority, usually in a charismatic way, leading by inspiration while being grounded in their own truth.

"Manipura's willpower, self-discipline and self-control offer the drive to commit to whatever decisions they choose in the context of healing; for example, to exercise, give up addictions, change behaviours or pursue new social settings. For those with a balanced Manipura, energy is spontaneously generated and instead of reaching exhaustion like many others, they can spontaneously manifest vitality in moments of need. Even on a mental level, there is a vivacity and ability to overcome laziness and procrastination by making firm decisions and carrying them out.

"Strength and courage are key features of this chakra. People with an active Manipura are often strong defenders of justice, providers of charity and protectors of those less fortunate.

"Humour and laughter are also associated with this chakra, which can manifest as a genuine playfulness."

Sofia contemplated that Manipura had the potential to be a vital chakra on both the horizontal and the vertical paths. It also had the power to corrupt everything and cause massive destruction. Such is the Fire element.

Sofia had a tendency to think that she was alone in how she felt, but living in *ashrams* was slowly changing that. She started to notice that there was a collective subconscious where many people would experience the same feeling simultaneously. Currently, there seemed to be a wave of restlessness; other times, it would be sadness, anger or something else. She once asked Ron how to protect herself from that influence and he taught her a protection technique but it did not seem to be working for her currently… Perhaps because the restlessness was her own.

Sofia took Paulo to her favourite café in Lisbon to eat her favourite *jesuita* – a specific Portuguese pastry tart with egg custard in the middle and sometimes almonds on top. The waiters seemed bored and unhappy, which used to feel normal to her, but now that she had been to New Zealand, where people were happy in their jobs, encouraged to follow their dreams and working on what inspires them, that was exceedingly difficult to bear. They also bossed each other around instead of being supportive, enquiring, or teaching more. Sofia was trying to find inner joy but could not shake that feeling of restlessness. People did not seem to care about one another; instead, they focused on what they wanted for themselves. The food in the *ashram* was the same every day. Devimar, with whom she shared a room, kept picking on her for seemingly unimportant things. Everything felt negative.

Seeing Sofia in distress, Paulo, in his infinite care, kindness and generosity, bought an enormous quantity of mushrooms, pasta and cream and cooked creamy mushroom pasta for everyone, surprising Sofia with one of her favourite meals. He couldn't fix the world, but he could offer her a delicious, comforting meal. Sometimes, she felt his presence like a gentle light in the midst of darkness.

Another thoughtful surprise he had set up for her was enrolling them both in an introduction to meditation course with a Buddhist monk he had known for some time. The course would take place over four Saturday mornings, starting in two weeks. Paulo said it had helped him with meditation many years ago and he would be happy to revisit it with her as a refresher. The idea felt exciting to Sofia.

That week's biodanza class was quite different. Agnes teamed up with a male Portuguese teacher from Lisbon, plus there were considerably more people in the class, which was a different – yet no less enriching – dynamic. During the class, Sofia noticed how much avoidance she felt towards men. She became aware that whenever there was a shared exercise, she gravitated towards women and skipped the men. Even if she did not find an immediate solution for the issue, she appreciated that she discovered something new in each biodanza class. She marked that aversion as a topic to keep deepening.

On the second week, Ananda elaborated on the manifestations of an imbalanced Manipura chakra. He explained that the main imbalances revolve around power and control dynamics. If the disruption is on the *yang* side of the spectrum, people tend to have issues with being powerful in disruptive ways: by controlling, dominating, abusing, provoking and manipulating. If the issue is on the *yin* side, they might feel powerless, standing on the receptive end of those tendencies.

On the *yang* end of the spectrum, people can exhibit feelings of superiority, such as arrogance, entitlement, self-aggrandisement, stubbornness, selfishness, recklessness or ruthless independence. In contrast, on the *yin* end, they can experience victimisation, inferiority, lack of courage, self-doubt, dependence, shame, fear or self-neglect.

The Swami explained that people with an imbalanced Manipura often experience a lack of self-esteem, self-confidence and internal states of not feeling good enough. To compensate for that, on the *yang* side, people can show ambitiousness, competitiveness, praise-seeking and a desire to conquer social status or business positions, while on the *yin*, an incapacity to assert solid internal values, shyness, introversion, isolation, withdrawal, lack of boundaries, inability to say 'no', and vulnerability to abuse.

Ananda added that the core emotion at the heart of this chakra is anger – in all its various forms, such as aggressiveness, rage and conflict. Such a strong energy often manifests as anxiety. The fact that Manipura chakra relates to both anxiety and humour explains why human beings often laugh when they are anxious.

Lastly, he articulated that the weak willpower characterising an imbalanced Manipura involves a lack of self-discipline and self-control. The resulting reduced internal dynamism impairs their ability to change, transform, make decisions and adapt. One can experience a certain passivity, lack of follow-through, self-sabotage and low motivation.

Before the class ended, Ron requested that each student ask their families if they could spend the following week with them. The goal was to reflect on one's family dynamics and see how they have shaped their own. Sofia felt very hesitant about what she might discover about herself through that reflection; that was one of her biggest fears. As such, it made sense that it was happening – she had heard that our fears tend to come true because the Universe does not hear the word 'no'. So, if we say, "I *do not* want to be confronted with my deepest egos," the Universe will hear: "I *do* want to be confronted with my deepest egos." Which makes sense according to the law of resonance, she thought, as we attract what we are emanating. Sofia contacted her parents, who were very welcoming in receiving her in a week.

During that week's biodanza class, Sofia noticed that she was planning her every move; she was thinking about which ways to dance, where to and towards whom, and then mentally executing that instead of allowing her body to express itself naturally and creatively. Through that, she realised that most of her human experience was lived through the mind, thinking rather than being embodied. Sofia could see just how disconnected her body and mind were and how the mind did not have access to how the body was feeling or what it wanted or needed. Essentially, she lived in the mind. When she discussed that with Paulo, he told her about a Gnostic teaching that states that human beings have three centres: physical, emotional and mental. If one of them is overused (in Sofia's case, the mental one), it draws too much energy to itself and away from the others. The excessively active mental centre causes the physical and emotional centres to be depleted, unbalancing the entire system. It requires conscious effort to transfer the energy to the underused centres. Sofia found it helpful to gain that awareness, though she intuitively knew that was yet another topic for her to deepen over time.

In the meantime, Paulo was also struggling with his own issues at the *ashram*. Until that point, he felt very stable; in fact, over the last few years, he thought he might no longer be capable of crying. Yet one day, he went to the Eduardo VII Park with Sofia, close to the *ashram*, and sobbed until he had no more tears to cry. There was no known reason. Sofia was witnessing

85

what she had recently been told about *ashrams*: that the pull towards consciousness was so high that spiritual growth was accelerated and unresolved issues bubbled up much faster and more powerfully. She booked a hotel room, filled it with candles, rose petals and incense, plus some food she had arranged and then brought Paulo there as a surprise. They enjoyed a bath together, relaxed to some soft music and rested for the night. However, as their intimacy increased, so did Sofia's distress. While entering more intimate stages of love-making, Sofia felt her PTSD increase, her grief and anger rise, and her fears surface. They navigated that exploration together, with care and vulnerability. Through every moment, Paulo was adamant that he did not want Sofia to do anything she did not feel like. That alone was helpful in shifting Sofia's beliefs. Though she could also feel her self-pressure starting to rise, telling her that while he was patient, he would probably not wait around forever. She felt like she needed to heal soon or conjure up some sexual energy so she would not lose him. Paulo's genuine acceptance highlighted that the issue was no longer that Sofia's lack of sexual desire was not accepted by men – it was not accepted by herself; the belief that there was something wrong with her was too ingrained.

On Monday morning, the group met for Yoga class and talked about family and how we learn our patterns from them from a very young age – that is how we first understand how to operate in the world. We assimilate what love looks like by seeing our parents or caregivers love each other. To use a stereotyped example: if Dad is violent towards Mum, we get the implicit message that violence is a part of love. If Mum is manipulative towards Dad, we learn that manipulation is acceptable in love. We may even rebel against that once we start to question the world, but we are still likely to have normalised those behaviours, which makes us biased and desensitised to aspects that other people might more easily notice. He explained that these patterns are usually totally or partially unconscious. Still, our consciousness wants to be free, so it keeps attracting people (partners, friends) who will lead us to face those patterns so that we can overcome them. That is why we keep having similar types of people coming into our lives cyclically and the same situations repeatedly happening through different people or environments. The teacher stated that as we transcend those patterns, we will stop attracting partners who represent the unavailable Dad or the emotionally distant Mum. Sofia made a note to try to identify those patterns in her family and herself.

The class finished with the *asana* practice as usual, plus another posture for the current chakra. Manipura postures were related to endurance or abdominal compression, elongation and twisting.

After class, each person went to their parents' place, except the students whose families were far away, like Anney, who was from the USA, or Elixir, from Argentina. Even Merle, who was from France, flew to Paris to see his mum. Anney was disappointed by that, as she was slightly attracted to him, and they could have otherwise stayed in the *ashram* together. Merle was a young man with a lone-wolf vibe, slightly removed but remarkably observant. He was stunningly beautiful and thin, with long dark-blond hair and piercing blue eyes.

Sofia arrived at her parents' house. They were welcoming as usual; her mum made the food she liked and they played their traditional card game. They talked about superficial things, which worked well because there were no arguments. With more awareness, Sofia could now consciously see the things that used to annoy her unconsciously. The rigidity, the judgement about what she was doing with her life, the pressure to act in certain ways, the questioning of her decisions, the subtle manipulation, the lack of ownership, the underlying criticism, the assumptions, the aggressiveness in speech, the disconnection from emotions that were acted out instead... Sadly, those were not even the most difficult elements. The most painful part was realising that all those things existed within herself; Sofia had somehow learned and integrated them. Seeing them in others was triggering because it was a *mirror* of the aspects she hated in herself. While talking about this on the phone with Paulo, he reminded her: "Things can only trigger you when they are already inside you; otherwise, you would feel indifferent or see them with compassion." He continued, "There is a story about an incredibly angry man who came up to the Dalai Lama and started yelling and cursing at him. The spiritual leader's followers looked at him attentively to see how he would respond. The Dalai Lama patiently listened to the man and then broke into a smile with great love and compassion for his suffering. Because he had no internal mirror for the man's anger, he did not take it personally, feel disrespected, or have the need to respond, as he could see it was entirely the man's projection." Sofia was inspired but could not imagine a reality where she would see all these things around her with equanimity, recognising that they were simply not about her. Regardless, from that point onwards, that became one of her highest aspirations.

One day that week, Sofia had a very challenging conversation with her father. He accused her of being irresponsible for leaving a successful job when the market was so down, abandoning a good long-term relationship for no valid reason, travelling when she could be working, and joining some crazy group of kumbaya people whose intentions were unknown but undoubtedly not good. He was furious at her. Unfortunately, at that moment, Sofia did not remember the Dalai Lama, compassion, or anything else. Instead of recognising that those were merely perspectives stemming from his fears, belief systems and social conditioning, she took them personally and got very triggered. She felt defensive, identified and humiliated. No questions were asked, just assumptions and accusations thrown at her. Nothing positive was mentioned; only what was perceived as wrong, stated as an absolute truth. Sofia felt like crying or screaming, so she walked away and did both. Afterwards, since no one had any knowledge of how to repair relationships in the immediate family, they all just pretended like nothing had happened and continued to have their lunches and dinners, hoping that the heat would blow over. Sofia felt crushed, not only by his claims but also by her own response – becoming angry and taking things personally. She had failed miserably at her aspiration to be equanimous.

Later she spoke with Paulo again, sharing that disastrous experience. He replied, "I have another story for you. More of a question, really. Let's say I have a friend who is holding a pen in his hand. He asks me to take the pen.

I don't want the pen, so I refuse it. He asks me again: *Please take the pen; I really want you to take it.* I still don't want it, so I refuse again. He asks again, more firmly and assertively: *Please take the pen; I need you to take it right now.* Stubbornly, I still don't take the pen. At the end of the day, who has the pen?"

Sofia answered, "Well, he does, of course."

Paulo concluded, "That's exactly right. If someone tries to give you anger, offers it to you over and over again in different forms and you simply won't take it, at the end of the day, they are still left with it." "You're right!" she reflected. "I don't have to become angry just because someone is angry at me. If I do, no matter which argument I win with them, I've already lost with myself."

Over the weekend, Sofia's parents invited her siblings for a family lunch. Whether what followed came up organically or if there was an intention to expose Sofia is not known. Either way, her father again got terribly angry at her at the lunch table, making new and unexpected accusations and insults. As usual, no one defended Sofia; not her mum, who would always agree with him, as they were a team; not her siblings, who were forever afraid to rock the boat. Everyone expected Sofia to defend herself, as usual, to be angry and push back. Yet Sofia had the light of her soul on her side, and she would not be broken by anger. She tapped into a force inside her that was beyond space and time – an almost imperceptible echo within her, telling her she was more powerful than any external events that could ever happen in her life. Sofia took it all, quietly. Since she was not fighting back, her dad continued to elaborate, thinking she might not have understood what he meant. But she understood it, all right. She felt humiliated, outraged, wronged, misunderstood, furious. On top of which, she felt complicit for staying quiet instead of defending herself, which she felt horrible about. Still, it was clear to Sofia that none of that was more important to her than acting in integrity with herself, so she refused to react in anger. The longer and louder he spoke, the more her siblings looked frantically between him and her. Sofia could almost hear them in her mind, screaming, "Why won't you defend yourself?" An enormous part of her wanted to, but that part was ego and she refused to feed it. She would feed her conscious wolf, which so desperately needed nutrition. At the end of all that, she simply responded, "I hear your perspective." And ate the rest of her food. He seemed even angrier, but he kept his damned pen!

Sofia could pinpoint that as one of the most significant moments in her life. After lunch, she went to her room, sobbed, and grieved for the rest of the day. She cried for all the times that she became angry when she did not have to; for all the despair she felt in her adolescence, with no one to protect or support her; for how the hatred had consumed her and distanced her from her true self; for all the violence she had experienced, and the anguish, suffering and agony she withstood – so many years of carrying that. What she also realised, though, was that she was the one doing the carrying, which meant that she also had the power to let it go. The events that happened over lunch were indeed a shock and extremely difficult to bear because they marked the breaking of the pattern. The following times got easier and easier; she could more effortlessly observe rather than react, increasingly tuning into the relief of not becoming angry, plus her ability to not take things personally increased exponentially. In time, she would learn to feel entirely at peace as people threw their anger at her – which, she realised, makes for a perfect mirror for others to witness their own violence.

It was an intense journey at her parent's house and Sofia was pleased to be heading back to Lisbon. Instead of going to the *ashram*, she spent the night with Paulo; they comforted each other and shared experiences and insights. Sofia got to know his apartment, which was so beautiful and wonderfully designed, with striking orange and brown colours. She felt right at home there – especially with him.

On Monday morning, they were back at the *ashram* for class. Sofia realised, in being away, how much it meant to her to live in an environment where everyone aspired towards the same philosophies and values and was held by a shared container, like the school of Yoga. The feeling that she was part of something, rather than alone in life, was more precious than anything she had ever encountered.

The theme for the class was ego, which they had touched on before, but now Ananda elaborated: "What is ego and how does it actually work? The ego is a mechanism of *compensation* for the lack of consciousness. For example, if we can only access a fraction of the capacity to love in our being, our ego will fill up the rest, for instance, with attachment. Likewise, it will compensate for our lack of safety with control, our lack of self-esteem with pride, and so on.

"If we can access the higher emotions and divine qualities of our being, we will no longer need the egos to compensate. In fact, while the ego starts off wanting to help, it ends up forming a major roadblock in accessing the self, because we become so identified with the *persona* we created that we forget who we truly are."

Someone asked, "But egos can be useful, right? If a lion comes to eat me, isn't it useful to feel fear, to motivate me to run away?"

The Swami replied, "Egos are never necessary. If your consciousness is awake, you will simply determine that you don't want to be eaten by a lion and leave. You don't need fear for that. In fact, fear could lead you to freeze or panic; all the while, you would have already been eaten."

Ananda continued, "Egoic traits (for example, anger, fear, jealousy, greed, arrogance, stubbornness, impatience, self-deprecation, lust, martyrdom, as well as countless others) not only take up the majority of our thoughts but also cause us to look at reality with tinted glasses, typically of very low resonances, hence hindering our connection with our higher self. To put in perspective how much ego we have: Gnostics believe that a regular being has ninety-seven per cent of ego and only three per cent of awakened consciousness.

"We can tackle ego on two fronts simultaneously: Connecting with the qualities of our higher self and exploring our psychology. In other words: light work and shadow work. One will connect us with our higher frequencies and resonances and the other will bring consciousness to what is in our subconscious and why we are feeling and acting in the ways we are.

"By transcending our ego, we reclaim our sovereignty. We can wake up in the morning and decide: *Today, I will feel unconditional love* – and indeed feel it all day long."

Hearing that, Sofia wondered if some people who go to therapy actually regress if they focus primarily on shadow work and not enough on their higher self. Surely that could increase the resonances of ego and set them back. She figured that if she ever did somehow become a psychologist, she would be a holistic one and cover not only the psychological dimension but also the spiritual and physical ones.

Agnes continued to co-facilitate the biodanza classes. In the current class, Sofia looked into her avoidance of men, which she had recently become aware of. She realised it was more profound than an avoidance; deep down, in a secret place in her subconscious, she actually felt disgusted by men. If Sofia even sensed a man's sexual energy, that brought up imaginary strings to all the past situations of abuse she had experienced and all the men who sexualised her or wanted to take her sexual energy for themselves, irrespective of what *she* wanted. She had been unconsciously suppressing that aversion, but it was now coming to the surface in a way that could no longer be ignored. When she discussed that with Paulo, he asked her how she felt about women. Sofia said that sexually, they excited her much more than men. Their bodies were typically rounder, softer, sweeter, gentler and with less hair, plus they were probably more inclined to prioritise pleasing the other rather than gratifying themselves. She had shared some kisses with women in the past, mostly under the influence of tequila, but had never experienced sexual interactions beyond that. He had asked that question simply out of curiosity, yet it stayed on Sofia's mind. She wondered if there would be opportunities for her to explore that. Devimar told her about a type of workshop called a 'temple' that was happening that week, hosted by a nearby community. In that temple, people could be naked or with as many or as few clothes as they liked, exploring interactions of any nature with whoever would like to explore with them. She thought that could be exciting and asked Paulo what he thought. He was open to it though not very invested, but willing to explore it with her. Ron and Devimar were also going. Sofia had only recently discovered that they were lovers.

The four of them arrived at the community and were taken to a big venue; a sensually dressed woman was at the door burning a sage incense stick and welcoming each newcomer. As they entered, they walked into a mystical, loving, candle-lit space with flowers on the walls, tapestries on the ground and a beautiful altar with various crystals and sacred artefacts. There was a circle of cushions where people sat and some soft background music playing. The two facilitators explained that each person there was encouraged to make a commitment to honour and look after themselves, to be clear to others about their boundaries and to explore whatever they liked. Everyone agreed; the atmosphere felt safe and free. They all stood up and the facilitators placed the cushions in different corners of the room to make way for people to start walking, exploring and gravitating towards whatever or whoever they felt attracted to. Sofia felt happy that Paulo was there; she felt safe with him. Being there enabled her to observe her acute aversion towards most men, from whom she steadily but discretely steered away. Paulo was there mainly to support Sofia, so he stayed close to wherever she was. He did not seem too interested in engaging with other people and only exchanged some touch here and there. On the other hand, Sofia felt extremely excited about that permission to explore women. She started by touching hands with another woman, then softly caressing her arms and enjoying the feeling of receiving gentle touch in return; their hands moved over each other's chest, to their bellies... Their faces came closer to each other and their cheeks touched softly; they kissed the corner of the other's lips and could feel each other's breath deepening. They kissed softly on the lips, tentatively at first but then with more confidence and passion, enjoying it completely. Their hands gripped firmly to each other's back, waist and legs; waves of pleasurable energy started to move through them. Sofia explored the feeling of the different parts of her body touching the different parts of the woman's body; the back of her hand on her forearms, her shoulders gently on the woman's back, her forehead on her neck... They explored each other sensually and very presently until, eventually, they naturally drifted away from one another and went on to discover new sensations. Sofia had a few more experiences of kissing and caressing with women, which felt vastly more exciting than with men. When men even walked in her direction, her body gave her a clear 'no', and she moved away. That also happened when Ron came close to her – she did not even look back to see his slightly disappointed expression. As she moved on, there were two women gently touching each other. They looked at her with a subtle invitation to join in. As Sofia approached them, they began to interact with her gently. Being so softly touched by two women at the same time, with so many different sensations arising in multiple parts of her body, Sofia noticed that at that moment, there was only presence, with no mind getting in the way. Her body was overtaken by desire; waves of pleasure were moving through her, her lips were on one of the women's shoulders and then her neck, the woman's hands were on her chest and breasts, her arms were pulling the woman closer, their legs were crossing... Their whole bodies came into contact with each other, sometimes soft and sweet, other times passionate and fervent. Their rhythm would accelerate, then slow down and accelerate again... At some stage, it did not matter whether they were touching, kissing or breathing; they were all involved in an energetic bubble of ecstatic pleasure, with their bodies organically moving together into thoughtless, delightful orgasmic states in waves of pure bliss. Sofia had never experienced sexual energy flowing as naturally and freely as there and then. She felt safe, relaxed and open. There were no shadows of trauma, fear, anxiety, or overthinking of what she should do. There was only ecstasy, sensuality and enjoyment. She was not *forcing* herself to be there; she *wanted* to be there and wanted that moment to last longer, as opposed to hoping for it to end as soon as possible. Perhaps that was what sex felt like to non-traumatised people. No wonder they liked it so much. Gradually the energy became less intense, the rhythms became slower and their bodies gained more distance. They carried on in different directions. Still under the influence of that sexual energy, Sofia approached and began caressing Paulo, who caressed her back. She was suddenly struck by a wave of excitement, realising that they were allowed to make love just there, in front of everyone.

That excitement also carried him; in that instant, it did not matter that Ron was only three or four metres away or that Devimar was looking at them through the corner of her eye. All that existed was their excitement and love for each other. The passion was immense, as was the thrill of doing something so taboo; neither of them cared about anything else at that moment. Sofia felt enormous freedom in not having to hide her pleasure and not having to comply with rules. Doing what she felt like doing on her own terms was liberating and exhilarating. At that moment, there was no psychic door closed by trauma, no PTSD and no past... There was only her sexual self, fully present, joyful and ecstatic. They moved in sync with each other until they moved as one, their beings slowly dissolving into the bliss of oneness.

That night they slept at Paulo's apartment. It was not until Sofia was lying in bed, left to her own thoughts, that she started to process that evening. She could no longer deny that her desire *existed*, so the possibility of her being asexual was off the table. Though it was with women that her desire came out – perhaps because she felt safe; she had no sexual trauma with them. The temple also showed her that Sofia might be bisexual, or even pansexual, a term that she had recently learned that meant being attracted to beings for who they are, regardless of gender. Irrespective of how she labelled herself, she thought how incredible her relationship with Paulo was that they could have sex with other people in front of each other without feeling threatened. Of course, that had happened within a particular context where no romantic feelings were involved – who knows what that might feel like under different circumstances.

To Sofia's dismay, as the energy of the night faded, she noticed that the psychic door to her sexual self had closed again and the PTSD returned. As powerful and insightful as that experience had been, it had not healed her.

The following day, Sofia and Paulo began their meditation course. The Buddhist monk was fantastic and took them on a journey through what meditation was, how and why to do it and different types of practices. He explained: "Our mind is typically active all day. We live a situation once and then tend to relive it in our mind over and over again, creating different scenarios, labelling how good or bad it was, and elaborating on ways it could have been different or how it relates to other stories in our lives, etc. We don't live a painful situation once; we live it a thousand times.

"Usually, all the mind knows how to do is to remember the past and imagine the future based on past patterns. In other words, it keeps regurgitating what it already knows. Over the years, it starts to identify with those thoughts, creating a sense of I – "I am, I do, I think" – with its own sphere of tendencies, desires, patterns and impressions that reinforce that sense of I. At some point, it completely forgets that the I was its own creation and assumes it to be the only unquestionable reality.

"So why meditate? During meditation, the mind quietens, yet we remain awake and alert. Detached from our past, future, thoughts, ideas and emotions, what remains is the awareness of who we truly are. In other words, when our mind is silent, our spirit can manifest. The spirit knows exactly what it needs in order to awaken and heal; all we need to learn is how to silence the mind.

"Additionally, in meditation, a door to our subconscious opens. Beyond it lies the root of our emotions, patterns, behaviours, belief systems and memories. By accessing our subconscious, we can enter that shadow world. From there, our consciousness may have enough force to directly resolve the issues we are facing without further involvement of our mind. Or, for more complex problems, it may have to take alternative paths, like bringing the issues to our conscious mind so we can gradually understand and deal with them, intuitively giving us the answers to deal with those issues or guiding us towards situations that might help."

Sofia was finding the course very insightful and felt excited about meditating.

In the following Yoga class, Ananda talked about power and control. He claimed that power comes from within, from the strength and force of our being. Unfortunately, most people are disconnected from their inner power and as he had previously mentioned, the ego works by compensation.

96

That means that to the extent that people are disconnected from their inner power, they will look for sources of power outside themselves, attracting or being attracted to others with power or exerting their power over others.

Hearing that, something clicked in Sofia's mind; she realised her motivations for wanting to know their next country in advance. She rushed to journal her findings: *I try to find safety outside because I don't feel it inside; to control because I feel out of control; to find power because I feel powerless. I don't trust the laws of the Universe to bring me what's holistically best for me; I think I (this arrogant I) know what's best and should therefore have things my way. I wonder how many ways people do that – trying to control how they are seen, how their partner feels, what others are doing... The list goes on.*

Sofia had a feeling that if she started exploring that, those questions would be only the tip of the iceberg, as power was one of those subtle family dynamics that was still very unconscious to her, which she would one day have to look at... But for now, she was tired of the intensity and hoping for a smooth week. A sharing circle was scheduled for later that week, which Sofia was anticipating would be lovely and connecting. In all honesty, she was looking forward to the next chakra – leaving the struggles of the ego behind and connecting to her heart and soul.

The week started off wonderfully. Paulo asked Sofia to meet him in the Largo do Chiado, the old part of Lisbon, and to make sure she dressed in something fancy. Out of all the things she could have imagined, what happened next was not one of them. He came dressed in a fancy black suit and tie, took Sofia by the hand and they entered a beautiful building, perhaps Gothic or Romanesque. Many people were seated on long wooden benches, looking at a stage that was still behind curtains. He said, "I have to go, but stay here and enjoy the show." *Had he invited Sofia to watch a show by herself?* She was increasingly puzzled but had a feeling of wonder, trust and excitement. Coming from him, she was sure it would be something spectacular. When the curtain was lifted, she could see a majestic choir and a symphonic orchestra and to her disbelief, Paulo was among the singers.

97

They sang delightful classical music, which was so harmonious and perfectly tuned that it could have come from heaven itself. Sofia gazed at him in awe... *How many more hidden talents could that man have that he humbly kept to himself?* She felt gratitude for being alive.

When the concert ended, Sofia expressed how much she admired Paulo. Humbly, he acted as if he had not done anything out of the ordinary. They went to his apartment for the night. After such a delightful evening, they went to bed and were too excited to sleep. They embraced and kissed, and Sofia appreciated the cuddles and the intimacy. She could have spent the whole night like that. But as Paulo's enthusiasm grew, his kisses became more sensual and Sofia could feel the sexual excitement manifesting in his body. She had a glimpse of disappointment about his energy having escalated; she was perfectly happy and comfortable with how things had been up until then. But she believed that *his* response was natural – it was *her* trauma-based resistance and absence of libido that were unnatural, so any negative feelings she had were immediately turned against herself; shame, guilt, self-blame. Her old subservient patterns kicked in and she felt pressured to please him and act as if she was in the mood for sex. Over the years, she had developed a *sex actress* persona for that exact situation where she did not feel ready but still pushed herself to have sex – it avoided conflict, made things easy and kept up appearances. Plus, she was too disconnected from her body and her boundaries to know the extent to which she *was not* ready – which opened up just enough room for the possibility that she *might be* ready. The *sex actress* was so natural for her that it became an automated response rather than a conscious decision. Hiding underneath the *actress*, Sofia was silently pleading: *Please stop.* She brought the attention back to her surroundings and moaned in a pleasant tone – to buy herself some time to figure out if she could turn the situation around; it was all happening so fast. Responding to her apparent enjoyment, Paulo kissed her more intensely; he closed his eyes and his breathing became audible. The *actress* saw that as a queue to make her breathing audible too, to keep looking excited and help him sustain his excitement. After all, if that was to end up in sex, Sofia could not just act like a corpse, could she? No, if she was to put herself through that, she might as well do it right. She knew that sex was important for men, so she was afraid of losing Paulo if it seemed problematic or disappointing. *Please stop,* Sofia kept pleading. The *sex actress* looked sensually into Paulo's eyes and smiled, trying to push herself to enjoy it. Responding to her sensuality, he gently placed himself on top of her and started moving his hands through her body, passing over her breasts, belly, bottom and legs... Sofia tried to calm herself down, comforting and reassuring herself that she was safe, that they loved each other, that they had already made love before, that it was for the greater good and that she would enjoy it in the end. The *actress* knew the next logical move was to start touching him too, so she passed her hands over his back, bottom and legs. Deep down, Sofia still had a glimpse of hope that the pace would somehow slow down and revert back to comfortable cuddles. *Please stop.* Paulo's facial expression and body responses indicated that he was enjoying her touch. The more he embraced his enjoyment, the more she was struck by the fear that the present interaction would indeed turn into sex – but she was too unaware, dissociated and in her mind to access her feelings. As he got closer to touching her pelvic area, it was evident to her that she did not feel ready to be touched there. She needed to avoid it somehow while still keeping up the appearance that she was excited. To prevent him from reaching her *yoni*, the *actress* simulated a wave of enjoyment where she pulled his body against hers and breathed more deeply – that placed her *yoni* out of reach. *Crisis averted. Please, please stop...* Perceiving her enjoyment as a sign that she wanted to increase intimacy, he undressed his shirt and pants. Sofia suppressed a feeling of dread – they had passed an invisible point of no return where she could no longer stop that motion towards sex without creating awkwardness, rejection or disappointment. Her old fears arose; that he would get mad at her, guilt-trip her, or punish her in some way if she did not comply. That was part of sexual trauma – those things would have been true for her first boyfriend. It did not matter that they were not true for Paulo; her feelings still responded *as if they were.* It did not matter that Paulo did not pressure her at all. She had internalised all the pressure onto her inner masculine. She no longer *needed* a male to pressure her; she was perfectly

99

capable of executing that all on her own. However, all those processes were deeply unconscious. *Pull yourself together.* At that point, Sofia accepted that sex was inevitable. She fully handed over the reins to the *sex actress*, who accepted the challenge. *"I've got this!"* said the *actress*, motivating and reassuring her. The *actress* acted more sexually and enjoyed the resulting look on his face; she knew she was turning him on, which gave her validation. She undressed herself and they touched each other without the barrier of so many clothes. He undressed his boxers. Looking at his naked body, Sofia had a PTSD flashback of Rico's body. Suppressing her disgust and simultaneously making sure her facial expression did not give it away, she made a conscious effort to bring her energy to her heart and picture being one with him spiritually. She looked into his eyes, his joyful expression, his loving energy. For a second, she could feel love instead of fear. Then, he kissed her neck, her chest and then her breasts. He played with his tongue on her nipples. Fear was back. She could sense that he was expecting that to be pleasurable for her. While she felt no pleasure at all, she was well aware that women are supposed to enjoy that situation. *Sex actress, help!* The *actress* closed her eyes and breathed more deeply, to make it appear as if she was having pleasure. Paulo started kissing her belly and then going down, at which point she disguised her panic by pulling him up, faking extra excitement. *I beg you, please stop...* Sofia imagined that if he went down on her, she would also have to do the same for him, but she was just too overwhelmed to look at his *lingam* – even with her poor awareness of boundaries, she could tell that was too much. As an excuse for pulling him up like that, the *actress* said, in a sensual voice, "Would you like to come inside?" At least if they had regular sex, she would not have to handle his genitals. He put on a condom and got ready to enter her. She embraced him passionately and made a conscious effort to focus on how much they loved each other and how they could become one through sex. She would try her best to experience and enjoy that. She pulled him close and kissed him passionately, feeling responsible for renewing his excitement after putting on the condom – otherwise, she might not cope with his potential embarrassment of losing an erection. He placed his genitals at the entrance

100

of her *yoni* and gently started making movements that got him closer and closer inside. Perhaps as a precaution, suspecting that something was off, or sensing that maybe she was not a 'full yes', he asked her, "Are you sure you want to do this?" Sofia quickly reflected, so he would not suspect something was wrong. Despite his tolerance and acceptance, she did not feel entitled to *never* have sex with him, so, occasionally, she would have to do it – *why not now?* It was as good a time as any, plus she had already gone through all the horrible pushing herself process that takes place at the beginning of the sexual act; now came the easy part, a few more minutes and it would be over. She said, "Yes." He slowly penetrated her, which she recognised as a queue to moan, demonstrating that all was well and she was excited. At that point, Sofia felt a hint of *real* pleasure. She placed all her focus on that pleasure, allowing it to expand. That helped suppress some of her fears and doubts. Openly expressing her pleasure led him to experience a lot of pleasure too and she enjoyed the feeling of power that gave her. She realised that through her movements, she could give him extreme pleasure and likewise take it away – that gave her a sense of control, which alleviated her powerlessness. She restrained his hands above his head. She moved him so he would lie down, then sat on top of him. When his pleasure was peaking, she would slow down. When it was slowing down, she would bring it back up. She was enjoying the game. She was alert. Deep down, she was afraid that if she stopped being in control or he ceased being aware, he might hurt her. Fortunately, unlike Rico, Paulo kept his awareness and did not hurt her. But her trauma-based vigilance was there nonetheless. She felt powerful and in charge. She played the game until he begged her to allow him to come. She felt her own pleasure rise and she intensified her moves so that they could climax simultaneously. He was screaming with uncontrollable pleasure, fully enjoying himself and surrendering to her while being firmly held down. She allowed herself and him to orgasm, fully and intensely, until eventually, she laid on top of him and they rested. Sofia felt a sense of achievement and relief; she was on the other side of sex, Paulo was satisfied, and now there would be no pressure to do it in the next few days. She enjoyed the sense of connection and intimacy that sex had brought him. All the painful feelings she had experienced had been dissociated and forgotten. She felt relaxed and happy. Though her womb was slightly painful – a fact that she did not give much thought to.

The next morning, Sofia felt inexplicably sad. Observing her, Paulo asked how it had been for her to make love to him. She automatically reassured him that she had really enjoyed it. That felt slightly dishonest, so she added, "Well, in the beginning, I always have to push myself a little bit, but when I get into it, I end up enjoying it." Paulo was startled. He asked, "How does that work, *exactly*?" Sofia had a bad feeling about where that was going. Still, she was determined to own up to her actions, so she moved past her shame and explained, "I just don't have sexual desire in the beginning and because of past experiences, sex feels a bit scary, so I feel slightly hesitant at first, but eventually I get into the flow and enjoy it a lot." That "a lot" was not entirely true, but in her panic state, she manipulatively added it hoping that Paulo would focus on that and let the topic go. Sadly, he was not after reassurance; it seemed like he was out for blood. "So, you don't feel like it, but you push through it and force yourself to do it anyway?" – he asked.

"Well, when you put it like that, it sounds way worse than it is…" she responded, even though she was shocked to hear it reflected back. She did not like the implications of that conversation and just wanted it to end, but Paulo was like a dog with a bone. "I think it sounds *exactly* as bad as it is. But OK, let's clarify. Your body is saying no, by not feeling sexual desire. Your emotions are saying no, by feeling scared and not ready. Your mind is trying to cope and make excuses. Yet you choose to ignore all that and have sex anyway. Am I missing something?"

More than anything, Sofia wanted to tell him that something was indeed missing, but deep down, a quiet truth within her knew there was not. Not settling for that, he brought his argument home. "You realise that if anyone else were doing that to you, that would be called *rape*?" Hearing that word caused Sofia's entire body to shiver. There it was, the place where she did not want to land. She had a reasonably successful long-standing strategy, invoking the *sex actress* to push through her sexual trauma, offering exciting sex, keeping her partners satisfied and buying herself the relief of a few days with no sex pressure. Now the *actress* was being questioned and the word *rape* was being thrown around. Sofia was intellectually racing to dismiss his theory, but her sharp logical mind had no arguments to offer. She reached for whatever she could. "It's more complex than that; there is a part of me that wants to connect in deeper ways..." She was going to continue, but it felt like a lie, so she abandoned her argument.

He said, "Let me make this abundantly clear, as *my own* boundary. I never, under any circumstances, want to make love with you unless your being is a 'full yes'. I want no part in what you are doing to yourself. If that means never making love to you again, I accept that. Is that clear?"

Sofia said, "Yes, of course." She was shocked that he would willingly give up sex forever, but even more significantly, she felt grief-stuck. The *sex actress* was a familiar role, whereas a 'full yes' to sex with a man was completely uncharted territory; she was not sure she was even capable of that. It felt unknown, unpredictable and mostly hopeless and scary. But she could not blame Paulo; if the roles were opposite, she would not want to take part in that either. She had no choice here – she would either have to heal or never make love to him again.

In the biodanza class that week, a man asked Sofia to dance. She froze and said what she usually says in that overwhelmed state: 'yes'. Sofia noticed that she had an inner voice that imagined (or projected) what people expected of her and told her that she would only be loved if she complied. That ranged from trivial things, like smiling most of the time, to bigger ones, such as compromising her boundaries. She wondered what it would feel like to live by her own values without the constant pressure to sacrifice herself for the promise of love. Sofia took out her journal and wrote: *It's time to stop taking responsibility for what others want from me; it's absurd! I am not to blame for their feelings or obligated to meet their needs. What people expect of me is none of my business. I am accountable for being true to my values, taking responsibility for my feelings, communicating my needs and setting boundaries if I need to. That is the extent of my role and I will no longer be responsible for other people's feelings and needs.*

While Sofia was trying hard to integrate those realisations, she knew that they were not yet grounded in her and that she had a long way ahead. She felt like writing that on the bathroom mirror so she would not forget it. She set an intention to frequently check in with herself and tune into her feelings, needs and boundaries. That was scary; people-pleasing felt easier and far less risky. Yet it came at a steep price, one that she was no longer willing to pay: the cost of neglecting *herself.*

Finally, the sharing circle had arrived; Sofia felt excited and expectant. She imagined that people would be really kind, soft-spoken and accommodating towards one another – like a glimpse of the world she intuitively remembered. In her innocence and naiveté, she would not even have considered any other way. It was the first time that the facilitators were holding one of these. They were told there were no rules; the goal was for each person to find their unique voice.

The circle started with a lot of silence, during which Sofia tried to contain her excitement about hearing what people would like to share. A couple of people shared things like missing home or feeling uncertain about the future, which was less uplifting than she had imagined, but she adjusted her expectations accordingly. Then Devimar shared a story about how she had a difficult childhood, always feeling like an outsider; then got pregnant and had deep feelings of connection and hope about the future, only to miscarry and lose all of it. She sobbed and expressed her deep grief. Witnessing a story that was bizarrely identical to her own, Sofia felt profoundly seen, like she was not alone in the world – someone else understood her pain, a pain that others could probably not begin to fathom. She felt the urge to reach out to her and share her own story so that Devimar also felt that she was not alone and that someone deeply understood *her.* So, Sofia shared her story with the group, which was a vulnerable and tender act, but her determination to help Devimar was bigger than her pain. Sofia expected a similar response from her, of sisterhood empathy, relief and feeling seen. Yet that was not at all what took place that day. Instead, Devimar looked at her with hatred in her eyes and accused her of stealing her experience to take the spotlight. She talked to Sofia as if she were a monster.

Sofia was mortified. With all the creativity in the universe, she could not have predicted that someone could react like that. She felt profoundly misunderstood, exposed, ashamed, humiliated, overwhelmed... Like someone had driven a stake through her heart in a vulnerable moment. She could not do anything except cry the entire day, after which she entered a state of shock. For a few days, she could not speak to anyone or even process what had happened.

Sofia was inconsolable; she missed the Yoga class on Monday, where they talked about courage, willpower and determination. She also missed the biodanza class. Paulo took her by the hand and they walked to what looked like a very fancy hotel that neither of them could afford. Sofia hoped he did not think he needed money to impress her or bring her happiness. He called the elevator and pressed the button for the last floor. When the elevator doors opened, they found themselves on a stunning terrace overlooking all of Lisbon. There was a snack bar on top where they could get some appetisers and drinks. The fresh air felt good and Sofia was happy to be up so high. She had jumped off aeroplanes and bridges and loved the silence and stillness of high places.

Paulo asked her, "How can I best support you? By holding you, listening, comforting you, bringing you food, brainstorming solutions, giving you space, showing you funny cat videos, or something else? What do you need?" She paused for a moment. No one had ever asked her that question before. People had always assumed what she needed, rather than asking her, and she had done the same to others. She had not realised that different people might need to be supported in distinct ways or that she herself could need different types of support at various times. That caused Sofia to recall the sharing circle situation. She wondered if, unlike her, not everyone who shared wanted to hear similar experiences to feel less alone.

Some people might prefer to have their story acknowledged, to have others observe with respectful silence, or to receive advice. Sofia shared with Paulo that she had been doing a lot of thinking and journaling over the last few days. With tears gently streaming down her face, she realised that because of the anger she had felt most of her life, she subconsciously felt like a *monster*. When Yoga came into her life, she disavowed the *monster* and created a new persona: a lovely, conscious *Yogi* on the spiritual path. Nevertheless, the new identity was also a mental construct and a fragile one at that. In her revision of herself, she had not yet gone deep enough; therefore, the *monster* still lurked underneath the *Yogi,* ready to rear its head at the first sign of confrontation, claiming: "I am who you *really* are." Devimar's anger was based on a projection that Sofia was trying to steal her spotlight, and while that in itself was not true, when she accused Sofia, it 'exposed' her as a *monster*. That incident shattered her *Yogi* identity and completely crushed her ego.

Paulo looked at Sofia with admiration. Her depth of introspection was something that had always fascinated him. "Sweetheart," he said, "you are a beautiful, kind-hearted person; that *monster* identification is absurd."

"Maybe," she contested, "but I can't just dismiss the *monster*; I have to question and dismantle it from within – only from there can I change my perception of who I am." Once Sofia had made sense of that, she felt enormous relief. Her identification as a monster was compensating for her lack of identification as the higher self. That was Ego 101. In fact, that had been a big ego lurking in the shadows, and as devastating and excruciating as it was to bring it to light, she could also see how that was needed. More than ever, she was determined to do anything to release her ego, no matter how painful, and step into her true self. Interestingly, that fierce drive to grow and change old habits fit perfectly into the theme of courage, willpower and determination discussed in that week's Yoga class.

The last week of the Manipura module had arrived. On the final Monday, Ananda spoke about the toxicity that anger generates in one's body, energy, emotions, mind and spirit. Given the anger that Sofia had felt and been exposed to growing up, she was already too familiar with its toxicity but found it an interesting discussion nonetheless. However, for Sofia, the most significant part of that 'teaching' actually took place later that week, during a sisterhood circle.

Sofia's decision to attend that circle was born out of a desire to continue her sexual healing journey. The circle was not hosted by the school; otherwise, Sofia would not have gone as she felt very unsafe around Devimar's attitude and projections. It was held in a Yoga centre downtown and facilitated by a woman who specialised in women's health issues, whom she had heard about through an old friend. The circle started with a beautiful meditation, followed by a space for emotional sharing. Sofia found it to be a very empathetic and bonding experience. Most of the stories that were shared were about sexual abuse. Some women cried, grieved or raged, everyone felt something, but at deeper levels, they all felt the same thing: the weight of masculine abuse. When it was her turn to share, Sofia shared the story of her sexual abuse, including details she had not shared with anyone before. Though she remembered the facts vividly, they were just intellectual memories; she did not feel or remember any emotions associated with them. Sofia expected as much, since that was how she had always remembered them. However, an interesting phenomenon happened. As she shared her story, though she could not feel anything, she noticed the women around her becoming restless. Sofia could see them twisting, moving uncomfortably, crossing their arms, adjusting their shoulders... There was a burning tension in the room and the only woman who could not physically feel it was Sofia. Watching them, Sofia realised she had suppressed her anger; she could not access it but those women were likely feeling it on her behalf. As a justification, she looked at them and said, "I wish I could be angry or scream, but I can't feel anything." The tension accumulated. Finally, out of the blue, one of the women could not take it anymore and screamed at the top of her lungs. Instinctively, all the others followed. Sofia was so shocked that something unblocked in her. She started to feel the tension in herself, the tiniest bit of anger rising. When enough anger built up, Sofia was ready to scream too. Strangely, her voice would not come, as if she were physically mute. The other women could feel that and screamed even louder; it became clear that they were not going to stop. Sofia had a feeling that they were screaming for themselves, for her, for humanity and for all the women and people that had ever been abused. Sofia closed her eyes and visualised the place of strength in her, the light of her soul that can create and destroy universes. From that place, her voice came. She unleashed a scream that was deeper, louder and filled with more rage than she had ever allowed herself to experience or express before. She yelled and bellowed and cried out all her pain and fury, unleashing not only her voice but also a part of herself that had been obscured until that moment. When she liberated the entirety of her anger, all the women, including herself, came to silence. After that release, Sofia never again forgot that she was not alone on her mission to heal the feminine; that there were women out there, everywhere in the world, going through the same journey.

That Saturday was the last session of the Buddhist meditation course. Sofia and Paulo learned more techniques and practised different meditations. The teacher said that even if they meditate only five minutes daily, they should already see some changes in their lives. Sofia felt inspired to try.

Agnes had announced that when the Yoga group moved on to the next country, she would be returning to South America. Sofia received such news with a lot of sadness, though she suspected that this would not be the end of biodanza in her life. So, that week's biodanza class had a flavour of sorrow regarding its end but also one of making the absolute most of the final experience with Agnes. For Sofia, the class was insightful, as usual. Perhaps as a result of the sisterhood release, she now found it possible to connect with men. Moreover, in the few times she chose to take that risk, she learned that she was capable of loving them unconditionally and experiencing beautiful moments together.

Despite the multitude of life-changing events in Sofia's life, she did her best to keep a vague sense of normality. She surprised Paulo by taking him on a light-hearted night out in the old part of Lisbon to a *fado house* – a typical tavern that plays traditional Portuguese music. Relishing a special meal while experiencing some first-class live singing, the universe had never been more beautiful.

When Ananda arrived with the tickets to the next country, Sofia felt proud of herself for not having asked where they were going next. She was determined to surrender to the cosmic intelligence of the universe, manifested in that case through the school. Her power should come from her connection to herself and Spirit; she should not need to control the reality around her to feel safe. Safety was in the power of her essence and the immortality of her being. Not that she had fully integrated that yet, but as Ron would say, "Fake it, till you make it." Even if someone fakes it, they still create a resonance with the real state and then the law of resonance kicks in, deepening the connection. She remembered reading a scientific article saying that the brain cannot tell the difference between eating an apple and thinking of eating an apple; the same regions of the same hemispheres light up. Therefore, by living according to her new principles, she would start resonating with them, deepening and increasingly attracting them, even if they were not fully integrated throughout the process.

Sofia finally looked at the tickets and almost screamed as she read "India." She had heard so much about *India ma*, mother India, since joining the Yoga world and could not wait to experience it for herself.

Chapter 9 – Anahata Chakra

Rishikesh felt immediately like home to Sofia. *What a privilege to be here, in the world capital of Yoga,* she thought. Sofia felt exhausted after the trip from New Delhi airport via night bus – a bus with small bed compartments intended for passengers to sleep in, even if that was an improbable goal considering the driver drove like a madman. She found herself fascinated by everything: the colours of the bright t-shirts and Yoga pants sold on the little stands along the road, the aroma of teas and spices brewing in the food stalls, the smell of delicious curries coming from the restaurants in an entirely vegetarian city, the cows on the street that forced the cars to stop but remained highly respected by humans as they roamed free, the Yoga studios at every other door, and most of all... *Ganga ma*, the Ganges river, in its immense glory and magnificence. It was as if it was calling out to Sofia. She was mesmerised. However, further exploration would have to wait; it was time for class.

Ananda spoke about Anahata, the heart chakra – the bridge between heaven and Earth, between the upper and the lower chakras. He stated that it was located in the chest area and related to the element of Air and the sense of touch. The qualities of love and empathy were at the heart of Anahata. The type of unconditional love that Sufis (mystics from Sufism, another esoteric tradition) refer to as *agape*, namely a warm, affectionate, fraternal, caring and profoundly intimate, non-sexual love. That differs from the Swadhisthana love, motivated by the desire for pleasure; *agape* is motivated by the desire to discover oneself reflected in the other.

The Swami mentioned that at this level, people manage to rise above material matters, individual will and actions, and into who they truly are. In other words, it is the journey from doing into being. The Anahata-balanced person goes through an expansion of consciousness to a selfless level, which

110

frees them from their individual desires and personality, offering the ability to be in union with self, others and the universe through unconditional love. That should not be mistaken for docility, conformity or blind compliance. There is an emotional maturity that comes from experiencing the real sense of unity and interconnectedness present in the universe, which leads to a refreshed sense of meaning and a paradigm shift.

Ananda articulated that this chakra relates to friendship and its inner elements: care, nurture, appreciation, human closeness and a heart-to-heart connection. Love is experienced as an internal state of being, which one can *choose* to extend to another person, rather than a feeling that happens in the context of (and is restricted to) a particular person, or worse, a feeling one expects to get from them. This type of love brings enormous potential for healing early emotional deficits and past experiences. Additionally, at this level, people gain complete access to the depth of their emotions and vulnerability.

He added that compassion is also at the core of Anahata, allowing one to remain calm and peaceful throughout disturbing situations by being able to empathise with the wounded parts of others instead of being centred on the conflicts and defences of the personality. He said they would discuss compassion in more depth in the near future.

He described that an important quality of this chakra is that it enables a profound reconciliation of opposite forces and integration of opposite feelings or aspects of ourselves or others, leading to a deep state of inner peace, harmony and joy.

Lastly, Ananda argued that rising above the 'I' allows the person to become a silent and detached witness to their experiences, a key element of mindfulness. Yogis sometimes describe that phenomenon as being in the eye of the storm, where everything around the person may be chaos and devastation, yet they do not lose their centre. The transcendence of the ego experienced at this level enables qualities such as acceptance, cooperation, a state of humbleness and the ability to surrender. People with a balanced Anahata have the capacity to manifest these qualities in communal ways of living. They tend to express altruism, generosity, devotion, sweetness and

111

emotional gentleness. They can be noble, uplifting, inspirational, able to see wonders where others see banality, and capable of living in a state of amazement and bliss.

That felt like home to Sofia. It was the essence of the echoes in her subconscious, secretly influencing her throughout her entire life. It also explained why she suffered so much in a selfish, unkind, disconnected world or when she expressed those aspects herself. In hearing about unconditional love, she remembered the essence of who she was. The silent echoes that had previously been hiding beyond her conscious memory had now gained a blaring voice, and nothing would ever be the same again.

Sofia explored the streets of Rishikesh with the excitement of feeling at home inside and outside in a city that reflected her. She realised what she had been missing in every other place she had been: Spirit. She did not mind the chaos, the uncomfortable accommodation, the unreliable electricity or hot water, the lack of information, the disorganisation, or having to go to a dozen tiny shops to get some basic grocery shopping done; she even coped with their squat toilets and poor hygiene conditions. Yet she could feel spirituality in the air, which was priceless to her. She could feel it in the Hindus with their altars praying to their deities, the mantra chanting that could be heard from random streets, and the enormous statues of Shiva in various roundabouts or by the Ganga. That was a colossal contrast to Portugal, where she felt mainly materialism and did not see herself reflected. She sat with Paulo on the terrace of a café that overlooked the Ganga, with colourful cushions on the ground and Tibetan prayer flags hanging from the canopy. She shared with him what was on her mind and then elaborated: "When we don't see ourselves reflected in our surroundings for long enough, we can start to forget who we are… At some stage, we may not remember it at all; the reality around us is all we know, so we start to identify with it. But the memory of who we truly are remains within a timeless echo in our subconscious; it is too powerful to disappear. It manifests as a disconnection from the external environment, a sense that something is missing and a feeling of meaninglessness, which I felt my whole life. That does not happen

112

to torment us though; it's there so we can find our way back home to the place of timelessness, where our spirit dwells. So we can remember *who we are*." Sofia proceeded, "I see now why I had to be exposed to all the oppression, disempowerment, abandonment and abuse I have. I see all the events of my childhood, adolescence and early adulthood and understand exactly why each had to happen so that I could awaken and remember who I am. Without them, I would have lived an entirely ordinary life on the horizontal path without realising what truly matters. I can see how each tragedy awoke parts of me, and together, they made up the pieces of the puzzle of who I am. Sure, I could not see the whole puzzle at the time; I could only see the pieces, which felt like *I was* in pieces. That process was painful and confusing, yes, but now I see that it is not until the puzzle is complete that we can see the whole picture and why we needed the pieces. Not that I'm claiming that my puzzle is complete, but at least now I see the puzzle and not just the pieces." Sofia felt compassion for herself and every person and situation in her past, even the ones that hurt her deeply. They were all teachers who led her to find the pieces of her puzzle. With that realisation, she felt a sense of forgiveness and gratitude in her heart.

Feeling the unconditional love emanating from her essence, Sofia emanated a powerful energy, feeling in love with life and all there was. The feeling was so immense that she went to the shores of the Ganga to integrate that state of being and ground herself in nature. She found herself sitting in a place of wholeness within herself; a place where polarities collapse, masculine and feminine are one, love lives in every cell, the heart rejoices, the soul pumps life into one's being, and the body is relaxed and at peace. Nothing was needed from others for her internal well-being and self-sustained joy.

From the abundance of Sofia's cup, a person appeared, a green-eyed man whose gaze met hers. Nothing was required from the other; nothing was expected at all. They could easily have met for one second or not at all. Yet their souls had a different agenda. Their bodies came closer, their arms embraced and she enjoyed feeling his essence; the warmth of his skin on hers, the pleasant smell of his neck, his heartbeat on her chest. Time moved

113

slowly and presence was heightened. Their breaths naturally aligned and it felt like only one being was breathing. Sofia could no longer understand if she was breathing him or if he was breathing her. Outside, the birds were singing for them and the wind caressed them with its gentle touch. As some light rain started blessing them with its sacred waters, their intimacy deepened, a glimpse of sexual energy arose and Sofia noticed a slight discomfort; her avoidance mechanisms got activated for a moment, questioning whether to end the experience. Whether that was the fear of intimacy with a male or the lingering psychological restraint chains of a monogamous stance she no longer followed, it was not clear. She checked in to see if her feelings for Paulo had been diminished, but her love for him remained untouched, which reassured her. Unconditional love was a bright light that obliterated all egos, and it had infinite room for all souls. To consciousness, what else was relevant in the universe if not that moment… So, pacifying the mind, she softened and surrendered to the experience. He also did not seem to let the rain or mind pull him away. Sofia found herself appreciating the feeling of his skin on her hands and allowed herself to explore that slowly and timidly. Her shyness was gradually overcome by light curiosity, consistently attuned to the permissions and consent his body language was expressing; no words needed to be spoken. Sofia invented ways in which she could hold him closer and learned that he could do the same. As their bodies found ways into each other, their breath deepened and their energy flowed in sync. She could feel his breath on her neck and his body pulling her in. As his face came in close proximity to hers, she could feel the intensity but also the discomfort and avoidance again. Sofia reassured herself that she was safe. While she noticed that some parts of herself still felt closed off, she reminded herself that it was within her power to set boundaries if needed. In the end, it was not needed because they were one; he could feel everything she felt and was completely attuned to her. Having transcended that fear, the separation between their bodies started to melt away and Sofia could no longer feel where he ended and she began. Or where the whole world ended and she began. She could feel her being opening up, her aura expanding further. Their breath continued as one, their

114

bodies interlaced, the energy spiralled up. They journeyed from stillness to slight movement in a dance of polarities and exploration of possibilities. As their faces touched, she could feel his breath on her cheeks, chin and lips. Sofia felt the shadow of discomfort again, a glimpse of an old fear of someone taking something she was not ready to give. Once again, she navigated through that and found more intimacy and excitement on the other side. It was as if she could see the distortions of the ego as well as the possibilities of consciousness. Sofia felt her body fully receptive; she gave him energetic permission to come further into her field. She could feel the vulnerability, tenderness and preciousness of that moment. He listened and brought her closer to him; all their energy points aligned. Feeling the depth of his energy rising, she welcomed him into her inner world and their breaths accelerated. Rays of energy penetrated them from all sides. Pressing her hand against the back of his heart, she could feel a bright light between them – the type of light that could heal timelines and transcend universes. Time stood still. Space disappeared. Separation dissolved. There was no longer a *her* or a *him*. Existence stopped and gave place to divine union. Ahh, the ecstatic meeting of the divine feminine and masculine, from where whole universes are born and fall back into…

Gradually, their breathing slowed down and as their bodies loosened their grip on one another, they relaxed into stillness. The rain had disappeared, the grass was still lying under their bare feet, the Ganga was still murmuring, and mother Earth was still holding them in her cosy womb. Sofia placed her hands on his chest as he held her back. They rested in the oneness of their beings. Their hands found their way into each other's; as their fingers interlaced, the sacredness of touch bathed them in delight. Having lost the sense of time, Sofia had no clue if two or three hours had gone by, but they could both intuitively feel that the time to part was upon them. Their noses and foreheads came together in a timeless *hongi*. They shared the breath of life. There was a silent recognition that they were one and the same. Their energy remained connected long after their bodies gradually disentangled. Standing in front of each other with their eyes closed, they could still feel each other's presence. The birds sang once more;

115

the wind gently touched their skin. Their eyes gently opened as they gazed into each other. She admired how beautiful he was, whoever he was; how his green eyes shined, how his smile made a sweet facial expression. Words could have been spoken or not; it was not important.

In the end, he did choose to speak. His name was James; he was part of a group of Yogis staying in a nearby hostel for one month. They were practitioners of a different Yoga tradition and did a lot of singing and chanting with musical instruments. He invited Sofia and her friends to a *kirtan* (a meditative chanting practice with traditional instruments) they were offering that week. Sofia had realised through biodanza how much music was a part of her life and how it could be an effective tool in connecting deeper with herself, so that practice felt appealing to her. They parted without knowing if they would ever see each other again. Either way, it did not matter. They felt complete. Their souls had touched and nothing else was required.

After Sofia had integrated what happened, she decided she would soon share it with Paulo. While it was true that they had decided to try polyamory, it was also the case that the only way she was willing to do it was with complete honesty, transparency and consent. Sofia felt slightly afraid that he would get mad at her, but she reassured herself that those were old traumas speaking and it would not be the case. If there was one thing that Paulo had extremely grounded in him, it was the belief that a person's feelings are *their own* responsibility. Our external reality is not happening to us; it is *responding* to us – to who we are and how we feel. To blame others for who we are or how we feel is absurd, seeing as no one can "make us be" or "make us feel" anything. *Internal locus of control*, he would have invoked, meaning that one's external reality is a result of one's own feelings and actions. Paulo would never blame her for however he felt, as he believed that humans are fully accountable for their responses, as they come from no one but themselves – such as the example of the Dalai Lama and the angry man. Other people cannot create egos inside of us; only we can. Others can only trigger suffering based on egos that already exist within us. So, would it not

116

be absolute madness to blame them for our suffering? Therefore, we should not project shame or guilt onto others but instead acknowledge – and hopefully transcend – our fears and egos. Others already have *their own* job: to work on *their* egos. So, despite some historically-based fears, Sofia knew he would never accuse, argue or be violent with her. He would either be OK with what happened or not, but either way, he would own how he felt and what he needed. Plus, she had never seen him insecure or upset about anything she had done, so she reassured herself that she might just be overthinking.

As it turned out, Sofia was right about Paulo's internal locus of control response, but it did not seem like he was OK with the situation. Sofia's encounter had come to him as a shock, and he was not quite sure how to handle it. Perhaps even more unsettling than the encounter was the fact that she seemed *excited* about him. Paulo asked for some space to think and retreated into himself. Sofia noticed her feelings of abandonment when Paulo withdrew, but part of her also respected that he was able to set boundaries (something she was substantially less brave at). *Well, this was not a smooth introduction to polyamory, was it?* Sofia thought to herself.

The following week, Ananda talked about the imbalances of Anahata chakra. He explained: "One of Anahata's imbalances is the inability to feel the interconnectedness of all things. Imprisonment by egos can trap the person in an enormous sense of aloneness and separateness, with recurring feelings of meaninglessness, hopelessness, aimlessness and purposelessness.

"The unhealthy experience of love can manifest as emotional insecurity, fear of rejection or abandonment, defences around love and emotional intimacy, and an inability to either offer or accept love (or both), which can lead to the person appearing cold and distant. Jealousy also relates to this chakra, even if it is also a typical imbalance of Swadhisthana, though Swadhisthana-type jealousy relates more to sexual intimacy, whereas Anahata relates to emotional intimacy.

"An imbalanced Anahata can also manifest as a lack of self-love and disregard for one's own feelings. Often the person may show a lack of

117

emotional boundaries, resulting in relationships where unhealthy co-dependency and emphasis on the other is out of balance (by either giving or needing too much), and emotional abuse or manipulation may be present.

"The imbalanced experience of feelings can lead to emotional hypersensitivity, confusion around feelings, inability to reconcile opposite emotions, emotional indifference, superficiality, lack of depth or mind-emotion dissociation (clinically called alexithymia).

"Another expression of the imbalance of this chakra is emotional selfishness and considering only one's feelings as the referential. One can become self-preoccupied and lack consideration for others. It can also be related to non-acceptance, inability to forgive and martyrdom.

"Fulfilment is absent when this chakra is imbalanced, allied to the impaired ability to experience love, which can be characterised by profound loneliness and painful longing and sadness. Grief is often strongly manifested in this chakra, as is the wounded inner child."

Sofia thought to herself that she had many of these imbalances and was grateful to have an asana practice to help with that; it felt very empowering.

After a few days of distance, Paulo and Sofia progressively connected again. Paulo told her he felt jealous, and while he reassured her that she did not do anything wrong, he also admitted to being unsure whether he was capable of polyamory. Paulo had started to doubt the framework of relating they had chosen. That was not to say that he was opposed to it or had given up on it yet; he was sharing how he felt but it was OK for their relationship to remain open for the time being.

In the meantime, Sofia had organised for a few students from the school to go to James' *kirtan*. Whether it was because of the nature of the kirtan or its facilitator, Paulo was not interested in attending. Merle, on the other hand, was incredibly excited, as he felt very connected to music. They were gathering in a big hall in the hostel where James' group was staying. The hosts were happy they joined, but Sofia and James did not greet each other with a hug. They were both secretly avoiding it, as they knew just how many hours that might last.

118

The *kirtan* was spectacular; Sofia felt at home with devotional chanting, live music and acoustic instruments. The songs were based on Sanskrit mantras, which were very profound. It is said that Sanskrit words are not based on random sounds like most languages; instead, they are made of sounds that correspond to the resonance of the object (or aspect, deity, etc.) that they refer to, which in mantras tends to be objects of the most elevated resonances. There was an extra djembe, so Sofia played it. The vibration of the drum as well as the Sanskrit chants took her to a place where time and space did not exist, where there was just soul. It was a state of natural trance and bliss. Merle also seemed to be in his element and even played on James' digeridoo – he was incredibly talented. Anney was especially impressed, of course.

When the *kirtan* ended, people started going home. Sofia thanked James for the invitation and expressed how much she had appreciated the experience. He said he enjoyed hearing her play the djembe and mentioned that she was welcome to borrow it if she liked. She caught herself about to say 'no' unconsciously. That got her to realise how much harder she found it to receive than to give – which was an Anahata blockage! Whether she had copied her mother's readiness to give yet not to receive or felt compelled to endlessly give back to make up for the *monster* (and, by the same token, not receive because she felt unworthy) was unknown at that stage. Either way, she was not about to give in to her ego or say 'no' to life's abundance, so she accepted and appreciated the offer. They exchanged numbers so she could return the drum when he needed it. As they said their goodbyes, they were both aiming for a short hug, but as it turned out, their bodies were in less of a hurry. With each passing second, the rush dissipated and there was more surrendering to the moment. Their minds started to run out of restlessness and excuses, and electricity began to flow through their beings. Another journey followed, similar to the first one. Once again, it lasted an unknowable amount of time – certainly a few hours. In the end, they left without words, yet with their beings united.

Sofia went to sleep as soon as she got to the *ashram* and was not looking forward to the conversation with Paulo the next day. She had not yet seen

119

him when Merle appeared and asked her if she wanted to jam; he had his travelling digeridoo and she had her voice and the djembe. That sounded like a wonderful way to keep music in her daily life. Also, she had a very lively cupid in her being, secretly in the background, hoping to find ways to connect Anney and Merle. Jamming with him could provide her with some opportunities to do that.

Sofia walked along the streets of Rishikesh to what had become her favourite *chai* stand. *Chai* really just means tea in Hindi, but it is also a specific and delicious tea that Indians seemed to drink as much as the Portuguese drink coffee. She ordered her usual *chai* without sugar, which cost next to nothing and offered her a world of pleasure. Sofia was admiring her *Ganga ma*, amused to observe some teenagers throwing themselves in and getting dragged downstream by the strong current. *That looked like so much fun.* Sofia made a mental note to do that one day. In the meantime, her phone beeped with a message from James. For a moment, she had forgotten that they had exchanged numbers because of the drum. "So lovely to sing with you last night. Feel like going out for *chai*?" he asked. *How synchronous*, she thought – receiving that message while holding a cup of *chai* in her hand. She was excited about the idea of connecting with him but chose not to reply until she spoke with Paulo.

Sofia found Paulo and told him about the *kirtan*, the hug and the *chai* invite. He seemed quiet once again but not unprepared. She tried to reassure him, saying that inviting her for *chai* did not necessarily mean that he was interested in her; it was not as if he had asked her out on a date. After taking a moment to process, Paulo said that a *chai* invite felt even sweeter than a date, which was more hurtful for him. Sofia realised that people's insecurities make them paint whatever story they need to paint to justify feeling however they feel. Paulo said that while he acknowledged the purity and beauty of polyamory, emotionally, he did not feel ready to handle the jealousy, fear and anxiety it brought, so he was no longer happy to continue trying it. Sofia felt slightly disappointed, especially now that she had met James. Still, her relationship with Paulo was absolutely precious to her, whereas she had never even heard of polyamory until a few months ago. So, they agreed to have a monogamous relationship from that point onwards – though, of course, one aimed at being as conscious as possible.

The following Yoga class was about love and attachment. Sofia was puzzled by that choice of topic. What was happening in the classes seemed to be reflecting what was happening inside of her, as well as manifesting in her external reality. The first few times it happened, she just brushed it off, but the more it happened, the more she started to see how everything was interconnected.

Ananda asked the class, "What goes through your mind when you think of love?" People offered different answers regarding how they felt about people in their lives, animals, nature and the qualities of that feeling. Ananda responded, "Exactly, we tend to think of love as a *feeling* we have for something or someone. Typically, we don't think of love as a *state of consciousness*, which is what it really is. We also have all these conditioned ideas about how it should manifest. For example, a mother should love her son more than other people's children; a wife should love a husband but have no other romantic connections; a brother can love a sister and his wife at the same time; a person's love for a partner is sexual whereas for a friend it is not, etc. These vary according to the society, country, culture and time period people live in. In other words, we created these concepts ourselves. They are not objective; they are *judgements*. *Biological* aspects are objective; for example, a *lingam* fits into a *yoni*, but it does not fit into another *lingam*. These are facts; the rest are subjective concepts. If we break out of this conditioning, we will be able to discover the state of unconditional love.

"In its pure state, love is absolute. It has no duality, limits, reasons, requirements, or conditions. It is a state of being, a way of living. It is not conditional on how much other people give back to us or any other external factors. It does not require anything. From that place, we simply are love, and we can also extend our love to other beings by loving them as a whole (as opposed to loving the parts we like and aiming to change the others).

"Surely, it would feel much nicer if our relationships were based on that pure love, right? So why aren't they? The answer is fear. Fear of being hurt, taken advantage of, or countless others. However, that raises a pertinent question: aren't we *more* hurt by *not* living in this state? If something is overshadowing that love, we should address and transcend it so we can return to our natural loving state.

"In the state of unconditional love, we experience true empathy (intuitively feeling how the other is feeling) and connect to people from our hearts to theirs. That makes it so that – regardless of the distance – we have a feeling of union and inseparability.

"We become altruistic, happy to share and care for other people's well-being unconditionally (not just for whom we like, when it is convenient to us or based on their behaviours). We listen to others attentively, with great wonder for their beautiful being, and are open to assisting them in reaching their potential. When we love, we find ourselves in everything and find everything in ourselves.

"That causes us to expand beyond the ego, to infinity. There is no room for egoism any more since we are not separate. We live in a state of communion with the world, in harmony and inner peace. We know we are complete.

"Sadly, we don't normally operate from this state of consciousness, as we don't realise that the source of love is inside. Instead, when an enjoyable someone comes into our life and a state of love and grace involves us, our heart opens – it's a beautiful feeling, but because we didn't feel that way before, it seems like the source of that happiness is related to the other. We don't realise that it was *our own* state of love that shined forth, so we externalise those feelings and see the other as a personification of our love. We even say: *You are my love*. Because love gains a human form, we think it is limited and finite, so we don't want the other person to leave or share it with anyone else, as it puts it at risk. The mind sees losing the object of our love as losing love itself. So, of course, when they are with someone else, we feel threatened and insecure; when they are gone, we feel devastated and incomplete. That is attachment. Surreptitiously, it moves the relationship from the heart to the mind, where love decreases and ego increases. Once that happens, it is all downhill from there. Control comes, appreciation goes, and before we know it, we have moved further away from our nature instead of towards it – this defeats the point of a conscious relationship and can even make it toxic. Eventually, new relationships come, but the cycle repeats itself because we will be attracted to the same patterns until we learn the lesson."

Love is a state of being, Sofia journalled. *We've externalised it and distorted it as a feeling for others, which generates fear, which in turn moves us away from our natural state.* She hoped to never lose sight of that and vowed to always choose love instead of fear.

Sofia's relationship with Paulo returned to its usual beauty and light, for which she felt enormous excitement, peace and joy. She had only felt like that once in her life – when she was pregnant. It must have been because that little being's resonance awakened her state of unconditional love. With that thought, a realisation struck her. He must have been a very elevated, heart-centred being. He never came here to live; he came to give his life so that his mother could live – *really* live, as opposed to carrying on with the mediocre existence she was in. Tears rolled down her eyes and immense gratitude filled her heart. She felt expanded, elevated… Even Ron, who had passed by, paused momentarily and expressed how shiny she looked. She noticed the love in his eyes. At that moment, it also clicked for her why Devimar was constantly projecting onto her and bickering for no reason. It had never been about Sofia's messy bed or occasional forgetfulness. It was plain old jealousy. She turned back to Ron and asked if he had a couple of minutes to talk. He said yes, as they sat on a bench in the garden. Without delay, she asked him directly if he could think of any reason why Devimar had been picking on her for months. That question seemed to catch him off guard. He smiled, slightly embarrassed, carefully choosing his words. "Don't feel like you have to share anything, if you don't feel like it." Sofia reminded Ron, to put him at ease. He took a few more seconds, then sighed. "In my life, I try to apply a philosophy of radical honesty. If we really want to develop a resonance with the truth of who we are and what the universe is, we can't be pretending to be someone we are not. That includes all the little white lies and excuses designed to avoid owning our reality and experiencing uncomfortable feelings. The uncomfortable piece of reality that you're touching on is that I feel attracted to you. I've never said anything to you because I could feel your body language and energetic boundaries saying 'no' whenever I got close, so I kept my distance. Regardless, I know it and Devimar knows it too because we are open about everything."

Sofia pondered for a moment, trying to be mature and transcend her discomfort. She replied, "Thank you, I really appreciate you being honest, expressing how you feel, plus having picked up on my boundaries and respected them; it means a lot." She then asked him, "Is Devimar into this radical honesty thing as well? Because if she is indeed jealous, should she not come to me or you and talk things through rather than acting them out?" Ron smiled.

He said, "Astute observation, which would only be true if she was conscious of – and owning – her jealousy, which she probably isn't. We should talk to her; radical honesty begets openness." Sofia cringed, considering that suggestion.

"Even if she does own it, what possible solution could we come up with?" she asked.

Ron answered, "Well, we would discuss that together. In our philosophy, the solution is typically internal; it involves us working through our issues and the other person – or people – being there only to support that process. With a previous lover, I made it a point to sit and watch them kiss and caress each other so I would be faced with my jealousy." Responding to Sofia's shocked face, he smiled and said, "Yes, it was hardcore, but I grew from it."

That's impressive, Sofia thought. She paused to reflect and said, "I think it might feel shaming for her if we both show up to confront her. With her tendency to project onto me, I'm concerned she might think we are ganging up on her and feel threatened. Perhaps it's best if you talk to her in private. I don't really need to hear her confess her jealousy or be sorry for it; I would just like her antagonistic behaviours to stop." Ron smiled again and said,

"You are naturally compassionate, even towards those who hurt you. That's a very elevated quality. You can see why I'm attracted to you." For Sofia, it was new to hear someone own their attraction to her so candidly. It was undoubtedly awkward and uncomfortable, but she could also see how it could become normalised and appreciated if she managed to get on board with that radical honesty concept. More importantly, it would encourage her to fully own every feeling, enabling its transcendence.

Ron did talk to Devimar about her acting out, though neither of them ever reported the outcome of that conversation back to Sofia. Yet from that day onward, there were no more antagonistic behaviours. Was there a nearly-imperceptible vibe of hostility cloaked underneath a higher aspiration to treat Sofia with decency? Sure, but that was good enough for Sofia.

Sofia was slightly apprehensive about Paulo's possible reaction to Ron's attraction, but he seemed absolutely fine with it and said, with the most incredible smile, "Of course he is attracted to you; what is there to *not* be attracted to?" She was impressed with how secure he was in himself when the relationship was monogamous. Her hesitance had been because of the James situation, though that was about *her* being attracted to someone, on top of which it was probably mutual and they had permission to pursue it… which was a whole different ball game and totally understandable. In all fairness, Sofia would have probably felt the same way.

The following week, Ron was teaching the class. He talked about empathy, explaining that it was one of the superpowers of the heart chakra. Through empathy, we can feel another person's emotions to the extent that empathy is awake in us. Ron also talked about judgement, calling it a poison of the heart. He explained that when we judge, we assign subjective properties of right and wrong to things, or better and worse, mostly coming from cultural values and social conditioning. Sofia felt triggered by that and asked him, on an impulse, "Then you don't think that rape is wrong?" Ron looked at her compassionately. He could see through her past with more awareness than she wanted him to have at that moment. Gently, he replied, "It's not that it's *wrong* or *not wrong*. In Yoga, we see things under a

125

different framework altogether. Instead of the lens of right and wrong, we realise that the universal law at play here is actually action and consequence, or in other words, *karma*. If I slap you in the face, you will probably be upset at me, so I will not do it, not because it's *wrong*, but because the consequence will be upsetting you and causing pain, neither of which I am interested in or want the karma for. If I want to receive kindness and grace, I need to act in those ways, not because they are the *right* ones, but because my actions will bring more of that into the world and ultimately back into myself." Sofia could accept that but was not entirely convinced. "Can't judgement be useful, though? Surely, if we judge others for really bad deeds…" She paused and corrected herself, trying to not use the word 'bad'. "I mean for deeds that cause a lot of suffering, it will dissuade them from doing them, right? We can't just have a society where everything goes and no one gets criticised for anything, can we?" Before Ron could respond, Paulo intervened, "May I tell a story that happened to Ajahn Brahm, an Australian Buddhist monk?" Ron nodded affirmatively.

Ajahn Brahm recounts that one night, he was in his monastery sleeping upstairs and heard a noise in the hall below. As he came downstairs, he saw a burglar holding the donation box in his hands. He said, "The box is locked, but the key is in that first drawer; you can open it and help yourself to whatever is there. There is also some fruit in the bowl on the table; you are welcome to take it too."

Visibly angry, the burglar said, "Is this a trick? Does it trigger an alarm, or a hidden camera somewhere, to catch me stealing from you?"

The monk said, "This is not a trick; there are no cameras. And you are not stealing; I offered you these things. The donation box is for those in need and you are clearly in need." Hesitantly, the burglar opened the drawer, indeed there was no alarm and the key was there; he opened the box with it, took the money and the fruit and left. Ajahn Brahm did not give that a second thought until a week later when he read in the paper that the same burglar had been arrested for stealing someone's house. Evidently, someone less compassionate than the monk. The burglar was sentenced to five years in jail. Five years later, the monk was sleeping upstairs and heard a noise in the hall. He came downstairs and saw the old burglar standing next to the donation box again. He said, "Oh well, the key is in the same place; you know what to do; help yourself."

The burglar contested, "I did not come here to help myself; I came here to ask you to help me. Every day for the last five years, I thought of the only person who had shown me kindness and acceptance. That was you. I came here to see if you would help me become a better person."

"Kindness and acceptance can often change things that judgement never could," concluded Paulo.

Ron agreed. "Precisely, wonderful example. There is certainly no lack of judgement in our society. Don't you think that if judgement was going to work, it would have worked by now? Judgement points out the worst in people and asks them to be ashamed. Kindness points out the best in people and asks them to be inspired. Only you can decide which strategy you would rather use." Sofia had no doubt which one she would rather use. She had been using judgement because it was the only strategy she knew to stop others from causing suffering and influence them to be better people. However, looking back on the people who judged her, she could see that they had not actually contributed to her being a better person. Yet the ones who showed her kindness definitely had. Now that she had learned a new way to create a better society, "Not *better*," she corrected herself, trying to avoid saying 'better' and 'worse' – a society that resonated with her so much more, she needed to let go of judgement. *Besides*, she decided, *the world has more than enough judges; it doesn't need me to be one.*

At the end of the class, Ron taught the posture of the week; as usual, they practised the asanas – some for this chakra and others for the previous ones. Postures for Anahata tended to involve chest compression and elongation (engaging the front, back and sides of the chest).

That week, Sofia jammed with Merle again. Or rather, they spent an increasing amount of time discussing philosophy, psychology and the secrets of life and the Universe. She tried to set him up with Anney a few times, but he did not react much. One way or the other; it was not looking promising.

Another day, Sofia and Merle went to an event they thought was a jam but ended up being a sharing circle. It was small and personal, lasting an unexpectedly long time. Sofia had a commitment with Paulo but felt stuck there, as people were crying and sharing deep intimate issues, so it felt rather tactless to leave. However, it felt equally disrespectful to be extremely late to meet Paulo. Multiple times she hoped they would finish, but the circle went on for hours. By the time Sofia left, she was three hours late for her appointment with Paulo. She stared at the clock, livid. Sofia had a terror of being late, having grown up with severe punishments for that. So, she ran as fast as she could to meet him and was tremendously anxious when she arrived. Sofia was sure he would be extremely upset at her, *and rightfully so*! She immediately apologised, justified herself and expressed her guilt about being so late. Unconsciously, she was expecting to be punished. He looked at her with a neutral expression, which broke into an enormous smile. He said, "Sweetheart… I'm so happy to see you!" That was so out of Sofia's reality that she had to take a moment to process what was happening. She asked, "You're not angry that I'm three hours late?"

He instinctively replied, "You being late is a fact. Me being angry is an optional response! It would be insane not to accept that you were late because a fact is what it is. My resistance to it would only bring suffering." That was another life-changing experience for Sofia, the moment she learned what true acceptance felt like. It was also one of the greatest gifts that Paulo consistently gave her: his unconditional acceptance and ability to hold in mind what *really* mattered. Regardless of the topic or tone of the conversation, he would always hold perspective. *Is it more important to be right or to look after the other's well-being? To punish or to be compassionate? To get what you want or to be kind?*

The days continued, and Rishikesh was progressively fascinating – the contrasts of peace and noise, prayer and violence, organisation and chaos; the random animals on the streets; the locals insisting on taking photos of the foreigners (usually without their permission); the multiple rituals and celebrations.

One day Sofia was feeling very joyful and inspired, doing her *sadhana* by the Ganga, when a shockwave of sadness hit her: her heart contracted and shrank, and she felt hopeless for no reason. She took some time to process what was happening, which proved utterly unsuccessful. Then, her phone rang; it was Paulo. He had just gotten off the phone with his father; they had a big argument, because of which he was feeling incredibly sad. She listened to the whole story and supported him. It was not until they hung up and she restarted her Yoga practice feeling joyful again, that she put two and two together. The wave of sadness she had felt was not her own; it was Paulo's sadness, which she felt through empathy. As Ron had said, it was part of the true potential of the heart to feel the other through empathy, regardless of whether they are together or apart. That was evidence of the quantum physics claim that energy particles can be connected in entirely different places in the universe. She could not wait to share that with Paulo.

Before they knew it, the next week had arrived. In the Yoga class, Ananda spoke about compassion, which he described as an antidote for violence, anger, judgement, non-acceptance, hatred, ill-will and many other egos. He argued. "*Ahimsa*, compassion, or non-violence, is one of the *Yamas and Niyamas* (guides to human conduct, universally applicable to all people, times and places). These are part of the eight limbs of Yoga (aspects we can develop within ourselves to awaken our consciousness and become fully aligned and self-realised), described in the Yoga Sutras (the foundational texts of classical Yoga, compiled by sage Patanjali around 400 CE, based on five-thousand-year-old Yoga traditions).

"To embody *Ahimsa*, we first need to become aware of the different forms of violence we are creating in our lives and replace them with compassion. Identifying the roughest, more obvious types of violence, such as the physical ones, is usually fairly straightforward. However, the subtler ones can go unnoticed, such as violence in thoughts, violence against non-human beings, self-righteous violence, violence as a response to violence, or violence in speech. Take the latter, for example. If we say something harmful to someone, while there may not be physical contact, the violence can be extreme. We are being violent when we criticise people because they did not meet our expectations, ridicule, slander, undermine them, or gossip behind their backs. There is an old saying: Before you speak, ask yourself three questions: Is it true? Is it kind? Is it necessary? If the answer to any of those questions is 'no', then refrain from speaking. When we bring *Ahimsa* into our speech, it naturally permeates through to our thoughts and actions, and we naturally start to resonate with higher states of consciousness.

"There is also violence towards ourselves. We can be our biggest critics, judges and perpetrators. We can push ourselves to the point of exhaustion and still judge ourselves for petty things we did wrong along the way. We can expose ourselves to a harmful situation for years yet do nothing to change it. We can criticise, undermine, disempower, hurt, humiliate, pressure, neglect and oppress ourselves in ways we would not dream of doing to another human! The principle of compassion needs to be applied to ourselves too. That includes love, forgiveness, understanding and appreciation. Only when we are able to apply compassion to ourselves will we truly be able to experience it in its greatest sense: for all beings.

"Violence is essentially a manifestation of power through force rather than consciousness. The violence we manifest externally is an expression of our internal violence. We act all-powerful because we feel powerless. "That is where shadow work comes in. If we can identify the feeling that is generating our violent reaction (for instance, fear, shame or guilt), we can transcend it through consciousness instead. Regardless, even if we fail at transcending how we feel, we always have the power to *act* consciously. For guidance, we can ask ourselves: "What would compassion do?"

"Our biggest resistances to being compassionate tend to be that people might take advantage of us, get away with whatever they have done, or receive solidarity they don't deserve. But compassion is not about what the other deserves; it's about what *we* deserve. We harm ourselves more with the negativity from the ego-based feelings we hold on to than any of these reasons ever would. That is not to say we need to keep the person in our lives; we may choose to or not. Either way, rest assured *karma* will be there to deal with their actions. Fortunately, that is not a burden *we* need to carry."

130

Before the end of the class, they performed a *Metta Bhavana* (Buddhist loving kindness) meditation, then the usual *asana* practice. As homework, the students were recommended to reflect on the types of violence they are manifesting in their lives and replace them with compassion and loving-kindness.

While Sofia was in a wonderful state of love and connection, not everyone shared that same feeling. Anney, her soul sister and best friend, was one of them. She seemed slightly hostile and annoyed – Sofia was unsure if it was at the world or at *her*. She asked Anney if anything was troubling her or if she had done something to upset her. Anney, who was very honest and self-aware, said that it seemed like Sofia and Merle were growing increasingly intimate; Anney was jealous of their connection as he was not as receptive towards her. Then, she bluntly asked Sofia whether she had any romantic intentions with him. Sofia was caught by surprise and felt secretly indignant that her loyalty towards Anney had been completely missed. She replied, "Of course, not. I've been trying to get him to like you!" That simple statement was enough to convince Anney. After that, Anney returned to her old self as if nothing had happened.

It did get Sofia thinking, though... Polyamory seemed like such a perfect philosophy, with elevated ideals and resonance. *Why did the people practising it not seem to be in a high vibration but instead involved in ongoing drama and suffering? Could it be that vibrating in the resonance of fear and jealousy keeps them trapped in lower states of consciousness, thus preventing them from ascending to higher ones?* In which case, polyamory could potentially work as a manifestation of an *already elevated* state of consciousness (once it is reached), but not really as a way to get there (unlike Tantrics argued). Sofia remained quiet about her findings. *Who was she to claim that a five-thousand-year-old tradition such as Tantra was wrong?*

In any case, both Sofia and Paulo felt like they could do with less intensity for a few days, so they left the *ashram*, rented a motorbike (a big Honda cruiser) and went for a weekend road trip. They rode down to the Kerala state and stayed in a town called Varkala. Varkala was on a cliff looking out into the ocean, with eagles flying over the beautiful green nature, hostels, Yoga and surf places all around. Sofia and Paulo surfed, practised Yoga and enjoyed the beach and each other. Varkala had the most stunning sunsets Sofia had ever seen and would probably ever come to see in her life. As the sun approached the ocean, people everywhere on the beach would gradually stop talking or swimming and stand in awe, facing the descending sun, in silent recognition of something sacred taking place.

With the calming influence of Varkala and the total absence of stress and responsibilities, Sofia and Paulo's nervous systems calmed down; they felt completely relaxed. One afternoon, Paulo was sitting down in a cross-legged position and Sofia sat on top of him, wrapping her legs around his back. Their arms embraced, their chests joined and their eyes closed; she could sense his heartbeat in her chest, feel the sun burning her skin, hear some drums at a distance… The noises of the beach started to quieten as if they were moving away and only the drums and their beating hearts remained. Suddenly she had a vision of what seemed like a different life, as clear as if it was happening right in front of her: there was a bonfire, a tribe sitting and dancing around the fire; their clothes and ornaments looked old and traditional, perhaps African, Native American or South American. Sofia was there but her body looked different; her skin was darker and the shape of her body was not the same, but she knew it was herself. Paulo was also present; his body was slightly different but she recognised his essence. *They knew each other back then.* The tribe was chanting, dancing and celebrating; there was a lot of spirit in the air. Her feeling was one of connection, intimacy and joy. Sofia wanted to explore that life but got too excited, lost focus and felt herself being pulled back to the present time. She felt the heartbeat and the sun again. She whispered to Paulo, "I think we know each other from another life." His scientific mind could not prove or disprove such an allegation, but he was open to the possibility.

Sofia told Paulo about Anney and shared that she felt hurt that Anney thought she was trying to steal her beloved – loyalty was one of Sofia's main character traits, so it felt like Anney did not really know her. She was reacting to Anney's ego instead of feeling compassion for it. Paulo could see that and replied with another story from the Australian Buddhist monk. A man was walking down the street and bumped directly into another person. The man was furious; he turned back, ready to yell at the other, but as he faced them, he noticed the other was blind. Struck by regret and compassion for the blind man, the man felt sorry for his own unawareness of where he was going and apologised.

After telling this story, the Buddhist monk usually enquired: "Why do we not treat ego like a psychological blindness and show the same amount of compassion as we would for a physically blind person?" Paulo added his own thoughts: "People will always have their egos and blindness – that is on them. Reacting against that, however, is entirely *our* choice." There it was again, the acceptance theme, which Sofia was struggling with and Paulo seemed to excel at so naturally. That would be a long journey, she thought, sighing in dismay…

During their time in Varkala, Sofia and Paulo saw some people drinking and wondered if they should enjoy a drink too. After all, alcohol had been a part of their lives for so long. Yet when Sofia tuned into her body to see whether that felt attractive, she received a definite 'no'. Her body was rejecting alcohol, which she was so happy about. She only wished it did the same with meat, which she had not stopped craving thus far. That quest was easier for Paulo, whose body had stopped desiring meat and alcohol.

Varkala felt soul-nourishing for Sofia and Paulo. They felt so free away from everything and everyone, with no chores or responsibilities; it was heavenly. After those beautiful days, it was time to head back. The road was long and they wanted to make the most of the trip, so they returned to the *ashram* around three in the morning on Sunday, leaving them very little time to sleep. That did not matter to Sofia, though, because now that they were practising Anahata chakra, she was only sleeping four to five hours a night. Ananda claimed that Anahata was the chakra that regulates sleep and, if it is highly active, substantially less sleep is required. Though Muladhara is the one that controls vitality, so if Anahata is active but not Muladhara, one can

133

still feel tired occasionally while not experiencing sleepiness. Sofia's experience confirmed that.

Two weeks before the end of the Anahata module, Sofia was already dreading leaving India. So many places she still wanted to visit, Dharamshala, Varanasi, Munnar, Tamil Nadu… Though her heart was not too heavy, she knew she would return one day. Mother India would call her back – she was sure of it.

In class, Ananda spoke about trauma and how it could shut down the heart and our ability to love. He said that trauma happens when something so violent or difficult takes place that our psyche does not have the ability to process or integrate it. For example, a child may not be able to process why Dad hits Mum, a sibling dies, or Mum abandons them. So, our highly intelligent psyche puts the trauma in a bubble and shoves it into the unconscious to protect itself. After that, we function normally, for the most part, except that the trauma bubble unconsciously influences us in the form of feelings (say, a lack of trust in men, irrational terror of death, or fear of abandonment). As a result, we create projections, get triggered by circumstances that would otherwise not matter, or make choices based on unconscious needs. Plus, we attract things based on those unconscious feelings. So, our work is to bring the trauma bubble safely and kindly to the surface and, with a lot of love, integrate it back into our psyche. The Swami said that extensive research behind Trauma-Sensitive Yoga (a new-age type of Yoga) shows two common characteristics of people who experience trauma: disconnection and disempowerment. He claimed that trauma survivors are on a journey to rediscover their power, their internal sense of safety and the unconditional love inside their hearts. Remaining small does not keep us safe; it keeps us disconnected – from ourselves, others and the universe. Anney, who had a lot of trauma in her past, asked, "How do you reintegrate the trauma bubble back into the psyche, *exactly*?"

Ananda replied, "A commonly used approach is *inner child* work, reconnecting with the younger version of oneself that was affected by the trauma. There are multiple ways to perform it, one of which is to meditate with the inner child, figure out how they feel and what they need and then have the adult part give it to them. That is often a painful process because as we integrate our inner child, we inevitably feel their feelings as if they were ours (which is called regression). Those are, of course, excruciating, which is why we block them in the first place. The key is to trust that while we as children had no tools or strength to face, contain and process those feelings, our adult selves do. They can do all that for the child." At that exact moment, a song was playing at a distance that Sofia used to hear on a loop in her early adolescent years. She felt like crying; she knew she had some critical and probably painful inner child work ahead of her.

Ananda said that their homework was to discover in which ways each person's prior traumas were affecting their life. Sofia was not sure if she was ready to open that box. Yet boxes have a way of opening themselves up anyway. One day, Klaus, one of the Yoga students, passed by. Klaus was a sweet, brown-haired, brown-eyed, strong-bodied Chilean man of average height who was very thoughtful, generous and caring. Perhaps recognising her tenderness, he said, "Hola, *Sofi-ita*" – (*Hi, little Sofia*). She was struck by that sentence somehow. She went out for air and sat on the shores of the Ganga. Sofi-ita was the name that her mother used to call her when she was little; she had not remembered that in years. Somehow, she had rationalised her mother as someone who could not express emotions, but she had forgotten how sweetly and caringly she would call her name, Sofi-ita. Sofia felt lost and alone at that moment; tears rolled down her face. Somehow, in her heart, she felt only despair. Then she realised those were the feelings of her inner child; Sofia was experiencing regression! So, she remembered what Ananda had said and invoked her adult self to support her. As the adult self, Sofia asked the younger one, "How do you feel?"

The child promptly said, "Sad and alone."

Sofia knew that the current conversation was taking place in her mind or imagination, yet somehow it felt very real, as if she was not making that up and there was actually a different part of her psyche responding.

"What do you need?" the adult self asked.

"I need you to stay with me," replied the child.

"OK, I will." She reassured the child. The child was hesitant to trust her but could see their potential to heal together somehow. Which was extremely difficult, as Sofia felt only despair due to her regressed state. Nevertheless, she had to *trust. Trust what?* She did not even know. That there was a light inside her that would steer her towards healing; that she would have the wisdom to find answers; that the Universe would support her; that there were timeless echoes inside of her that would always guide her Home – not to a house, but to her higher self. At that moment, something touched her foot. It was a little flower with a candle on top, floating in the Ganga. Then another one came, and another, and then there were three. The situation seemed improbable because even though she had seen those kinds of little flowers floating around (she assumed they were offerings to the Gods), the current was very strong; they should have been pulled out rather than calmly floating by her legs. It did not seem *physically* possible. While trying to rationalise this, Sofia heard a voice inside her head. If that possibility were not so crazy, she could have sworn it was the voice of the Ganga. The voice said, and she would never forget it. "You are not lost and you are not alone." Suddenly her despair was replaced by a feeling of hope and trust in the universal mysteries. Her inner child felt relieved and held. That was when Sofia realised that human beings are held, supported and uplifted by powerful forces, which they often cannot see. She felt grateful and humbled by those forces as she walked back to the *ashram*.

On Sofia's way back, she recalled half a dozen other sweet names that her mother used to call her. With that, new memories emerged, such as actions her mother had done for her, or sacrifices she had made. How Mum told her interesting stories about historical events to help her study History – a paper which she found extremely boring; how Mum cared for her after surgery more attentively than the nurses at the Hospital; how Mum cooked her favourite meals when she was sad. In light of her current understanding of love languages, Sofia realised how much her mother actually loved her, in so many ways that she could not see at the time. She was overcome by a feeling of warmth and love but also regret for the times she had been cruel, rash or insensitive to her mother. Sofia realised what that meant: she had

136

forgiven her mother. So, she wrote her an email apologising for all the suffering she had caused her. It was not that the overbearing and controlling patterns that caused Sofia so much suffering over the years had been magically forgotten to make things OK; things were made OK because she was unwilling to keep on carrying all the pain. Despite her many attempts, her mother would never acknowledge those patterns and the harm they caused. For Sofia to heal, she had to forgive someone who was not sorry for something they would never regret. She did not do that for her mother. She did that for *herself*. The past is meant to be a stepping stone for us to trample, not a boulder for us to carry. It was time for her to let go of the boulder and set herself free.

Every week a different life-altering realisation. Sofia did not know how much more she could cope with, yet the thirst for her divine essence would not let her rest until she was Home.

The last week of the Anahata module arrived. Ron spoke about kindness and generosity, stating that when one truly gives from the heart, there are no strings attached. They would not expect a gift or service in return; the other person is not required to give anything back (not even their appreciation), and there is no *karmic* debt. He said that most people do not even know what that feels like. Sofia thought of Klaus, how he sometimes arrived at the *ashram* with yummy organic ice cream for everyone, bought board games so the group could play together, or made a special Chilean meal for someone's birthday. Somehow, she felt like those were completely detached gifts – his only desire was to *offer* them. Even the wish for people to appreciate them could have been a hook, but she did not feel that from him. They felt like truly detached gifts. Ron continued, talking about Karma Yoga, the Yoga of service, where one offers selfless service out of that purity of heart. He claimed that Karma Yoga was one of the most elevated spiritual practices one could perform and that some people in their school had achieved enlightenment through that.

Altruism was very present in Sofia's relationship with Paulo. If they were to argue about anything, it would be who would get to give the most delicious piece of food to the other or clean the dishes to let them rest. Anney was also very selfless, but somehow in a unique way, which felt more merged... As in, "Sofia can use my personal things because she is *a part of me*," as opposed to "because she is a *separate human being who I love*". Maybe as a result of considering her personal items and food to be fully available to Sofia, she also felt welcome to take whatever she needed of Sofia's, as if it were her own. That contrasted with Sofia's more individualistic view of friendship, where she was generally open to sharing but did not see her friends as an actual part of herself and would not have expected them to help themselves to anything that was hers. Sofia embraced that new perspective and possibility; Anney inspired her.

On her last day in India, Sofia finally gained the courage to jump into the Ganga. She climbed down one of the ropes along the banks and let go, surrendering to the exhilarating current and enjoying the adrenaline, the freshness and the speed. Sofia remained conscious of catching the next available rope so as to not float recklessly into something dangerous. With great excitement, she managed to catch the rope and climb back up. As she sat on the bank of the river to dry, she looked at the imponent, enormous brown and green mountains across from her. The inhabited part was only the very bottom – what looked like five per cent of it, at best. Noticing that led her to contemplate how enormous the Earth is and how tiny human beings are, yet how self-important they feel in comparison. That gave her perspective on how small her problems really were.

She got some *chai* for the last time and sat back down, drinking it and eating a banana. Unexpectedly, a monkey hanging from the tree on top of her took the banana from her hand and ran away. Sofia found it hilarious but started walking away just in case he decided to take the rest of her bananas. She was on her way to meet Merle for one last jam by her beloved *Ganga ma*, yet her monkey adventure was far from over. Halfway up the street, a group of monkeys came and started climbing onto her to reach for the remaining bananas. She tried to shake them off, but they were unafraid and would not leave. Sofia froze and could not think of a solution. Seeing the scary scene, a local guy on a *tuk-tuk* (a three-wheel motorised taxi, typical of India) stopped and told her to get in. As she ran towards the *tuk-tuk*, the monkeys started to leave and he told her, "Never carry food on the streets, especially bananas!"

The seemingly random situation of the right person arriving at the right time, in addition to many other synchronous conveniences, started to convince Sofia that the Universe constantly had her back. She and Merle laughed a lot about the monkeys and shared experiences of funny past situations. At some point in the conversation, Sofia thought of casually dropping Anney's name and seeing if she could gauge if there was hope for him to be interested in her. However, inspired by Ron's radical honesty, Sofia realised that was a shady, manipulative way to get that information, which was not needed nor acceptable to her. So, she asked, cheekily but more candidly, "How are things going with Anney?" He looked at her as if she was implying something highly unexpected. "You mean *romantically*?" he asked.

"Could be, why not?" she replied.

He answered, "Absolutely not, I mean we have fun but I'm not interested in her in that way at all." He was very definitive about it, which to Sofia felt like a punch in the gut – he might as well have broken her own heart. At least that was clear, she told herself, trying to put a positive spin on the situation. That left her with a different problem, though. Whether to betray Merle's trust and tell Anney he was not interested, betray Anney's trust and tell him she was interested, or not say anything to anyone and let Anney potentially become increasingly interested, only to have her heart broken later on. Sofia panicked and then thought to herself: what would radical honesty do? She let the topic go for a moment and inspiration came naturally once she stopped thinking about it. She told Merle, "Sometimes when I become close to someone, especially from the opposite sex, I think we are just becoming friends, yet the other person is gradually falling for me. I've learned that if I know that I'm definitely not interested, it's important to be clear so that I don't hurt the other person in the long run."

139

After reflecting, he asked her, "Do you think that might be happening with Anney?"

Sofia replied, "You spend the most time with her, what do *you* think?" She was profoundly relieved to have found a way to address the situation that did not involve giving her own opinion or betraying anyone's trust.

"I think it's possible. Maybe I should have a conversation with her. Wouldn't that be awfully awkward, though?" To which, remembering what Ananda had said, Sofia replied, "*What would compassion do?*" Merle understood and said he would consider it.

Before Yoga came into Sofia's life, she saw love as a feeling that only happened in the context of relationships. Not being able to access the infinite source of unconditional love inside of herself meant that her relationships were unconsciously aimed at filling those gaps and fulfilling mutual needs – needs that are established through expectations and enforced through control and demands. She now understood that love was a state of being; it should stem from the connection with her own true nature and emanate from herself, like an inner light that extends to those around her. She recognised that most of her needs, expectations and demands were compensation for her inability to access *her own* state of unconditional love. Additionally, she realised that only when she acts from her place of wholeness does it leave other people free to fully embody their true nature and shine their own light without conditionings... Only then can they connect soul to soul – which was the only way she wanted to connect.

Ananda came over with the tickets for the next country, but Sofia was not excited to see where they were going next... She felt like a part of her heart would always remain in mother India. The tickets read: *Bucharest, Romania.* "What's in Romania?" asked someone. Ron answered, "The Yoga school's home base and international camp."

Chapter 10 – Vishuddha Chakra

As the class travelled East by train from Bucharest to Mangalia – a Romanian beachfront village – Ron shared that they would be staying at the guru's base *ashram*. The school had Yoga *ashrams* in countries worldwide, housing students and teaching Yoga classes. He said that the guru was physically gone but still present in the astral planes, guiding and protecting the school, helping students and holding the consciousness field of the *ashrams*. The class was told that if they felt inclined to connect with him or ask for guidance or inspiration, they could do so psychically, especially from that particular *ashram*, since his energy was so present. Sofia was excited about that mysterious field supposedly held by the guru from the astral. Like most of her fellow students, she had a critical mind that needed proof and was not prepared to believe things out of blind faith. That fit the approach recommended to her in Yoga: to do the practices and experience the results for herself.

When the group arrived at the *ashram*, they were faced with a locked gate, with a volunteer guarding the door. That caught Sofia by surprise; she had idealised the school's home *ashram*, having an expectation that it would be some kind of elevated utopian place. That frosty reception confronted that idea. The volunteer called two other helpers from inside the *ashram*, one of them searched people's luggage (one could only assume for hidden weapons?) and the other had a form for them to sign, fill out their contact details and take personal responsibility for any damage they create in themselves, others or the school property. The students seemed slightly surprised and uneasy about that, but coming from the Western world, they were used to bureaucracy. Plus, they had not really been given a choice not to sign it, so they complied. Nevertheless, Paulo seemed very reluctant to sign. He posed a lot of questions and did not seem comfortable with the process at all. In the end, he did sign it but was clearly unsettled. Sofia was curious, as she had never really seen Paulo agitated. He argued. "If the school trusts the state of consciousness it is creating, it shouldn't need any of these measures, and if it doesn't, shouldn't they be questioning their teachings in the first place?" He said he would let that go for the time being, but Sofia could tell he was starting to question the school.

As they entered the ashram building, Sofia felt a specific consciousness field very strongly, as if entering a different energy bubble. Permeated into that field was indeed what felt like the guru's energy. On the one hand, that felt very clear to Sofia; on the other hand, she was always the first to doubt what she perceived, especially when it concerned extrasensory things. Conversely, Sofia's friends were much more trusting of her perception; Paulo certainly believed her and was uncomfortable with his energy being intermingled with that of some guru he had never heard of. He was nothing if not true to himself, so he left the *ashram* and found a place to camp close by, in the courtyard of a nice lady who had some Yogis from the school camping there. That situation rattled the whole class, like a mirror that reflected their readiness to blindly follow authority.

Ron showed the class around, pointing to the building where the canteen was, as well as the hall where they would be taking the classes and two more *ashram*s. As they left the gate, the volunteer searched their purses, presumably to ensure they had not stolen anything. Most of the students were shocked, especially Paulo.

It was time for the Yoga class. Ananda shared that the Vishuddha chakra journey would differ slightly from the previous ones. The current class would be their only regular (theory-based) lesson for the current module, after which, the structure would change. First, one of the teachers from the school, trained in non-violent communication, would offer a four-day course on the topic the following week. It was optional, but he said that typically students found it very insightful and transformational. After that, what they called the 'school camp' would start. It included lectures and daily practices

142

for a whole month for students all over the world. Sofia was puzzled about why they called it a camp, as it seemed more like a retreat. She supposed it was because most people who attended the event were camping.

The class was told that during the camp, Ron would meet with them once a week at the regular class time to practice and share a new Yoga pose and offer support. Apart from that, students were still expected to practice the two hours of daily *asana sadhana* and keep including the new postures. There would be one last class at the end, where they would do a special spiral meditation.

Ananda explained that each student needed to sign up for the Yoga camp and do some tests to get in. "What kind of tests?" Paulo readily asked.

"Blood tests," the Swami answered, "to ensure that everyone is free from diseases. You can get them from a lab here in town."

Paulo replied, "What happens if people choose *not* to take the blood tests?"

"The blood tests are there to ensure this is a safe environment for everyone. You cannot join the camp without doing the tests," replied Ananda.

Sofia felt her blood temperature drop; she had a bad feeling about the situation.

With no further questions asked, Ananda began with the theory on Vishuddha chakra. "The expansion beyond the limits of individuality and into the greater whole continues with Vishuddha, located in the throat area. This chakra is connected to the element of Ether – the energetic tapestry of the universe, through which all things interconnect. A key faculty that emerges when Vishuddha is balanced is intuition, through which the person achieves a sense of cosmic connection, making it possible to live in tune with the universal current of life, of which synchronicity is a resulting common experience.

"At the level of Vishuddha, intuition offers direct access to the universal archetypes, mysteries and the collective unconscious. That enables an alignment with the internal and external natural rhythms, which results in a harmonious lifestyle. One of the foundational ideas in spirituality is that each

143

of us is like a drop of water in the ocean; when we realise that, we can tune into the ocean and harmoniously ride the waves instead of being constantly struck by them. In other words, we can live in sync with the universe."

The Swami continued, "A question I almost inevitably get asked in this course is, how do we know if we are aligned with that universal stream of consciousness? For that, we need to be able to discern if our emotions, behaviours and intentions are coming from a consciousness-driven place or an ego-driven one. A critical factor in that is precisely our intuition; it is a paramount tool to hear our internal wisdom. The issue is that our intuition is often very weak, like a muscle that has not been trained. Through awakening and balancing Vishuddha chakra, the intuition becomes pure and enhanced, allowing for that discernment.

"Another essential feature of Vishuddha chakra is expression. A clear, persuasive and melodious expression, able to channel fundamental truths and elevated states in clear and concise ways. That happens through active listening, which enables access to superior guidance and divine grace. People who are active at this level can access their power of expression through words, singing, melodic music, rhythm, art, beauty and other forms of inspirational creativity. Swadhisthana chakra also enables creativity, but it is a type of creativity that is motivated by pleasure, whereas Vishuddha's is driven by intuition and inspiration.

"Purity is another important element of this chakra; an aspiration towards more elevated levels of consciousness and the consequent state of harmony and plenitude.

"Common-sense capacities concerning day-to-day situations are also related to this chakra, such as knowing what is considered appropriate, and more subtle aspects connected to the sixth sense, such as the sense of timing and the ability to discern what is aligned with spirit. The latter relates to the element of Ether and our capacity to feel the essence of objects and people, meaning their underlying substance."

Ananda gave the class a secret technique to connect with that divine wisdom and check whether the choices they were about to make or actions they were about to perform were aligned with it. That sounded like a key technique to Sofia, which she was keen to practice diligently; she felt that knowing if her choices were aligned with the universal wisdom would be a major asset on her spiritual path. After that, the Swami spoke about the imbalances of Vishuddha chakra: "When this chakra is imbalanced, one may experience impairments in communication, such as the inability to speak or express, or chaotic, disorganised, and disharmonious forms of expression. It is also common to make detrimental or superficial use of expression, such as disregard for others, gossiping, stuttering, loudness or antagonism.

"Lacking the receptivity and active listening ability characterising a balanced Vishuddha chakra, one may experience an impaired ability to listen (physically, interpersonally or intuitively).

"Additionally, one may feel unable to access or understand intuition, creativity and artistic expression. With impaired intuition, one may experience a disorganised, compromised or discernment-less access to the sixth sense, the collective unconscious or common sense.

"If imbalanced, the purity associated with this chakra may result in bitterness for all that is imperfect, plus judgement and disappointment towards the world. Withdrawal, detachment and rejection of the outside world are not uncommon. One can live in a state of metaphysical concern, manifested as a tendency to deny life.

"Impairment of the Ether element can result in the breakdown of one's holistic communication (such as between body and mind, internal parts of the self, or external connections).

"People who are imbalanced at this level often lack the inspiration that comes from being connected to the universal mysteries, cosmic energies and natural rhythms. That can also give an impression of separation from the environment or a sense of futility caused by prioritising spiritually insignificant matters."

At the end of the class, there was a meditation; a practice with Vishuddha chakra. While Sofia was meditating, she felt herself being lifted. She realised that she was no longer in her body but on top of her body. With her eyes closed, she noticed she could still see things, which became clearer and clearer. Sofia saw millions of bright colours and lines forming specific

145

shapes, including the shape of her body and the things around her. She wondered if that was the astral, but she had no framework to understand that experience at the time, as fascinating as it was. Either way, at the very least, it meant that her consciousness was capable of transcending her body. That, or she could be delusional, of course. For the duration of the meditation, she remained in awe of the magical world around her. She was so delighted to have the opportunity to see that; perhaps most human beings would never get to see it in their entire lives! As the teacher called for the end of the meditation, she reluctantly came back into her body and opened her eyes.

After class, Paulo caught up with Sofia. She wanted to tell him about her mystical experience, but he had something more important to share. He said that the course was not really resonating with him and he needed to consider his options. Sofia was struck by a shockwave of fear, imagining what life would look like without him. He was so supportive; she felt so safe with him… Though in that moment, she also realised how much of her sense of safety and support she was outsourcing to him. Maybe the Universe was forcing her to bring those qualities back onto herself by removing Paulo from her life. *Wow, if that is the case, the Universe is as caring as it is ruthless, and the transcendence of the ego comes at a great cost,* Sofia thought to herself. She went to Ron, seeking advice on the matter. Ron smiled kindly and said, "Look, I've seen this happen many times over. Romania is the top school, the highest tests will be here. Many people can't handle the energy and leave almost immediately, often for seemingly unrelated reasons. That seems to be happening with Paulo. We call it a *spiritual test* – it can come in different shapes to see if we are ready to take the next step in our spiritual evolution. I'm afraid he will need to overcome the egos he is facing, or he will indeed leave."

Sofia had approached Ron with no expectations about what he was going to say, but she could have definitely not predicted that answer. Were these indeed *egos* that Paulo was faced with? It seemed like his principles were higher than the school's, but could there be some grey area she was not seeing? If he had no ego, would he not just see all that with compassion and

146

stay in the school to keep learning? Because really, they were not harming anyone with any of those rules… Then again, they did not seem very elevated either or even necessary. Or were they necessary in ways that they were not aware of? The situation seemed very complex and Sofia did not know what to think. Regardless, ultimately it was his decision; she could only support him – in whichever way she could that was useful to him.

To add to the list of complex things, Merle spoke to Anney and had a conversation along the lines of, "*I know that sometimes friends get attracted to each other, and while I'm not trying to imply that is the case between us, I just want to make it clear that I don't see you in that way.*" Anney felt sad, of course, but also relieved, as if he had lifted a weight off her shoulders by removing the uncertainty. She felt gratitude for him being clear instead of allowing her to fall for him deeper. She was surprisingly fast at recovering! Anney was highly effective at transcending her emotions, which Sofia admired and felt she could learn from.

Mangalia was bathed by the black sea, which Sofia was surprised to see was not black at all, but instead of a clear, greenish turquoise colour that she adored. The water temperature was noticeably colder than Jamaica yet warmer than Portugal, so she was not overly disappointed. No surf, though. During the day, she would walk on a scenic walkway along the cliff, appreciate the little touristy shops and stands, and do her *sadhana*. She no longer had her borrowed drum to jam with Merle, but they gladly replaced that with enjoyable conversation and bubble tea, a drink he had introduced her to. She realised he was exceptionally skilled at self-care, continuously checking in with himself to see whether he wanted to do things or not, and willing to set boundaries – aspects which Sofia could definitely learn from. She found boundary-setting excruciating, as she felt responsible for other people's feelings and had a perception that setting boundaries would hurt them. "It's not about hurting others," Merle said, "it's about honouring and respecting *yourself*. You can't give to others if you're breaching your own boundaries, because you'll give from a place of resentment, drain yourself and ultimately do more harm than good to both yourself, them and the relationship. In the end, it helps no one. Plus, if they are indeed hurt by your boundaries and would have you please them rather than respect yourself, would you really want them in your life?" Words of wisdom that would take Sofia a long time to digest, practice and integrate.

Sofia enjoyed what could be her last days with Paulo in the foreseeable future, should he decide to drop out of the course. He seemed visibly dissatisfied and bothered by being there. Sofia encouraged him to stay in the school and take advantage of its teachings while disregarding the aspects he disapproved of. However, deep down, they both knew his mind was made up; their hearts just needed to accept it.

A few days later, Paulo finally told Sofia he was leaving the school. The guru's energy field, how they were treated at the *ashram*, and now having to do blood tests was too much for him. He could not stay in a school he did not trust. He decided he would do the upcoming non-violent communication course and then leave. That felt like a substantial change for both Paulo and Sofia. She shared how insecure she felt about life without him in it. He shared with her a story about a woman who was very joyful and content with life. One day, the woman was happily walking down the street and saw a diamond ring she really liked through the window of a jewellery shop. She went home, contemplating whether buying such an expensive ring was a responsible thing to do, but instead, she started obsessing over it and fearing that someone else would buy it. She raced back to the shop. Luckily, the ring was still there and she bought it. She was so relieved and excited to have it on her hand; she spent days feeling its energy and admiring its beauty. One day, she went swimming and lost the ring. She looked everywhere, but it was nowhere to be found; it had been lost to the ocean. She was devastated; she cried every time she looked at her bare hand or passed the jewellery shop. She could not find her joy and felt incomplete without it. The interesting thing is that before discovering the ring, she felt whole, joyful and complete. Paulo concluded, "You were joyful and complete before I arrived; you felt safe, brave and excited about life. If you have outsourced part of these qualities to me, life may be asking you to reclaim them." Sofia knew he was right... She probably did not even know how to be in a romantic relationship without outsourcing parts of herself. She felt sad; they were both grieving. To Sofia, that all felt very unexpected; the Yoga course meant everything to her – she could not imagine leaving; nothing in the world made more sense than that path of enlightenment. She realised she had been projecting that onto him, maybe to all students; perhaps he did not feel the same way. Either way, she chose to trust the cosmic intelligence, where everything happens for the greater good.

The non-violent communication course started. There were two facilitators, who began with a small theatrical play, acting as spouses.

The wife said, "Unbelievable, you spend all your time on social media!"

The husband replied, "Who do you think you are to control what I can and can't do? I'm spending time because I need to, plus I reckon I will not be finished for at least two more hours."

Then, they did another small play, where the wife said the same sentence, "Unbelievable, you spend all your time on social media!"

The husband contested, "Look who's talking! You're the one who is always on social media, and you're talking about me?"

Lastly, they performed one final play, where the wife said, "I've noticed that you've spent three hours on the computer today and I feel fragile because I have the need for connection and affection. Do you think we could go out for dinner later?"

The husband warmly responded, "I would love that! Sorry, I was just decompressing from work, but you know what? I miss you; let's spend some time together right now."

After that play, one of the facilitators asked, "What do you think happened in the first two examples that differed from the third?"

Someone replied, "The wife accused him rather than share her feelings?"

The facilitator agreed, "Exactly. When we judge or blame others, they feel threatened, which leaves them with two options, *defend* or *attack*. In the first example, the husband defended himself; in the second, he fought back.

149

When we use non-violent communication, people are more likely to be receptive and work towards a positive outcome."

The other facilitator continued, "So what is the difference between regular and non-violent communication? In regular communication, people tend to make assumptions, projections and distortions – often stated as *truths* – and blame others for our emotional landscape. In non-violent communication, we state real facts, own our feelings, communicate our needs, and find solutions. When we share our feelings instead of making accusations, the other is likelier to empathise rather than become defensive or fight back. Most humans will be able to feel empathy and compassion towards someone who is scared, jealous, ashamed or hurt. That vulnerability is the key to establishing the connection, rather than increasing the disconnection."

Those were just the first fifteen minutes of the course, and Sofia already felt like it would change her life. She had been taught that vulnerability was shameful and exposing, whereas they were arguing that it was beneficial and bonding. That explained why she could not connect with the other children at school when she was younger – she was doing the exact opposite! It also showed her how little knowledge of emotional intelligence has been passed down to her.

Four days passed, and Sofia and Paulo's entire framework of communication had changed; they felt much better equipped to communicate with other human beings at a deeper level. However, there was also sadness in ending that course. It meant that Paulo was about to leave. For their last night together, they had dinner at a popular restaurant amongst the Yoga students and then Sofia surprised him by booking a hotel room for the night. They cuddled in bed and felt tremendous love within themselves and for each other. They looked back on the beginning of their relationship and their time together. How much they had learned, shared and grown together. It felt like they loved each other so deeply that they would not be apart even if there were time or physical distance between them. While they obviously had separate bodies, somehow, it felt like there was no separation between them – as if they were energetically merged. Being very sensitive

150

to energies, Sofia enjoyed that sense of union. They sat cross-legged in front of each other, looked into each other's eyes and felt the depth of each other's being. Holding their gaze, they could perceive different facial expressions in each other – some younger, others older; it felt like a peek into different lifetimes. Without a word, they tapped into a multitude of experiences and learnings that the other had been through, including many cultures they had lived in and many lives they had touched. Sofia closed her eyes and could feel him as if they were touching. Then she opened their eyes again to verify that they were indeed not touching, as it felt so real. Their fascination and passion for each other were palpable. They felt as one emotionally and energetically, even though their physical bodies were not expressing that oneness. Suddenly Sofia had a sense of loss, realising that the oneness was not complete; it was not being manifested in the physical reality – their bodies were not together. She felt a sudden attraction to him, a desire to merge with him physically. Sofia undressed herself, as did he. Paulo remained seated and she slowly sat on top of him, with her legs interlocked behind him, while his legs interlocked behind her. He did not have to ask questions; he could clearly sense that she was feeling a 'full yes'; her whole being was receptive to him. She adjusted her position in a way that his *lingam* entered her *yoni*. At that moment, they were one, physically, energetically, emotionally, spiritually… Their minds were fully present and in sync. They were completely still, yet a powerful flow of energy was circulating through them – from him into her through the genitals and from her back into him through the heart. They felt vibrant and fully alive. There was a bright light involving them, coming from within. It felt as if they had no beginning and no end. The energy was pure ecstasy; their hearts expanded to infinity; love was everywhere; it felt as if they were the whole universe and the whole universe was in them. They iterated between slow movements and stillness, never letting go of each other. Sofia felt safe. She could feel the divine feminine creatively and intuitively manifesting through her, and she could see in Paulo a perfect expression of the divine masculine; they were *yin* and *yang*. The blissful and orgasmic energy between them was so powerful that Sofia could feel how that same energy could birth universes

151

and create new life. Their whole bodies and the entirety of their beings were vibrating in pleasure. She felt whole, complete and filled with an immense desire to love him – physically, emotionally, mentally, spiritually and in every way possible. Her ego dissipated and her individual will surrendered to the cosmos; they were one and the same – it was as if he were just another expression of her. Their white light encompassed all space and time. They may have been there for minutes or hours; it was impossible to tell as time stood still.

The following day, Sofia reflected on the previous night's experience. It was as if the Universe had graced her with the experience of what trauma-free love-making could look like – and it was *so* beautiful. However, she could not conceive of how to achieve that again – she felt her fears and resistance returning. She remembered Ananda saying that sometimes the Universe gives the person an experience that shows them their potential. That happens not by their own merit but purely by grace. Then, they have to earn their way back to it through their process of healing and awakening. At least now Sofia knew what to hope for.

Paulo woke up and packed his bags. Sofia took him to the train station and felt every single emotion available in the human spectrum, all at the same time. Before leaving, Paulo told her, "I thought a lot about what I'm about to tell you, and I decided I want you to be completely free. I can see that this course is changing your life, which can only continue to happen if you are fully available to experience whatever you need to – even if some of it doesn't fit the monogamous standards. I'm very keen to stay connected; I love you deeply, there is no question about that; I know you love me too. We've experienced incredible things together and I hope we'll continue to do so many times over. But while you're in the course and I'm away, I want you to know that from my end, you are completely free to do whatever you want, to be with whoever you want if that arises, and experience everything you need to." Sofia felt shocked again, though, at that point, she should no longer have been surprised about anything that came from Paulo. It was the ultimate act of altruism and unconditional love: to renounce his attachment to her and encourage her to be fully herself, regardless of the consequences for him. Sofia tried to argue against his resolution, but he was steadfast. He contested, "I would not be in integrity with myself if I held you back from becoming who you truly are. And not being in integrity with myself is not an option." Suddenly, the train arrived and the conversation was over. Sofia was left on the platform, overwhelmed and waving goodbye to that being she loved at a depth that still astounded her.

Sofia went to the ocean and cried. The waves brought her the comforting words of the Ganga: *You are not lost and you are not alone.* She felt like the ocean had always held and supported her. More poignantly, she was now conscious that she was crying tears of ego – she knew that true love did not hurt. There was another part of her that, even with him gone, still felt fully connected to him due to the presence of unconditional love. Heavy-heartedly, she recognised that she could not have identified the parts of herself that she had outsourced unless he were to leave. She sobbed even harder, trying to be angry at the universe but failing. Her ego was inconsolable, but she could also feel her consciousness at peace. How could she feel two completely opposing states? Moreover, how could she hate a universe that kept on giving her exactly what she needed…

Ron gathered the class and offered some recommendations on how to approach the upcoming Yoga camp. He said that the daily qualities they were being initiated in would remain in them as a small seed of consciousness that would gradually unfold. Therefore, it would be productive to assume a state of receptiveness while receiving them, being open and attentive. He also explained that if people felt so inclined, they could psychically tune into the guru during that process. Ron also recommended setting an intention for the camp. He claimed that whenever someone sets an intention, they put a request out to the Universe to receive what they are asking for, and if it is a genuine aspiration and they are ready for it, the Universe will assist them. He argued that the most powerful days to set intention were on the full moon and new moon, as the moon is closest to the Earth, and the gravitational pull and influence of the mysteries were most present. Ron added that he always works with an intention; he writes it on a little whiteboard on top of his bed to be reminded of it as soon as he wakes up and just before he falls asleep. "If you have this effortless, free and powerful tool at your disposal, why not use it?" he concluded. After careful consideration, Sofia decided on an intention for herself: To become aware of her most significant ego.

The Yoga camp began. There were hundreds of people, many from different countries, though the majority were Romanian. Each day was an initiation to one of the qualities of the self, such as unconditional love, peace, acceptance, willpower, courage, transcendence, etc. In the mornings, they had meditations and practices, and in the afternoons, they were left to their own accord yet still encouraged to remain focused on the quality that was being awakened.

Sofia learned many things from getting to know more students in the school, particularly the Romanian ones. The most pertinent one explained why the ashram had so many rules. A Bulgarian student told her, "There is a lot of violence, mafia and theft in Romania and its surrounding countries. The population is impoverished and education is not at the level of Western European countries. You can see that in the rubbish all over the streets and people drinking everywhere. Some people are kidnapped or robbed, the organ trafficking black market is huge, there are a lot of rapes and physical assaults... You must be careful here, especially at night, even more so if you're alone." Whether he was exaggerating or not, something clicked in Sofia's head. The extreme measures at the *ashram* were not school-related; they were culture-related. They were actually *appropriate* to the state of consciousness of the countries and the people visiting them. Too bad she did not realise that while Paulo was still there, maybe it would have made a difference... Then again, maybe things needed to have happened that way and it was indeed a spiritual test, which would explain why that information was only arriving at this time. Who knows. Either way, rightfully or wrongfully, she trusted the Universe. That thought led her to remember an occasion when she asked Paulo, "What if you trust the Universe your entire life and at the end of it you realise it was all bullshit and there is no Spirit at all?"

He replied, "If you've lived joyful, excited and at peace your entire life, does it matter?"

Sofia started to pay more attention to her surroundings. Indeed, she noticed that the streets – even the beaches – were full of rubbish, there was extremely loud music every few metres, people were drinking at every hour of the day, and there was a multitude of individuals roaming around who did not seem particularly conscious, respectful or in any way concerned about other beings. Observing her thoughts, Sofia noticed herself judging the people of that place and positioning herself above them. She wondered how to not place herself above people having such unconscious attitudes. Was she not *indeed* above them? Despite some logic there, that felt arrogant to her, so she meditated on it. What came to her in meditation was that she was reacting to those actions because she had *been* one of those people, or maybe to a degree still was, and she rejected those parts in herself. The truth was, all of those parts were there, even if just in potential. Although she had been blessed with teachers and experiences that led her to awaken certain parts of her consciousness to a degree, others were still going through the phases of unawareness around those specific aspects. Who knows, they might even have other parts awakened in themselves that she did not. Considering that possibility unblocked Sofia's empathy and compassion. She could feel their suffering and disconnection, plus their areas of wisdom which she could learn from. She no longer felt superior to them; in fact, in some ways, she was exactly the same – a person trying to do their best, suffering and seeking happiness.

Regardless of her empathy, the conversation with the Bulgarian guy shook Sofia, causing her to feel scared. She noticed herself avoiding going out on her own, staying out past sunset or approaching the locals. A few days passed, and Sofia observed the fear closing her off. She witnessed first-hand how our thoughts and feelings perpetuate our reality. Because of fear, she shut down and therefore appeared closed off. People responded to that by not being very friendly to her, which maintained the reality in which she

155

should be afraid. She realised that was an example of how fear manifests itself. Yet she did not quite know how to bring herself back.

One day, she went into a shop, expecting to be treated with indifference or discourtesy. Instead, the employee gave her the greatest smile and warm look and said some kind words. Simply with that smile, the employee's spark ignited Sofia's. She remembered her essence as love. After that, while the streets were the same and the people were the same, *she* was different, so her whole reality was different too. She was no longer afraid, which made everything seem relaxing and joyful. People mysteriously started being friendlier to her. Sofia considered that very eye-opening – a clear example of how a person's internal reality shapes their external one.

As Sofia started reclaiming the parts of herself she had lost or outsourced, she started feeling more inspired again. The school's daily initiations into the qualities of the higher self were also elevating her into increasingly more subtle frequencies. She felt more and more elevated every day. She decided to communicate psychically with the guru in a meditation to see what would happen. Not only did Sofia feel like she succeeded, but she also felt as if that meditation (and subsequent ones where she invoked him) resulted in immensely powerful experiences in which she felt as vast as the entire universe, as timeless as eternity, and as vital as source energy. From that, she concluded that he must be powerful; otherwise, he would not be able to initiate students with such elevated energies.

Passing by the place where Paulo had been camping, Sofia ran into one of the Romanian students from the school. He had seen her pass through there before, so he greeted her and asked how she was. She said she felt 'peaceful' and 'inspired' (consciously using descriptive adjectives in an effort to avoid using the word 'good') and mentioned that she was going to the beach. The young man expressed that he was looking for an excuse to go to the beach, implying that he wanted to tag along. Sofia's head felt fresh and clear, so for once, she did not react from auto-pilot but instead asked herself, "Do I *want* him to come with me?" She froze and noticed her tendency to say 'yes' not to hurt the other person. Having caught herself in that instant, she had something new: a choice. Unfortunately, the frozen state kept her from pondering on the issue with the necessary clarity and efficiency. She was, however, prepared for that exact situation. She had memorised a quote for when she felt frozen and needed to buy herself time to tune in instead of feeling like she had to make a quick decision: *"Please give me a moment to tune into myself; I need to check if that feels aligned for me right now."* She was almost surprised when he naturally agreed, reflecting just how unentitled she felt to make that decision for herself. As she abstracted from that and tuned in, she recalled Elixir's philosophy on saying 'yes' to life, as well as Merle's one on respecting oneself and setting boundaries. She felt into her body, which was opening up rather than closing down, relaxing rather than contracting. She interpreted that as a 'yes'. That man had a certain innocence about him, an authenticity that Sofia intuitively felt she could trust. She said, "OK, let's go."

They started to engage in fascinating conversation. They realised they had opposite signs and elements in their astrology; Sofia was Air and Water, while he was Earth and Fire. She felt at home in the upper chakras, while he was grounded in the lower ones. Not only did they find that fascinating, but after a brief conversation, they could also see how they were complementary in their perspectives. She made a mental note to explore more about astrology in the future. He suggested they do a meditation together. Sofia loved the idea; it felt original and refreshing. It was a mirror to her Western culture, where people mainly get together to talk or eat – often both – and she had not realised there could be many more ways of connecting.

They sat cross-legged in front of each other; his left hand was up, receiving from her right hand, facing down, and his right hand was down, giving to her left hand, facing up – that created a closed circuit of energy between them. They closed their eyes and opened up to the experience. Sofia felt like she naturally went to her place of comfort, up there with the higher frequencies, but she soon sensed that he had not managed to follow her up, so she came back down and gradually pulled him up. She managed to do so for a short while, but at some stage, she felt a lot of resistance from him. After some more attempts, Sofia gave up and went all the way up by herself.

157

Up there, she felt the divinity of the entire cosmos and eventually drew on that light to come back to him and pull him up. It worked; they went higher than he had gone before, even if not as high as where she had just come from. Their meeting up there was incredibly beautiful and beatific; they dwelled in that bliss for a few moments. They had not agreed on how long the meditation would last, but they finished it at the same time. What Sofia had experienced felt very vivid; she wondered if he had had a similar experience or if she had imagined it all. She was always keen to verify spiritual mysteries, so she asked him, "How was your experience? Would you like to share? 'No' is a valid answer." She liked to give people explicit permission to say 'no' since often they did not give themselves that permission – she was certainly one of those people. He replied, "Sure. Well, I felt like you went up very quickly and I tried to follow you, but I was faced with my fears and demons. I felt like you came back down to try to pull me up, but initially, I had too much fear and resistance and was not able to. You were wise enough to respect that and leave me to find my courage, which I eventually did, at which point you came back and we went up together." Sofia looked at him in stupefaction. What were the odds that they had imagined the exact same thing? She told him that he had just described her experience to a tee. He seemed happy, though not too surprised, and said, "Do you have any messages or feedback for me?" He seemed to trust her intuition and embodiment of the divine feminine very strongly. He saw her in the priestess and initiator archetypes; she could tell he was asking in that capacity. Sofia tuned in. What came through her was that *he had not dared to show himself to her*. She was surprised as those words came out of her mouth, as that was not something she had thought about or felt until then; it was as if that message had just been channelled *through* her. He asked her to give him a moment to integrate that. Sofia also learned from his response just then that she can ask for time to integrate things rather than expecting herself to always appear certain of things and *have it together*. He responded, "That message made a lot of sense and is a recurring theme for me; I know I'm too in the *yin* and not enough in the *yang* – it's something I've been working on." Sofia was pleasantly surprised that the message made some sense to

158

him. She wondered what it meant about the channelling phenomenon and her ability to do it. They went for a swim in the warm, green, welcoming ocean under the sun and then returned to the towel to dry.

The Romanian young man asked Sofia if she wanted to do another meditation, which she accepted. They sat down in the same position as before and closed their eyes. Sofia felt herself in a priestess archetype, but more grounded and less spacious. His fervent, earthy energy started approaching her, which felt slightly scary – her fear of the masculine was showing itself. She drew on the light of her soul and focused on the timeless essence within her, which could not be harmed by anything or anyone; fear was an illusion. She felt herself opening up and him slowly and pleasantly embracing her with several energetic arms. She felt as if she had multiple arms too, which in turn enveloped him. They started a sensual, provocative, connected dance of Shiva and Shakti, masculine and feminine, consciousness and energy. That dance was full of vitality and movement; Sofia could feel herself vibrate. Their bodies were connected in all chakras and holding each other in a firm embrace, which got gradually deeper and slower. She was the sacred feminine with a hint of masculine; he was the sacred masculine with a hint of feminine. Their energies intertwined like *yin* and *yang*, merging until they reached absolute stillness, union and wholeness. They were one. Eventually, as the feeling became less intense, they parted and gradually opened their eyes, once again at the same time. Sofia controlled herself to wait a moment before asking, but she really wanted to know: "What did you experience? If you'd like to share, of course."

He said, "I felt like I was ready straight away, but it took you some time to get past your resistances, which I respected. Slowly you opened up and we involved each other in powerful, energetic movements, connecting and flowing together. Then we slowed down into stillness and oneness. That was no less powerful for me than a physical love-making experience."

Sofia was at a loss for words. What were the odds that they had made up two identical experiences twice in a row? Was there indeed an astral space in which encounters could be had, or was it all just imagination? They faced the ocean and sat with their own experience, which they both felt humbled by and grateful for. They left the beach without exchanging contacts and never saw each other again.

The school's daily quality initiations continued and Sofia started experiencing an ongoing state of wholeness. It did not feel like something she had achieved or imagined, but rather an absolutely natural state, *her* natural state. Perhaps even everyone's if they had no blockages. She realised that human beings did not need to *learn* that state, only to *remember* it – by removing the things that were blocking it. That was the work of the light and the shadows.

Merle had messaged her: "Bubble tea?" However, Sofia felt whole in herself and wondered why do anything in the world. She also felt that talking with him would probably bring her energy down to a Swadhisthana level, forcing her to descend from her current elevated frequency. She checked in with her body; it was contracted. Recognising that as a 'no', she replied, "Sorry, just had lunch." She sent the message without a second thought. Half-jokingly, he messaged back, "Is it true?" Starring at her phone screen, she was struck by a profound realisation: what she had said was actually *not* true. Not in a *Satya* sense (one of the *Yamas and Niyamas* – truth). It was not a lie *per se*, seeing as the fact itself was truthful (she did indeed have lunch recently), but that fact was completely unrelated to why she did not want to meet him. She realised she had manipulated the facts to obtain her desired outcome and lead him to think or feel what she wanted without having to own up to her feelings and needs – regardless of whether she told herself that her excuse came from a kind place or was designed to prevent suffering. She had no doubt learned that from her family, but more importantly, she had done it countless times, with innumerable people, on a myriad of topics. Thousands of memories flooded her brain at the same time, of ways in which she manipulated others. They were memories of subtle patterns, such as talking more than other people, over them, for lengthier periods of time, or in a slightly louder tone of voice (often pleasantly masked by being inspiring, eloquent, intelligent, interesting or self-confident). Not

160

fully listening, meaning listening to a point but ignoring the parts that did not match her views. Cherry-picking the information she shared in order to achieve her goals (usually driven by good intentions, which were believed to justify it). Not requesting people's feedback on occasions where communication could lead to opposition. Interpreting situations based on what she wanted to see (for example, uncomfortable hesitation interpreted as mild acceptance). *Gaslighting* (influencing others to doubt their version of the truth). Asking very few – or leading – questions so that her views would not be questioned. Having strong views and being convinced she knew the truth rather than recognising her views as a perspective. Giving unsolicited advice. Being defensive when her worldviews were challenged, sometimes bordering on aggression. Using her authority when she needed to exert power or control over others. Being seemingly cooperative but, if there was no agreement, not hesitating to impose her will (because of feeling entitled and believing she knew what was best). Talking about topics that she did not know about as if she did and seeming so sure of her decisions that others would comply.

Sofia realised all that in tears and despair, feeling everything that everyone had ever felt on the receiving end of her ignorance and control. She felt other people's feelings of disempowerment, feeling unheard, fear of challenging her authority, self-doubt, silence, discomfort, avoidance and shutting down. Sofia felt how many people she had lost, exhausted or depleted. How many times she led them to dim their inner light, passion, creativity, authority and ability or motivation to be themselves. She felt like a narcissist, an arrogant, manipulative monster who had ruined countless moments and caused immense suffering and disruption only to preserve her fragile ego. The agony and regret she felt were unbearable. She would have torn her heart to pieces if that were physically possible or annihilated her own existence if that would undo all those interactions and the suffering they had caused. She felt as if she could serve humanity for the rest of her life and that would still not be enough to make up for the pain she had caused. *How could she do that? How could she have been so ignorant and unconscious…* She felt way more unconscious than the people littering the streets. She cried herself to sleep on the sand. She was cold at night, but a self-destructive part of her believed she deserved to suffer, so she stayed there, where at least the ocean waves would comfort her.

Sofia woke up in the morning, freezing after hardly any sleep, and undid the only situation she could: The last one. She messaged Merle, saying, "I'm really sorry; that was untrue and manipulative. I just felt like being alone. I'm deeply sorry for lying. I regret it and hope to never do it again." Merle was not bothered by that at all; what he valued the most was her honesty and self-awareness. But that did not matter to Sofia. In a way, it felt even worse – she *wanted* to be punished. She returned to the *ashram* feeling inconsolable, but it also came to her that she got what she asked for – her intention had been to be shown her biggest ego.

Sofia knew that when she managed to close her open wounds, she would ultimately find gratitude for that ego having been brought to her awareness; she needed to face it. Ron was at the *ashram* when she arrived. Looking at her troubled expression, he asked, "Are you OK?"

She asked him how the spiritual path could have so many ups and downs; one moment, she felt on top of the world, connected to the source of all creation, and the next, she was in absolute despair and devastation. Ron replied, compassionately, "The path is indeed full of ups and downs. But worry not, as the ongoing trend is upwards."

Sofia spoke to Paulo on the phone. Despite feeling a tremendous amount of shame, she managed to tell him about her realisation. Once again, she expected judgement and punishment, yet he had nothing but compassion for her. He said, "Buddhists would say, take refuge in the *Buddha*, the *dharma* and the *sangha*. Meaning in our divine essence, the spiritual teachings and the fellow seekers who walk the path with us." She considered talking to some of her friends about her latest realisation, but she felt too ashamed. Nevertheless, she was determined to examine and journal about these patterns and, to the best of her abilities, never repeat them. She asked Paulo how he was doing; he said he was *doing well*. Now that Sofia was starting to deconstruct the concepts of good and bad, 'well' sounded vague and undescriptive; it could mean so many different things depending on the person's personality and culture, ranging from "not as anxious as last week" to "numb but at least not suffering", "generally content", or "happy about life", amongst countless other possibilities. She assumed the latter, as he was incredible at compartmentalising and focusing on his work. He also probably had a ton of good *karma* helping him through life – Sofia presumed.

For their last class of the Vishuddha chakra module, they were about to perform the spiral meditation. Only the people from the usual Yoga group were there, as the camp had already finished and most participants had left. First, they performed the *asana* practice and Ron shared the last *asana* for Vishuddha – postures for that chakra involved the compression and elongation of the neck (from the front, back and sides). Then, they formed a spiral for the meditation; students were placed in a specific position according to their astrology and biology. Ananda was at the centre, Ron was at the end, Devimar was outside assisting, and music was playing. The meditation started. Sofia did not feel anything at first, so she decided to be open to not feeling anything. However, a few minutes later, she felt a whoosh of energy passing through her, as if a wave of electrical current had been turned on. Sofia's head seemed like it was about to explode and her stomach felt as if it was about to purge. A few minutes passed, and she was doing her best to contain her increasing urge to throw up or empty her bowel. Trying to hold that energy, she started feeling lightheaded and afraid of fainting but reassured herself that she had never fainted before and was probably incapable of it. Moments after, everything turned black.

When she came to her senses, she was next to the spiral while everyone else was still in it. No longer feeling sick, she sat down to meditate. Even from outside the spiral, she could feel a powerful energy. She focused on that and relaxed her mind when she felt a tap on her shoulder. She was sure she had imagined it, as no one was close to her, so she brought her concentration back. Then, out of the blue, through her mind's eye, she saw the school's guru very vividly; he was looking directly at her and smiling. "Where are you from?" he asked her psychically.

She replied, "From Portugal."

163

He acknowledged her and disappeared. A few minutes later, the meditation ended. The first thing Sofia did after that was to look up photos of the guru online to see if they matched the figure she had seen. They did, but she could not remember if she had unconsciously seen pictures of him around the school; it was not impossible. She realised that no matter how many inexplicable situations she experienced, no amount of proof could satisfy her doubtful mind. The mind was simply too small to experience the divine; only the higher self was big enough to experience it. That was where she needed to experience it *from*. From that place, no proof was necessary.

Sofia was secretly excited to leave Romania. Despite her deep gratitude for all the incredible experiences she had been through, she was also extremely exhausted from all the intensity. She received the new tickets with enthusiasm. Peru was the next adventure. Yay to the land of Shamans, the Amazonian jungle and ancestral medicines! Merle was very interested in Shamanism; he and Sofia had spoken extensively about South America. She looked at him to appreciate his exhilarated face.

Chapter 11 – Ajna Chakra

The group flew all the way to Iquitos, Northeast of Peru, and headed straight for the Amazonian jungle. An old bus picked them up from the airport and drove about half an hour away from the city. During that time, the Swami announced that they were going to a Shamanic retreat place for five weeks, where they would experience different plant medicine journeys. He explained that, although Yoga is not typically associated with Shamanic practices, they had meaningful reasons to include them in this one-year course. Afterwards, he added, they would cruise through the Amazon River before making their way to Cusco for their last week, where a final ceremony would be held. He meant one final ceremony *for that module in Peru*, as opposed to for the end of the course, but when Sofia heard those words, she panicked and could not think rationally; her mind was frantically trying to remember if that was the last module and if the course was about to end. She realised she felt terribly unprepared to leave the school and face the world on her own. She quickly buried that feeling in a cold dark place, one that she would hopefully not have to revisit for another few months. The bus stopped, leaving them on the side of the road where there seemed to be nothing but trees. A Peruvian man came from the forest and signalled for them to follow him through a small path. Carrying their backpacks, the group followed him, venturing into the jungle.

Sofia expected to see some kind of jungle lodge just behind the trees, but they kept on walking for almost an hour before reaching their destination. She felt a heaviness in her heart, imagining how challenging that journey would have been for people with disabilities. That thought faded away as she admired the many colourful, almost psychedelic butterflies that came to greet them along the way. Seeing Sofia admiring a bright blue one, Merle commented, "Animals are drawn to particular places or people needing their

165

medicine. Butterflies, in this case, bring the medicine of change, transformation, metamorphosis, rebirth, lightness of being, among others I probably don't remember." Sofia had never considered that animals could hold a spiritual purpose, aligned with their environment and personal characteristics. She thought back to the animals that felt significant in her recent journey, the crows in the beginning, the eagles in Varkala and probably more that she had not paid attention to. She wondered what was their spirit medicine and regretted not feeling grateful for receiving it. "How do you find out what is an animal's spirit medicine?" Sofia asked.

"Well, personally, I look up the name of the animal online followed by the words 'spirit animal'," replied Merle.

"Interesting!" She observed, feeling like yet another new dimension of awareness had opened up for her.

After all that time walking with heavy backpacks in the sun, the group finally saw a wooden gate on their right-hand side, well ornamented with plants and flowers. The man signalled them to enter and gave them a tour. Several wooden huts with palm tree leaf rooftops were used for accommodation, with two rooms and a toilet each. A larger venue was also used as a kitchen, dining hall and library. There was one more big wooden venue, which they called *maloca*, for ceremonies and classes. A stream meandered alongside the retreat, passing right under the maloca – perhaps they chose that place precisely for its fresh water access. Everything was surrounded by beautiful vegetation, with carefully crafted little spaces for contemplation. There was no electricity, cell phone service or internet; they were entirely off the grid. They were told that the Shaman would come to meet them later and asked them to make themselves comfortable and choose their accommodation.

While Merle loved animals and nature, he did not get along with many humans. His combination of familial and cultural factors made it challenging for him to connect with others. From his family, he had suffered the trauma of rejection, and from French culture, he had learned strong judgement and negativity, so he either triggered or felt triggered by every person in the

166

group, usually both. Yet Sofia was all too familiar with the poison that judgement brought to the world, so she was determined to show love, empathy and compassion instead. That was enough for Merle to feel safe with her – a feeling that was quite precious to him. Sofia also really appreciated their friendship, even though she occasionally felt drained while interacting with him. He reminded her of a story of a man who had built a glorious wall in which he had mistakenly placed a brick of a different colour – all the man could see when he looked at the wall was that *one brick*. Especially when Sofia spent more time with Merle, he often started taking her for granted, being overly critical, complaining about the *one brick* – whatever that may be – and having expectations instead of just enjoying all the incredible things their friendship had to offer. She had once mentioned this to Paulo and confessed that it was sometimes hard for her to accept that he would systematically choose the path of suffering rather than the one of happiness. Paulo responded, "Why do you assume he sees two paths?" She held on to that image at times when she struggled to accept people's egos. She was privileged enough to see two paths, but not everyone else was – just as in some situations, she could not see them, while others could. Those people needed compassion rather than judgement – light rather than more darkness. Sofia was happy to share her light, which she felt so privileged – and unentitled – to have, to help Merle see the second path. Whether either of them could see it or not, the light she shared with him was having a significant impact on his life – a living example of a big heart, devotional spirit and unconditional support.

So, it was the logical choice for Merle to ask Sofia to stay in one of the two-bedroom huts together, which she accepted. Sofia enjoyed his sharp intelligence, dark humour, open-mindedness, emotional depth and sweet heart. Those were the conscious reasons why she accepted. She would not have been aware of the numerous unconscious ones, such as feeling protective of him, not wanting to feed into his trauma of rejection, feeling like she is connected to him and therefore not alone in the world, feeling special and unique with him, being afraid of losing love, and not loving herself enough to set sufficient boundaries even when she felt drained by him (and believing that she probably deserved it anyway).

That night, the Shaman came to meet the group and said that over the following five weeks, they would go through a journey of purification and transformation. First, they would be taken through some purification practices, such as *temazcal*, fasting, *kambo* and *rapé* (also spelt *hapé*) – these would be explained later on. Food-wise, they would have a *dieta* – a diet aimed at vitality, based on organic, biological food with no salt, sugar, meat, dairy or fat. Apart from the salt, that was similar to what Yogis called a *sattvic* diet – a pure, lifeforce-driven diet, mainly consisting of fresh fruits, vegetables, whole grains and legumes. They would also go through a one-week fast, drinking only the herbal teas they prepared. Then, he said they would experience three plant medicine journeys, for whatever work holistically needed to occur in their beings. He said that he understood that some of the students may not have heard of those sacred medicines but reassured them that they would all be carefully explained in time, and everything was optional, so they were welcome to reject anything they did not feel ready for. He also said he would meet with each student individually to discuss their medical and mental health history and determine which practices were appropriate for them.

The next day, the group had their first Ajna class. Ananda began: "Ajna chakra, also called the third eye, is located in the forehead and considered the centre of mental command. It relates to mental abilities such as intelligence, discernment, insight, meaning-making and understanding complexity. When activated to its full potential, it results in states of genius and induces self-confidence at a psychic level.

"People with a balanced Ajna experience a detached awareness and objectivity, lucidity and clarity, which allows them to analyse the world through a deeper consciousness stream rather than a self-conscious one and see reality from a big-picture perspective instead of being restricted by the constant conditionings of the past, belief systems and environment.

168

"Like Vishuddha chakra, Ajna also connects to intuition, but more to the parts that access wisdom and universal truths, rather than the ones that perceive the underlying essence of things and the sixth sense. Both forms of intuition can be used as guidance, but Ajna leans more towards understanding how the universe works, whereas Vishuddha relates to being able to sense it.

"Ajna holds the dimension of concepts, generalisations, universal laws, patterns, causality, logic and principles. People with this chakra activated typically have the ability to conceptualise, work with abstract or symbolic concepts and ideas, synthesise, apply judgement based on higher principles, make links between emotions and the lessons behind them, and correlate seemingly distinct elements of reality.

"At this level, people tend to show good self-reflection, self-awareness, introspection and the ability to access and explore the subconscious and make complex non-linear interconnections. That is helpful in shadow work, to identify damaging patterns and determine the roots of distorted beliefs. Ajna governs functions such as memory, access to dreams and the relationship between the higher and lower aspects of the self.

"In combination with Anahata chakra, Ajna governs emotional intelligence."

Ananda reminded the students that the Shaman would come to speak to them individually and that the schedule for the ceremonies would be communicated throughout their time there. Then, he talked about the purification phase they would be going through, specifying that *Saucha*, purity, was a crucial element in Yoga and one of the *Yamas and Niyamas*. He explained that by becoming purer (physically, energetically, psychologically), we release our denser energies and naturally resonate with higher frequencies.

Ron addressed the one-week fasting experience, saying that fasting was one of the most powerful practices he had ever experienced. This impressed Sofia, who thought fasting was about not eating in order to lose weight. Growing up, she had recurrently heard that a person would die if they did not eat for more than three days – a theory which, by the looks of it, would

169

either be proven or disproven in the next few days. Ron went on to explain that our body accumulates food leftovers, toxins, parasites and unhealthy bacteria for years, which creates and sustains diseases, blockages, energy leaks, poor organ functioning and an overall lack of health and well-being. Sometimes we need to purify our system, and fasting is an extremely efficient way of doing that. He said he knew several people from the school who had fasted for three months and even more. Ron also claimed that numerous people with cancer and other terminal diseases made full recoveries simply by fasting. He stated that they would align the fast with the full moon on Saturday, as – similarly to the new moon – when the moon is closest to the Earth, its gravity helps pull out physical, energetic and psychological impurities, plus it intensifies one's practices. Additionally, if one fasts with an intention, it directs a lot of energy towards that intention. The group energy also amplifies it. Both Ron and the Swami recommended that students set an intention for each of these practices. Ananda warned them that if they chose a particularly challenging intention, for example, to address one of their main egos, they might have an excruciating practice, so he advised moderation. He reiterated that all those ceremonies and experiences would be available (pending the individual physical and psychic evaluations performed by the Shaman) but were entirely optional. The Swami recommended that people use their intuition to tune into themselves and see if each feels right for them rather than joining because of peer pressure or fear of missing out. With that said, he mentioned that their first practice would be the *temazcal* in two days. The *temazcal* (which Western culture often calls a sweat lodge) was designed to help people face their fears, transcend boundaries, unlock emotions and free themselves from ignorant beliefs. It was also a strong way to purify, detox and heal the body.

The Shaman stopped by Sofia and Merle's cabin later that day. He was a Peruvian man in his fifties, whose humility concealed the decades of experience and hundreds of ceremonies he had led. His hair and eyes were dark; he wore a poncho over his simple clothes and had various amulets with crystals and feathers, which gave him an outlook of someone who was part

170

of nature. Having asked them about their physical and psychological health, the Shaman deemed them fit for all ceremonies. After that, he asked if they had any questions of their own. Sofia could not think of anything specific but asked him if there was anything he felt guided to share with them. She had learned that question from the Romanian guy she had meditated with. The Shaman paused momentarily, and then told them, "When you're participating in the ceremonies, consider your relationship with their plants and medicines. Are you using them to take whatever healing they bring, or do you respect them as sentient beings with gifts to offer? Do you take them for granted and expect them to fix you, or are you grateful for their abundance and generosity? Will you disregard or respect them? Ignore or acknowledge them? Will you be receptive, learn, understand and honour them, and integrate their blessings? That is just as valid for the medicines in the big plant medicine journeys as for the herbal tea you drink during the fast or the piece of mint you might collect from the garden. Do you take it without a second thought, or will you take a moment to connect with the plant, energetically ask for its permission, and express your gratitude?" That was another paradigm shift for Sofia. She was so happy she asked that open question! Sofia realised she was used to Western medicine, where a person mindlessly takes a pill and expects to be fixed. Conversely, the Shaman was opening up the possibility of establishing a respectful relationship with the natural world and consciously receiving its wisdom. That changed how Sofia would look at all plants from then onwards.

The group got together for their first experience, the *temazcal*, which most people attended. The *temazcalera* (person leading the *temazcal*) was called Antonia, a short but powerful and connected Mexican woman in her early thirties. She had feathers in her hair and emanated powerful *mana* with all her being. The *temazcal* was a dome, a hemispherical structure made of bamboo with blankets all around, covering it in such a way that made it completely dark on the inside – representing the mother's womb. In front of it was an impressive bonfire, where amongst a large amount of wood were some reasonably sized volcanic stones, which they called *abuelitas*, the little grandmothers. The intense heat was making them orange. The *temazcalera* had a big sea shell that she used to make a trumpet noise, indicating that the ceremony was about to begin. Antonia spoke in Spanish, but Sofia knew enough of the language to pick up that she requested the spirits of the land for permission for the ceremony, asked ancestors and guides for guidance and protection, and thanked the directions and the elements. Using *palo santo* and *copal* (natural incenses, one is wood from a specific tree, the other a resin), along with charcoals from the bonfire, the firekeeper cleansed the participants one by one as they respectfully entered the *temazcal*. People knelt and crawled inside, forming two circular rows around a hole in the middle. Sofia got in and ended up on the outer row. She sat down uncomfortably on the earth, slightly repulsed by the dirty, humid soil and weary of touching anyone around her. Once everyone was inside, the *temazcalera* entered and closed the door; everything went dark. She requested that the firekeeper bring in the stones, one by one, placing them in the hole at the centre. "*Piedra caliente!*" the firekeeper yelled out.

Antonia responded, "*Gracias abuelita*" – thank you grandmother stone. When enough stones were in, she closed the door. The inside of the dome was pitch black, and the stones in the middle emanated intense heat. Sofia had a heightened sensitivity to heat; she thanked the Universe for placing her on the outer row, further from the stones. Still, she felt like her body was almost on fire. Antonia explained that they were in the first of four 'doors' (rounds), each corresponding to one of the four elements (Earth, Water, Fire and Air). For each door, more stones would be added. Anyone who needed to get out could do so in the few minutes in between doors. Then, she asked people to do a round sharing their names and intentions. Some people stated intentions related to physical healing, others to emotional release. Sofia said she wanted to let go of what did not serve her. The heat was not decreasing, as the *temazcal* was very well insulated, and in fact, it would increase every time the *temazcalera* poured herb-scented water on the stones. Sofia tried to calm herself as the heat sank deeper into her body; she was too hot and eagerly looking forward to the door opening. When the last person said their name and intention, Antonia said, "Congratulations, you've made it through

172

the first door." No one got out. Sofia felt relieved but unconvinced that she would make it to the end. However, if she had anything left in her, it was a warrior spirit, so for the second door, she drew on that. The *temazcalera* called for the second door and the firekeeper brought another set of stones in, after which the door was closed again. Sofia thought she could stay sitting, but the heat was unbearable. She started to place her body closer to the earth, where it was slightly cooler, and drew on every bit of strength she had, but she was starting to feel truly scared – frightened of what might happen to her, of fainting, of dying. Antonia started saying some prayers in Spanish, asking for the blessings of nature, spirits, guides and ancestors, requesting protection and support, asking for their intentions to be fulfilled and saying words of encouragement and inspiration. Her voice was like a lifeline keeping Sofia tethered to this world. Nevertheless, with every passing second, Sofia thought of quitting. She kept saying to herself, "Just one more second." After what seemed like an impossibly long time, the *temazcalera* called the end of the second door. The breeze that came from outside was nothing short of a miracle for Sofia. Three people went out. She had planned to leave, but that breeze gave her just enough courage to stay in. Next came the third door; people returned and as soon as more stones were brought in, Sofia sorely regretted not having gone out. Antonia mentioned that that was the door of the Fire, the hottest of them all. Sofia's body was already hot, so the extra heat triggered a panic wave in her – she felt as if she was not going to make it. She looked around to verify that everyone was still alive, particularly the people in the first row. Not because she had the energy or the thoughtfulness to be concerned for their health, but to pacify her own desperation and reassure herself that she was not about to die, that it was only her fear creating illusions. As long as other people did not faint or die, she would probably not do so either. At that point, she had mud all over her body, yet she no longer cared at all; her arms and legs were touching the people around her but that did not even remotely matter; everything unimportant faded away. There was no past or future, just acute awareness of that excruciating moment and the vision of her imminent death. Attuned to people's heightened state, the *temazcalera* started playing loud rattles and instruments and singing songs, maybe evoking some pagan deities, Sofia was not sure any more, but it felt intense, yet sacred and ceremonial. The sound of Antonia's voice reassured Sofia; her lifeline was still present. Suddenly, it occurred to Sofia to ask her ancestors for help, so she psychically called them in and then released that thought too. Through the unbearable heat, she noticed that beyond her physical existence, she could peak into a place of stillness, where something in her was immortal. A place where her soul could not be touched, where no harm could be done. A place where time did not exist, neither did fear: Her true essence. She laid down on the ground and surrendered. Her panic was gone. If the choice was to live with ego or die, she was ready to die there and then. As she declared that to herself, the heat became less intense. It still felt incredibly hot, but in a more sustainable way. There was peace. When the *temazcalera* called the end of the third door, Sofia felt like she could have handled staying longer. More people got out, but she stayed. She endured the fourth door on the ground but with no fear. She had been reborn.

After the *temazcal*, the group bathed in the river and talked about their experiences. Not everyone had experienced a rebirth like Sofia; people had different responses of various intensities. Sofia and Merle discovered that it was gratifying and insightful for them to debrief about their experiences with each other afterwards. Merle had a warrior spirit, so the *temazcal* medicine did not feel too extreme for him. He said he envied Sofia's profound experience and wondered if it would happen to him with any of the upcoming medicines.

Saturday arrived, and with it, the beginning of the one-week fast, which was celebrated that night with a full moon ceremony. The group and the facilitators sat around the bonfire and played native instruments like flutes, drums and rattles. Each student wrote a piece of paper with what they wanted to call into their lives and what they wanted to let go of, which they then offered to the fire.

On Monday, they had the next Yoga class, where Ananda explained the symptoms of imbalances of Ajna chakra, which mainly manifest as a range of problems with mental abilities: lack of memory, concentration, discernment, mental clarity, objectivity, intelligence, awareness, insight and lateral thinking. The person can experience mental chatter, an agitated mind, ignorance, confusion, chaotic thinking and obsessiveness. There may be an impairment of the ability to work with abstract concepts and ideas, synthesise, and apply judgement based on higher principles, resulting in failures in logic, contradictory actions, incoherence and a lack of symbolic representation capacities.

The Swami elaborated that Ajna imbalances could compromise self-awareness, self-reflection, introspection and meaning-making. Distorted perceptions are common, on one hand of the spectrum having their views clouded by lack of insight, self-centred perceptions, denial or pathogenic beliefs and on the other end with delusions and hallucinations. The resulting lack of self-confidence at a psychic level can leave the person vulnerable to manipulation, blind faith and compromise. People imbalanced at the level of Ajna may have little or disorganised access to their subconscious. They often find it hard to remember dreams.

Lastly, Ananda mentioned that if either Ajna or Anahata are imbalanced, people tend to have low emotional intelligence.

The fast had been very surprising for Sofia. She was amazed to realise that her body was actually not hungry at all, though her mind kept bringing up food-related thoughts. It felt as if her body had enough sustenance for all that and much more, but her mind had immense resistance. The teachers had recommended that they meditate, go for walks in nature, breathe the fresh air and take in the sun as ways of receiving energy that did not require ingesting food. That was what Sofia did. The first three days were smooth; she hardly thought about food and did not feel less energy at all. She had read that sixty percent of the daily energy that human beings spend is on digestion alone, so she was saving sixty per cent of her energy by simply not eating (even if she did not gain some of it either). On the fourth day, her

175

mind started to bring up increasing resistance, and the fifth day was particularly challenging. She felt annoyed and irritated all day long; her mind was constantly thinking of food, she thought about quitting several times, she lost her joy and could not see the point of all that suffering any more. On her daily walk, she ran into Klaus, who was extremely excited about his fast. He said he felt a lot of energy and was considering doing a longer fast, like a month, if not now, then for sure when they ended the course. That broadened Sofia's perspective. All things considered, one week was a very short time in her life. Plus, more than half of it had already passed. She reclaimed her courage and felt motivated again. Something changed in her at that point. It was as if a switch had been turned off; she was no longer suffering from the fast. She was reminded of how Buddhists differentiate pain (physical, factual) from suffering (emotional, subjective) – it felt as if she had removed the latter from her current experience. By the time the following Saturday arrived and they were allowed to eat again, she felt like she could have kept going. Nevertheless, she was more excited about eating and happily chose to do so. She noticed that either the *temazcal*, the fast, or both had changed or cleansed something in her. She felt lighter and more energised, plus her main addictions had disappeared (chips and chocolate). More significantly, she realised she had spent her entire life eating far more than she needed out of unawareness, comfort, gluttony or addiction.

In the next Yoga class, Ron spoke about concentration. He claimed that *energy flows where attention goes*; hence our attention is a powerful tool for us to change our reality. We can choose to channel it towards the chakras (to stimulate and harmonise them), train it to obey our command, or use it for any other intention rather than having it run wild; either way, it's a significant achievement. He asked, "How many thoughts do you have per day? Five thousand? Fifty thousand? Now let me ask you this, how many of those thoughts do you *consciously choose* to have? Two? Ten?" He concluded, "Let's face it, our mind is constantly pulling the strings and our thoughts are random, unfocused and chaotic. Can you imagine the resonances we would attract if we chose only a few things to focus on instead of wasting energy on countless unnecessary things? That is why *Dharana*, also called steady concentration or single-pointed attention, is also one of Patanjali's eight limbs of Yoga that we discussed before."

Someone asked, "What are the other seven?"

"Well," Ron replied, "the eight limbs of Yoga are: *Yamas and Niyamas* (the moral codes we have been discussing), *Asana* (the postures), *Pranayama* (breathing techniques), *Pratyahara* (withdrawal of the senses), *Dharana* (concentration), *Dhyana* (meditation) and *Samadhi* (oneness)."

Ron taught the posture of the week and an exercise for concentration, after which the class ended.

At the end of the class, the Shaman joined them and explained that they would be having the *kambo* and *rapé* ceremonies that week. He explained: "*Kambo* is a medicine that purifies the body, boosts the immune system and treats chronic pain, drug dependence and other ailments. It comes from a frog; essentially, the person's body reacts to the frog's secretion as if it were being poisoned, releasing all the toxins it can in order to remain alive. The person can sweat, purge or have bowel movements if necessary.

"*Rapé* is tobacco medicine, where tobacco snuff, supplemented with other healing plants, is blown through a special blowpipe up the person's nostrils. It permeates through their mucous membranes and into the bloodstream, causing chemical reactions in the brain that cause the person to feel calm and relaxed yet awake and alert. It is also said to cleanse the respiratory system and clear the third eye. It can also trigger some more mild purging effects. None of these substances are psychedelic. If you have any questions at all, feel free to come to me."

Anney was terribly upset because the main ceremonies she wanted to attend were the plant medicine journeys, but the Shaman refused her because of her mental health history. Moreover, she did not feel called to participate in the other ones but had nothing else to do and feared missing out. Anney was having a tough time, feeling disconnected from the group. So, she took solace in the forest, which felt like her home, and decided to create a sanctuary there, in a place where the trees had allegedly asked her to perform a healing ceremony to release some trauma that had happened in that land in the past. Whether the forest *actually* spoke to Anney or she felt so merged with it that she projected her own feelings or traumas onto it, Sofia would never find out. Either way, her mission was to accept Anney as she was, so it did not matter. They had a lot of fun; Anney would tell Sofia about the roles of the plants and their medicines; animals would drop in to see the clearing they were creating; it felt very special. Sofia knew that sometimes she took solace in Anney, as Anney was very positive and uplifting, which recharged her after spending time with Merle. They felt more like sisters than friends. Sometimes they would lie on the grass and just enjoy the sun, with their heads resting on the other's belly, arms or legs. That evolved into *cuddle puddles* – people relaxing on each other in whatever uncanny positions they ended up forming. Elixir and Klaus were delighted to attend these on a daily basis since – much like Anney and Sofia – touch was one of their love languages. There it was, Sofia realised, another way of connecting that did not involve talking – simply resting comfortably on one another and enjoying each other's presence.

Merle longed for intimacy but had too many blockages to connect with people in that way, so at times, he felt jealous of Sofia's intimate relationships and resentful of her for being so open. Sofia responded to that with kindness; she had absorbed from Rico all those years ago that jealousy was also a love language, so she always received Merle with love, empathy and acceptance. Sofia would find herself in the mother archetype with him, probably because he was a decade younger than her, but also because of his wounded inner child that she could see distinctly through his pain, insecurities and fear of rejection. Under his many defences and protections, Merle had one of the sweetest, biggest hearts she had ever seen; she loved him dearly. When he was vulnerable, she wanted to hold him in her arms and never let him go. When he was angry, she worked on compassion and acceptance. Their bond was profound and complex, deeper than many relationships of a romantic nature, even though theirs was not. Deep down, Sofia knew that this relationship came at a cost – of often losing her energy, having to choose between him and her other friends, and being weighed down instead of uplifted. However, it also brought her a lot of meaning, depth and connection. Besides, she was simply unwilling to close her heart. *If we are indeed endless beings, I can give endless love,* Sofia thought, or at least she would try.

The time of the *kambo* ceremony had arrived. The class had been told to drink two litres of water beforehand. When they arrived, they were given a bucket each (for purging) and shown where the toilet was. The Shaman came with a cute frog on his hand, bright green with long toes that ended in big cartoon-like circles that stuck to his hand. He passed the frog to Merle, who he had taken an interest in since an occasion when he had heard him play the flute very harmoniously. Merle was the type of person who played from Vishuddha chakra, meaning by channelling his connection with nature and the divine; therefore, his music was very healing and inspired. What Sofia loved the most was hearing him play the didgeridoo right over her head. The frog seemed quite happy to go to Merle, who was very respectful of and connected to animals; he would make friends with all the cats in the places he visited. Sofia realised it was because he always focused on what the animal wanted rather than what he wanted from the animal. That approach was new to her – until then, she would typically only consider whether she wanted to pat a cat, not whether the cat wanted to be patted. Sofia stared at the captivating frog, making it a point to be grateful for its medicine. The Shaman pointed out that that was the frog from which the medicine had been taken (a gooey transparent liquid it secreted). He asked if everyone was ready. Having received affirmative responses, the Shaman disinfected each student's left shoulder, then burned the end of a little stick and, with it, burned three dots onto each person's shoulder. Then, he proceeded to scrape some of the frog's liquid onto each dot. Very shortly after, the students started to feel the effects. Sofia felt as if her entire system had suddenly been activated and on high alert. Her heart was racing, her immune system spiked through the roof, she felt hot and cold, and her body was sweating as if she were back in the *temazcal*. She started purging into the bucket. Lightheaded, faint, feverish, and frantically shaking, she raced to the toilet to urgently empty her bowel. She felt like her body was releasing

179

all the toxins it possibly could to survive. She did not even have the strength to see how other people were doing or to take comfort in them still being alive. Yet that process was not reversible, so unlike the *temazcal*, where she could get out, that moment presented no options. She was either going to die or not; either way, she had no way of influencing the process. That made it easier in a way – the only thing she *could* do was trust and surrender. Her focus was fully on the present moment: On feeling her heart continue to beat, not fainting, and managing to vomit roughly into the bucket. Fifteen minutes passed; her symptoms finally stabilised, then decreased over the following fifteen minutes. By the time it ended, Sofia felt utterly exhausted and the only thing she could do was drag herself to the hut and sleep for the rest of the day. Once again, some people did not have such intense experiences. In her debrief with Merle, he said he did not even purge, unlike everyone else. Sofia was so happy about his experience, while he was envious of hers. "Why on Earth would you envy such a God-awful experience?" she asked, shocked.

"Because I'm not afraid of intensity, I *want* to purge, cleanse and release everything already," Merle replied. He had a good point, though Sofia wondered if perhaps he simply had a lot less to release. She had learned that simple explanations are often the most accurate. Either way, she trusted that he was having the exact experience he holistically needed – even if it was not the one he wanted.

Sofia was unsure how many more of those intense experiences she could handle; she could only hope that the next ones would be softer. Fortunately, it was the case. When the Shaman arrived at the stream for the *rapé* ceremony, the whole group was already there, excluding Ananda, who did not participate in the ceremonies. The Shaman's helper delicately poured a bucket of flowers immersed in water over each person, honouring them with a lot of respect, care and devotion. It felt sweet and gentle, which mirrored how callously Sofia had always treated her body. Her body had literally carried her all her life and she had never done anything nice for it, except maybe a couple of massages, which had been mostly for pleasure rather than conscious offerings. Sofia had certainly not expressed any regret or gratitude towards her body either. She was essentially *using* it – it was not a reciprocal relationship; it was slavery. With that thought, her eyes teared up and she found it hard to swallow. Sofia voiced, once again, *I'm so sorry, body...* As the flower water poured over her with such love and gentleness, she felt a wave of grief along with it. Though the mirror was painful, she tried her best to hold her tears – she still carried the shame that comes with mistaking vulnerability for weakness.

Sofia felt terrified of the upcoming *rapé* experience, as her nose was one of the most sensitive areas in her body; she would not even let her friends or partners near it. She had psychologically prepared herself for that practice, but now that it had arrived, she felt broken and vulnerable from the flower water episode and, deep down, no longer felt ready for it. Unfortunately, she was not consciously aware of that, as she had not checked in with herself, so she was about to do it anyway. Looking at her, Merle asked, "How are you feeling?" This led her to check in with herself. She realised that she felt shaken and unsure. He reminded her that she did not have to do something just because she had previously decided to do so. In a way, he gave her permission to listen to herself and trust her own wisdom. That was one of his gifts, as well as a big mirror and inspiration for Sofia. She asked the Shaman if he could facilitate the *rapé* for her another time and he said he would be happy to do that. So easily fixed, the situation. All that was missing was awareness. Sofia felt relieved about having respected herself, though she was left with a poignant feeling about how close she came to not doing so. Luckily Merle was there to save her from herself. Disrespecting her body was highly normalised for Sofia, who could sense how challenging it would be to shift that. She stayed and observed her friends receive *rapé* through the blowpipe in their noses; some felt slightly startled for a moment; they spit the tobacco into the stream, then sat to meditate. Some claimed it was highly uncomfortable, which was the extent of what they felt; others said they felt a deep peace, entering a meditative state. Overall, it seemed vastly less extreme than the *temazcal* or *kambo*.

181

The following day, Merle asked Sofia if she wanted him to serve *her* *rapé*. *Rapé* had been one of his practices for a while but he had not attempted to offer it to someone else yet, so he said he would be honoured to do so. Somehow, she felt more comfortable receiving it from him, who was less experienced but knew her and her nose trauma. So, they went to the stream; he took *rapé* himself first, after which he served her. She felt a quick and powerful surge of energy shooting up to her third eye and then a state of extreme peace; no mind or thoughts, just silence and an elevated vibration. It was a similar feeling to jumping off an aeroplane at fourteen thousand feet or reaching the top of a high snowy mountain just before skiing down. From that place, Sofia could see the *karmic* links she had to past lives and even follow them to see what she had done in those lives – one of which was the tribal one that she spontaneously had a peak of when she was with Paulo, another one was in India as a Swami – which explained her sense of familiarity with Yoga – plus a few others. That state lasted a few minutes, after which Sofia felt that her body was becoming frail and slightly sick, so she was tempted to lay down, but Merle encouraged her to stay up. In doing so, she felt like some cleansing was happening but also perceived herself going away from her body and into mind space. At that point, Merle, who was very attuned to her, used his rattle to make some remarkably appropriate sounds, which felt like a lifeline back into her body. Sofia knew that some healing was taking place and she needed to be present for it. She held on for as long as she could but eventually had to lie down. Merle stayed there, holding space for her, attuned, making sounds exactly when needed. That lasted for about two hours, then she rested for another two while he went for a walk, then he came back for her and they went back to the hut. He advised her to tune into her body to see what she needed and honour that (such as drinking water, resting or moving), and alerted her that *rapé* may awaken her dreaming abilities.

When Sofia and Merle were debriefing about the *rapé* experience later that day, they realised a few things: That she could probably not have had that experience in the context of the group the day before, as she needed the individual support, and that he appreciated his role as a space holder and medicine man – something that would start its own journey. Sofia was fascinated by how the series of events since the flower water came together for the greater good. She journalled: *I can see how the past happened exactly as it needed to happen, for us to experience exactly what we needed to experience so that we could learn exactly what we needed to learn.* Just in case there were still any questions regarding whether there was a universal intelligence that had their back.

In the following month of Ajna classes, Ananda and Ron talked about the potential of the mind in unleashing one's natural and supernatural abilities. They explained ways in which Yoga could help a person unlock the power of their subconscious: "Through our unconscious, we can access the values, gifts and capabilities of our being, draw from the force and light that is in our shadow, bring awareness to our egos and unconscious patterns, intuitively access the answers we need, come closer to the realisations we need to experience in order to self-realise, awaken our psychic abilities that were once natural (such as telepathy, mediumship, clairvoyance, telekinesis), amongst other incredible gifts."

The class continued to practice one more Ajna posture per week, mainly consisting of inversions, balancing and resting poses. They also discussed topics such as the power of meditation, visualisation, attention, awareness, silence and other practices. Sofia intuitively knew that reaching the level of Ajna chakra, which was so subtle and elevated, would take much more than seven weeks, as those states of consciousness were typically very far from the ones that regular humans currently lived in. While the theoretical background was enough to give Sofia a sense of what that state of being could look like, she knew how far she was from having that lived experience. If someone indeed had Ajna awakened, they would be experiencing states of genius, accessing *akashic* records (the so-called memory of the universe), seeing past lives, *karmic* links and other dimensions, lucid dreaming, being fully intuitively connected, drawing on the full power of the unconscious and probably many other aspects that Sofia could not even fathom. She wondered if the school realised that too, meaning that while for the previous chakras, they used teachings and techniques to attempt to give students a glimpse of those states within a few weeks (which people could then deepen over the years), for Ajna, they would be more likely to achieve that through powerful short-term experiences and the help of plant medicines.

The time to embark on the plant medicine journeys was approaching. The class was excited about the upcoming days, except for Anney, seeing as she could not participate. Her sacred space in the forest was stunning; she and Sofia had put some mats on the ground and were hosting increasingly popular daily cuddle puddles. The relationship between the two of them was very precious. Anney had a history of childhood trauma and ongoing abuse, so she often felt unsafe with people; yet Sofia had an unwavering loyalty, warmth and almost devotional loving essence towards other humans that Anney felt relaxed and safe around. Sofia was like a sister she knew she could trust and count on. The two of them radiated unconditional love and were a magnet for people who wanted to be in that vibration. For Sofia, this relationship helped her confront her deep-rooted ideas that she was unlovable – because of feeling like a monster and also due to her inability to connect with people most of her life. Having that love and friendship now was gradually starting to shift those beliefs. Perhaps one day, she would even come to believe she was worthy of love instead of automatically expecting rejection from people. When Sofia was with the Yoga group, there was meaning, harmony and connection – it was the most at home she had ever felt in her life.

That morning, the Shaman came to talk to the group about the plant medicine journeys. He explained that they would be working with the grandmother plant, which consisted of a special brew of a vine and another main plant, sometimes adding some more Amazonian medicine plants in smaller quantities. It takes several days to prepare – a process performed ritualistically and delivered ceremonially. The grandmother plant is said to have the wisdom to detect, understand and fix anomalies in people's physical, energetic, psychological and spiritual bodies, and heal anything from body illnesses to emotional traumas and diseases of all sorts. For those

184

reasons, it is often called *the grandmother*, as it is meant to give the person what they need, as opposed to what they think they need. The Shaman stated that this was a psychedelic medicine; hence the experience could be intense, but his recommendation was to trust the medicine, as she knows exactly what she is doing. He explained: "You may need cleansing, insight, healing, feeling or experiencing something, which is what will happen. We will be having three journeys, in which I will be there to hold space, support you and be the bridge between the seen and unseen worlds. Your three journeys may be completely different from each other; just trust that whatever is happening in each moment is what your being holistically needs." With that, he scheduled the ceremony for six o'clock that evening.

On her way to the ceremony, Sofia could hear the crickets chirping outside. She asked Merle, "What is the spirit medicine of crickets?"

He replied, "I've heard that ancient civilisations believed they were mediators between body and spirit, and the vibration of their sound elevates people into higher spiritual states."

How appropriate, Sofia thought. They arrived at the *maloca*, which was modestly but beautifully decorated; there were some Peruvian tapestries, nature-based ornaments and candles. Several mattresses were on the floor a few metres apart, each with a bucket next to it. It was fairly dark. The students sat on the mattresses and waited for the Shaman. The Peruvian man who had welcomed the group when they arrived was assisting him in the ceremony and started burning some natural incenses. The Shaman played some native instruments, which set a calm, introspective mood. Then he uttered some invocations in Spanish and maybe some worlds of protection or appreciation, after which he asked the group to come and receive the medicine one by one. As Sofia sat in front of him and drank from the small wooden bowl that held a dark liquid inside, she remembered to honour the medicine, be open to receive its wisdom and feel grateful. She was not prepared for the highly unpleasant taste that followed, but she did her best to drink it appreciatively and welcome whatever she needed to receive. Her intention was for the *grandmother* to do whatever needed to be done in her

185

physical and subtle bodies, and she trusted its wisdom as well as the Shaman holding the space.

Sofia went back to her mattress and sat down. With her eyes closed and the space getting darker, she could hear some heavenly chimes around the room, which she later learned came from an instrument called a *koshi*. They used the *koshi* to connect to the four elements, raise the vibration of the space and begin the journey into the unseen. The sound resonated in Sofia's head as if the instrument were inside. She asked any ancestors, spirits and guides who wanted to support her journey at that moment for protection. Immediately she felt her spirit guide arrive – the one she had met in her adolescent years – as well as an ancestor from the Māori tribe that gave her the *pounamu*. She felt them standing beside her mattress and holding a protection field around her. Either that or she was imagining the whole shebang – as usual, she left ample room for self-doubt. Deep down, she was hoping for some mystical psychedelic experiences but also feeling sincerely open to whatever came. Yet magical experiences were not in the *grandmother*'s cards for that evening. Instead, Sofia started feeling sick… Very sick. She tried to contain the urge to purge, which only made her sicker. She began to sweat, feeling hot and cold and extremely uncomfortable. The Shaman started singing chants in Spanish, sometimes whistling or playing musical instruments. The songs felt very appropriate, harmonious and healing; Sofia had a sense that he was perfectly attuned to his environment and everyone in it. She laid down; it no longer felt possible to sit. Her body started shaking and feeling sore all over. All the while, she was getting sicker and sicker. She felt delirious because of the tremors and nausea. Sofia held the medicine in her stomach for as long as she could, but at some stage, she could no longer do that either, so she purged into the bucket. She kept on purging for a long time, though she had not eaten much that day or the one before. Where was all that coming from? Her body could no longer lie still; it was shaking, aching, and vomiting who knows what. She could feel herself between worlds and sense the presence of the Shaman, attentive and protective. He passed by and blew tobacco smoke on her and the others. Smelling the tobacco, she felt even sicker. They considered tobacco a healing and protective medicine, connecting humans to Gods. For a moment, Sofia could see the spirit of the *grandmother* herself; she was mystical, beautiful, powerful, intentional and connected. Still and calm, but with great life force, full of *mana*. She was part of the forest and embedded in its spirit. Sofia addressed her psychically, "I trust you. I welcome you. I thank you for your gifts." Then she felt a sudden bowel movement, which jolted her into the physical world. She could not fathom how to gather the strength and balance needed to drag herself to the nearest toilet, yet she had no choice but to try. Somehow, she found herself heading there, crash landing on the toilet and releasing the content of her bowels. She felt as though she was in a dream, not really there but not away either, profoundly sick in every way. Eventually, she crawled back to her mat, only to shake and vomit more for an awfully long time. After a while, feeling exhausted, sore and feverish, her body started to slow down until it gradually came into stillness. She no longer felt sick or shaky. She experienced only tremendous peace – as if her whole being was lighter.

Sofia had no idea how many hours had passed, but eventually, she brought herself back to her room. Merle arrived just after, sharing that he also had a very painful, shaky and uncomfortable experience. He had heard many people in the room vomiting and moaning as well, so maybe a lot of cleansing needed to happen.

Sofia was dreading the subsequent two plant medicine journeys; she was unsure how much more purging her body could take. She felt grateful for the retreat place they were in, the nature that felt so healing, the food that felt so nourishing despite the lack of salt, the stream that felt so cleansing. She also felt thankful for being able-bodied and reasonably healthy; it was an enormous privilege that she took for granted far more often than she wanted to. Those medicines had been a shock to her system; she felt a lot of gratitude for being able to rest and recover there.

The night before the next ceremony, Sofia had a vivid dream, which felt like more than a dream, just like the one she had of Sintra mountain at the very beginning. She dreamt that the spirits of the land had come to tell her that she was going to have a crucial journey that day, one that she could not miss. Something significant was going to happen to her. She woke up with a sense of urgency, as if it were important for her to remember the dream. Her mind was still slightly afraid of going through another intense journey, but the dream encouraged the part of her that was committed to healing and trusted that she was being held and supported by the Universe.

At the time of the ceremony, Sofia headed towards the *maloca* and surrendered with no expectations. The room had the same layout. She sat on one of the mattresses just as the ceremony began. The Shaman spoke. Sofia drank the medicine, ignoring its dreaded taste while focusing on opening up and feeling gratitude. Once again, she invoked all the spirits, ancestors and guides that wanted to support her at that moment. In response, an unexpectedly large group of spirits came, maybe a dozen, including the two that had come for her last journey, some spirits of the forest, a luminous woman that felt like an ancestor of hers, the spirit of the medicine, and some very elevated spirits that she sensed had come to assist in her healing process. That caught her by surprise, but it made sense as she recalled her dream – being warned that something significant was about to happen. For the first part of the ceremony, she felt sick; her body purged in multiple ways, similarly to the last time but less intensely – as if there was less to cleanse. She could tell that the Shaman had his focus placed on her; every song he sang or whistled seemed perfectly aligned with her process. When she felt blocked, he would play the same song repeatedly until she unblocked. When she felt the intensity, his music also had power and energy. When she needed comfort, his instruments held her in a melodious embrace. When she needed to release something, he would blow tobacco over her. In her increasingly delirious state, she wondered if she was attuned to his state or if he was attuned to hers. Either way, she knew for sure that there was a direct link between the two of them. She felt in between worlds again, but the spirits were guarding and guiding her. Then, when the time was right, she felt them taking her to an entirely different place in the spirit realm. She found herself in a type of medical room, under lots of lights, with the elevated beings that she did not know standing over her. Sofia could see the whole scene in vivid detail. She could tell they were about to perform some surgery, but not only on her physical body; it affected all her *koshas*. The beings conveyed a sense of trust and reliability; Sofia got the sense that that was what they did; perhaps, they were some kind of ethereal, holistic doctors. Regardless, at that moment, she felt totally vulnerable. She appreciated how important the role of the Shaman was, protecting the psychic space. She was mindful that something very healing was about to happen for her, but also that if less beneficial entities came into the space, they could inflict some serious damage on her subtle bodies, as she was totally vulnerable and exposed. She had seen that damage before on people who had been through plant medicine journeys; it was as if their aura was completely shattered, even though some were living their lives completely unaware of being in that state. She secretly vowed to herself never to have a medicine journey with a Shaman she did not trust. The light beings, for lack of a better term, picked up their tools, opened Sofia's belly and started operating. She could feel them in the area of her ovaries, cutting in and removing things, simultaneously affecting the corresponding psychological areas and subtle bodies, where trauma and feelings were stored. Sofia felt completely exposed but trusting and surrendered, especially because of the spirits she was already familiar with, such as her spirit guide and the Māori elder – she was sure they would not let anything harmful happen to her. She could sense some less elevated entities further outside the energy field and grasped how dangerous it would be if they made it in, but the Shaman was fiercely protecting the field, so they could not come close. The Shaman started singing a song about freedom from childhood patterns and kept singing it on a loop for what felt like many hours. Sofia could not believe how long he repeated the same song, but he did so over and over again until the surgery was over, at which point he halted. He stopped singing altogether, got up, came directly to her and blew smoke over her again. Sofia felt like that entire session thus far had been about her, but that seemed arrogant: How could that be if there were so many other students there? Sofia wondered if they also felt like the session had been about them, though it felt improbable. The light beings put away their tools and took her out of the operating room. She felt as though she had been healed from something, though she was not sure what. At that point, she purged again but had a bizarre sensation as she was purging, as if she was purging small sharp objects – which did not make sense physically, as she could not have swallowed anything like that. Perhaps it was simply a distorted sensation. She made a note to herself to look at her bucket later to verify that theory. A lot had happened, yet Sofia's journey was far from over. After purging, she felt an immense peace, wholeness and lightness. Her consciousness went to a place where everything was bright light and all things were made of energy – a subtle energy that connected everything in the entire universe. The colours of those energy waves were stunning and there was profound aliveness, intelligence and harmony in everything. She could see that the waves connected many different dimensions and universes, yet she was dwelling in the source of it all. She could trace a minor, almost imperceptible thread of energy back to her body and physical surroundings, through which she could also feel the entire forest – including many animals and trees holding space for the ceremony – the spirits in the room, the consciousness field held by the Shaman, the students on the mattresses, and the threads that connected everything. She also noticed how that was merely one of the infinite threads stemming from that place of divine essence where her consciousness was. She could feel the vastness, the absolute magic and perfection of it all. She could see the *karmic* links that were creating all the interactions on planet Earth and how perfectly balanced they were, how much wisdom there was in that, how each human was creatively unfolding their essence and exploring their potential, how it was all a manifestation of consciousness and how it would eventually be reintegrated back into consciousness. From that place of cosmic Source, she could feel everything from the beginning of Creation to its finality, to its various ends and beginnings, folding and unfolding. That place was outside of time. Sofia could see how time itself was part of the energy of creation, allowing for the unique manifestations that were taking place in it. She could see how everything, absolutely everything was God; there was no non-God – every single part of existence was a direct manifestation of the divine creation.

190

What Sofia was witnessing was far beyond human existence, physical bodies and emotions… Those were but a grain of sand in the great cosmic unfolding. The intelligence present in the creation of all that, the profound interconnectedness of it all, the light that united everything, the wholeness and sheer beauty of it was beyond inspiring; it was mesmerising. She stayed there in absolute bliss, dwelling in profound awe, reverence and appreciation of this divine Creation.

Meanwhile, pragmatically on Earth, a few hours had passed, maybe six or eight. Sofia intuitively knew it was time to come back into her human shape and continue her journey with that new inner knowing. Gradually, she brought herself back into her body. Before leaving, she looked at the bucket beside her to verify what she had purged. Indeed, the top layer was covered in small sharp dark pieces that seemed alien and had no logical explanation for having come out of her.

She went to her room and could see sacred geometry – incredibly bright, colourful, beautiful symbols and *yantras* (sacred geometry shapes) – regardless of whether her eyes were open or closed. Moreover, she could see the hysterical humour in everything. Humans had forgotten how divine they were. The paradoxes were nothing short of hilarious: how humans felt disconnected from themselves while being fully connected, how each ego contained the very source of consciousness that it was compensating for, how spiritual aspirants thought they needed to reach something that was already there. She laughed until morning and contaminated Merle with her expansion, joy and hilarious realisations about everything. Unlike her, he had gone through another very challenging purging experience, which he was disappointed by. While he envied Sofia's transcendental experience, she was in such a pure, elevated and inclusive state that he allowed her experience to fill him up, eventually rejoicing in it. In that state, Sofia could see into the future, from where she could tell his next ceremony would be as powerful as the current one had been for her. She was about to tell him that when she sensed that sharing that knowledge was not aligned and would not lead to the most healing outcome, so she stopped herself. Tapping into that foresight ability, she could also see into her own next ceremony; it would bring her a state of enlightenment again (for lack of a better word) but with no surgeries or purging beforehand. Lastly, the medicine told her to fast on that day in order to not feel sick. She fell asleep in pure gratitude for consciousness, the natural world, and all the beings, seen and unseen, that had been a part of her healing.

Over the following days, Sofia descended from that incredibly elevated state and felt tremendous grief for returning to a substantially less connected state with a minimal perception of divinity. Yet her being could never forget that timeless place. She now knew what was at the end of the Yoga path and that it was worth all her efforts, so she became even more motivated and inspired. She wondered if the surgery had been about her endometriosis and if it had been somehow healed. She would probably only find that out in her next menstruation.

Merle grew increasingly frustrated that week. He was in a state of disillusionment about how much effort he was putting in while getting so little results, disappointment with the medicines that did not bring him the experiences he wanted, and jealousy of Sofia and her friends who, in all their openness and cuddliness, mirrored his sense of disconnection. He was starting to feel annoyed at everything. There he was, in a paradisiac place among the exotic Peruvian jungle, surrounded by incredible humans, being nourished with home-grown organic food, undergoing extraordinary experiences, travelling around the world for a year at no cost, receiving paradigm-shifting teachings about life and the universe, and all he could see was his *one brick*. It was hard for Sofia to witness that, especially knowing that his healing and the experience he craved were so close. Regardless, she continued to sense very strongly that revealing that information would somehow not be beneficial. Besides, she could not be certain about the accuracy of her prediction and was afraid of setting invalid expectations or influencing the outcome. As a convenient side effect, it was also a priceless opportunity to verify it. So, she held him with empathy and compassion through his frustration. Inevitably, such an ongoing attitude of tender care from Sofia was very healing for him too. It showed him that he too could be loved, all parts of him, even his shadows, which deep down he felt were unlovable. Perhaps one day, he would come to love and accept those parts too.

Anney also needed a lot of support from Sofia that week, as she felt disconnected from everyone for not participating in the plant medicine journeys. Sofia held her with a lot of love too. She also realised something else when sharing with Anney: "We feel disconnected because we cannot feel the layer in which everything is connected. No one is *actually* disconnected, or we would simply flicker out of existence. Yet we *feel* disconnected. So, we fill that empty space with other people, friends, partners or family, and when they are gone, we feel empty and alone again. Except that the source of that suffering is not in people leaving, but in the unawareness that we are all connected, which led them to become attached to people in the first place." Sofia had felt alone and disconnected pretty much all her life, but now she felt more connected. However, it was hard to say whether that was because she felt the connectedness of everything or because she was filling that emptiness with the people around her. Only time would tell, she concluded.

Finally, the day of their last grandmother plant journey had arrived. Merle was still gloomy and discouraged in the morning and told Sofia he was sure that, once again, the ceremony would be a disappointment.

"I wouldn't be so sure if I were you," she responded, hiding an almost imperceptible smile that she hoped would not give away what she knew.

The group entered the *maloca* again; everyone knew what to do; the ceremony started, the room was cleansed, the Shaman chanted and the students were given the medicine – the same routine as the previous times. Indeed, Sofia did not purge. She went straight to a place of enlightenment, though a different one, perhaps more down-to-earth than the last one, but from which she could still access the fabric of the universe. She could hear Merle purging, but he stopped after a short time, after which there was silence. From that place of light, Sofia could *feel* him and knew that he had reached his own state of enlightenment. She was relieved and happy for him.

That is, if Sofia could trust that her intuitive perception was accurate. In that state of pure bliss, she could see how she was whole, how nothing was missing or needed, how perfect the universe was. Feeling less grounded in the divine source of creation and more grounded in her human existence, Sofia could see the divine creation in everything that surrounded her more distinctly. She could perceive the energy field of the room and the spirits and the Shaman in it. She could tell that the Shaman, though sitting in his place, chanting and whistling as usual, had his focus directed at Merle, who needed support in his process. She could hear the crickets outside, the trees, the wind and all the night creatures; how they all formed the most celestial background melody for healing, creating the perfect harmony for that moment. She perceived that – at the request of the Shaman – all the beings in nature would increase volume and raise intensity or facilitate quiet space and stillness. It was as if he was in full communion and cooperation with nature, spirits, music and the people in the room, leading a symphonic spiritual orchestra aimed at healing and consciousness. Even though Sofia was in a place of oneness, she could see that such a state was not as elevated and ecstatic as the last one, which to some degree, could have been a loss because she craved that pure light. Yet it brought something new, allowing her to see the divinity in the material world, which felt very special. Maybe there are stages on the path to enlightenment, she thought to herself – from disconnection to getting glimpses of the divine (whether it be through medicines, meditations or other experiences), to consistently seeing it manifested in the material world, to dwelling in pure divinity.

After an undetermined amount of time, she felt called to go to Merle. When she appeared from the almost complete darkness next to his mat, he told her, excitedly, "I swear I just called you psychically!"

He placed his arm under her head and they rested together; no words needed to be spoken. She was automatically in the place he was in, so they could witness it together. She could see him through her third eye, including his many lifetimes on this planet. She could also perceive her own previous lives, some on this planet but also others before that, in a subtle world with an elevated civilisation, where the luminous ancestor woman who had come

194

to her last ceremony was from. In that civilisation, everything was light and energy, beings were community-focused and worked creatively and collaboratively towards common goals, they honoured Nature as their mother and Spirit as their father, everyone felt connected and psychic abilities were an ordinary part of life, love and compassion underlaid every interaction, all species respected and honoured each other. Acceptance was not even a concept because everyone embodied their divine essence and intuitively manifested it in every action. *Had she dreamt about that before?* She knew immediately that that civilisation had been her home. Suddenly, she understood why she had felt so much grief on Earth – due to the contrast to where she was from. While she might have lost the memories of that place, the timeless echoes inside of her *remembered* and grieved for that loss. A wave of grief struck Sofia; her body was still, almost frozen. Merle found himself crying and asked her, "Suddenly, I feel so much grief… Is that what you are experiencing?"

"Yes," she whispered, feeling enormous relief that someone could feel her grief. She articulated that world to him and he could see it too. From there, he was pulled back to the place of light and divinity that he had been experiencing before she arrived. He also wanted to describe that to her, but he had no words. Suddenly, Sofia spoke, "You see the place of light, don't you? The place of pure consciousness, where everything stems from." He felt immensely relieved that she could put into words what he was seeing. Together in that state, without words, they travelled universes, explored multiple dimensions of reality and experienced how they were part of the oneness of all things. Sometimes the birds would call them, bringing their focus to the environment around them, experiencing its magic; other times, they dwelled in pure bright light and experienced the creation of the universe and the links between everything. Towards the end, Sofia could see him in front of her again and witnessed how they were one, too. They were Shiva and Shakti, divine masculine and divine feminine; consciousness manifesting itself so that it could recognise itself in each other and in oneself, again and again, through experienced reality. That might even be the reason for the whole Creation. Had there ever been a more beautiful encounter?

There were no barriers, separations, protections or obstacles; there was only pure connection. There was no armour, no unconscious parts or blockages; there was only recognition that they were the same. That powerful moment, facing each other, that acknowledgement, that recognition, felt like it was at the very core of existence. An encounter made up of the same source energy that gives birth to universes, that is at the core of sexual energy, maybe even Creation itself. No words could be pronounced; no description could ever do justice to that experience.

As they headed home, Merle asked Sofia, "You knew this was going to happen, didn't you?" Disarmed, she smiled without answering.

Over the days that followed, Sofia felt the painful comedown from that state again; the loss of awareness of the divine, the grief. Regardless, it was a small price to pay for what she had experienced. She realised through her Shiva-Shakti experience that she kept projecting the love she naturally emanated onto male partners. She could see that it had always been *her own love* that she experienced through them – their love was just a bonus. Her love was – in potential – accessible anytime and with anyone (or no one). She also discovered how profoundly special it felt to witness another being in their fullness and connect in that. Additionally, it was a revelation that the two beings did not need to be romantically involved to experience that.

Sofia and Merle discussed all these realisations and insights enthusiastically. He shared with her that he felt like the Shaman was completely attuned to him on that last session and wondered if others felt the same. Whereas the previous time, he had felt like the Shaman had been attuned to Sofia – which matched her experience on both occasions. Sofia felt immense gratitude for having Merle in her life. Only an extraordinary being could be brave enough to face his demons and expose his deepest vulnerabilities to another human being, as he continuously did towards her. So self-aware, even with the parts that seemed shameful, selfish, mean, needy or unlovable; so open, even with the voices of his trauma constantly advising him to shut down. Sofia loved him deeply, and he felt exactly the same way about her.

196

The time had come to leave the retreat place. Sofia put on her backpack and felt secretly excited about eating salt again. She thanked the Shaman, the other people from the retreat, the trees, animals, spirits and medicinal plants. She felt deeply grateful for everything.

They were taken to the pier, where they caught an enormous old ferry with nothing but local Peruvian people and merchandise. The Yoga group was to sail for a week, having the whole top floor to themselves and sleeping in hammocks under the stars. There was enough space to gather and do Yoga. The crew provided very simple food. For eight days, they saw nothing but the vast and expansive Amazon River, with jungle on both sides and occasionally some small villages where merchandise was dropped off or picked up. Sofia wondered how people get entertained in those places, with no technology and seemingly nothing to do. She made it a point to observe them carefully. They never seemed unhappy or bored; she saw them chopping wood, playing games, teaching the children, collecting plants, cooking food, exploring nature, talking or conducting other activities. She wondered if the exaggerated stimuli present in Western society are like the story of the woman's ring, where humans were actually happy and fulfilled when they had way less.

A week later, the group arrived at Pucallpa, from where they made their way to Cusco. Cusco was a city that felt very mystical to Sofia. Maybe the Amazon jungle or the river or Yoga had purified her or attuned her more to nature, but she could more easily feel the spirit of the land and the vibration of the environment around her. They stayed in a big house near the mountains. Another Shaman was there, older and more withered, who also received them warmly and humbly. One day he took the group on a horse ride, showing them the *Templo de la Luna* and the *Templo de los Monos*. Sofia was surprised that the temples were embedded into nature. She was used to the Western architectural approach, which was typically to wipe out nature and build whatever people desired, irrespective of the land. Conversely, the Incas built their temples in harmony with the land, with deep respect, cooperation and grace, which resulted in temples with innate spirituality and power.

The next day, Sofia and Merle visited the *Templo de la Luna* again. They ate some coca leaves the Shaman had offered, which were meant to help with concentration, awareness and introspection. Afterwards, they meditated and Merle played music. It felt very special; Sofia felt mysteriously connected to that place. She wondered if she had been there in a previous life. Regrettably, she was no longer in a state where she could verify that.

The Shaman explained that they would soon have their grandfather plant medicine journey. The grandfather was a cactus that was said to help people integrate the higher realisations of the grandmother plant journey into the physical world and day-to-day human existence. He described that it also helped with healing, self-awareness and feeling a sense of awe and wonder about the universe. He stated that it was also a psychedelic journey and reminded them it was totally optional – only those who felt called to should do it.

On the day of the ceremony, the group was advised to fast or eat only light food early in the morning. Given how well Sofia had felt in the last medicine journey where she had not eaten, she decided to fast again. They met in the *maloca*, which was smaller than the one in their last retreat, but also very beautifully decorated, with traditional ornaments, plants, crystals and elements from the land. The Shaman said that the day was beautiful, so they would take the medicine inside and then go for a walk through the mountain and the sacred sites to experience it. After some brief words of invocation and protection, the Shaman filled large individual glasses with a thick green liquid that he took from a big jar, serving one to each person and instructing them to drink it. Sofia was prepared for the medicine to be extremely unpleasant-tasting, so she was positively surprised when it seemed to taste slightly less dreadful than the previous one. Though when she looked at Merle on her left-hand side, his face suggested otherwise. Klaus, on the other hand, drank all of his in one go.

With various degrees of difficulty, the students finished their glasses. Together they made their way towards the *Templo de la Luna* and then further up the mountain. Sofia felt slightly indisposed, but nothing compared to how she felt with the grandmother plant. She was grateful that the cactus seemed like a gentler medicine, or there would have been no way that she could have walked while experiencing it. A couple of students seemed to be struggling, having purged the medicine early on. As Sofia walked, she felt like the colours were getting brighter and the trees seemed more alive, though the effects were very mild. As the group reached the top of the mountain, the Shaman asked each person to find a comfortable place to connect with the medicine more fully. When Sofia did that, the effects increased exponentially. At first, it was physically fascinating, as the colours became so bright and intense that it seemed like she was in an animated movie. When she looked at the big tree next to her, she perceived that it was actually alive and made of energy rather than rigid and unchanging as it had previously seemed. She wondered whether she was seeing the *actual* reality (that people are not able to see in their non-psychedelic state of consciousness, as the mind is constantly dimming their experience) or whether the psychedelic effects *distorted* reality. The latter seemed more probable, yet she would probably never have a definitive answer to that question. Sofia sat with her back against the tree and felt the life force of the tree in connection with her own. The tiny and mundane details that would usually bore her out of her mind, such as the skeleton of a rotting leaf or the carcass of a dead insect, now felt fascinating beyond measure. She wondered if the tribes living in the villages alongside the Amazon were capable of appreciating beauty like that, in which case it would certainly explain why they did not need further entertainment. When she closed her eyes and sat back, she could feel how she was an integral part of nature, just like the trees and the insects. She was not separate or different from the earth, the plants, the trees, or the air in the atmosphere. She could feel all the land expanding for miles and miles, the wind on the trees and the clouds in the skies. She could expand further and feel entire countries, even the whole American continent. She could zoom out further and feel the whole Earth, which she was a part of, just like a single cell was part of her body. In fact, she felt as though the Earth *was* her body. She was made of the same organic matter as everything else and united by the same spirit. She could feel the Earth as one organism with different particles everywhere, each person being one of them, just like the ocean is made up of its own different organisms and expressions of life even though it is still one ocean. She was having the embodied, lived realisation of how she was *actually* nature. At that moment, there was no question, no doubt, no need for debate. Sitting against that tree, Sofia would never again be able to deny that she was a part of nature. Whatever implications that might have could not be known at that stage. That was not a mental state with intellectual realisations; it was a *vivencia*. She remembered biodanza and could feel Agnes on the other side of the world, just like in our body, we can feel our hand or arm. That brought her happiness. She then expanded her consciousness beyond Earth, feeling herself dissolve into the entire cosmos, where she lay for the rest of the day – which felt like many days. Eventually, her perception of the cosmos started narrowing back down; she could experience nature again and was grateful that she still felt part of it. Slowly, her consciousness contracted all the way into her own body, at which point she walked back to the house.

On their last day in Peru, looking at the beautiful view from the Shaman's house, overlooking all of Cusco, Sofia felt deep sorrow in her heart. She could see why people sometimes go crazy with these psychedelic experiences. For some, they could be terrifying, especially if the person does not have a spiritual framework to understand what they are witnessing. Others could suffer dangerous attacks if not protected by an experienced Shaman. Plus, she could see how people with less resilience could easily get lost in grief and totally disheartened by coming back to this seemingly disconnected reality… Or completely addicted. Sofia could feel the deep pain of this world, which was so lost in superficiality and disconnected from the oneness. Or maybe it was just her own pain.

Sofia's grief was exacerbated when Ananda came with the next flight tickets. Regardless of where they were going, that would be their last module, which was heartbreaking. She looked at them through her tears and read: *Nepal.*

Chapter 12 – Sahasrara Chakra

Somehow, Sofia was expecting all of Nepal to be high mountains, stillness and fresh air, so arriving at Kathmandu was like a bucket of cold, dirty water over her head. There was so much dust in the air that she could hardly breathe, and the pollution, the sound of the cars and people, plus the overall busyness caused her a lot of resistance. She took comfort in the thought that the group would soon make their way to Pokhara, a smaller city near the mountains, used as a gateway to the Annapurna circuit, a popular trail in the Himalayas. *The Himalayas,* Sofia murmured, her eyes lit up with that prospect, sparking some excitement.

A bus was waiting to take the group to Pokhara. The bus was so old that even the universal mysteries probably struggled to comprehend how it was still running. Yet there it was, travelling at unreasonably high speeds while crossing absolutely stunning Nepalese mountains through narrow roads full of holes alongside the dramatic precipice. The holes were so many and so deep that the buses had their suspensions taken out; otherwise, they would constantly have to replace them. Occasionally, looking down at the steep drop, one could see other buses that had crashed at the bottom – clearly, ones that had not been as fortunate as to make it to their destination. The ride was bumpy and terrifying for Sofia, who felt extremely sick for the many hours it lasted.

The group stayed in a lodge in Pokhara for three days. During that time, they had the opportunity to appreciate the town's little Yoga centres, shops and cafes and admire the scenic Phewa lake, which had a beautiful little green island with its own temple in the middle.

They met for the first Yoga class of the module. Ananda announced that they would be trekking the Annapurna circuit over the following weeks, so they should prepare themselves by acquiring warm clothes and anything else they felt was necessary. He explained that they would not be trekking as a group, but instead, people could walk on their own or split into smaller groups, making their way to the place where the group would meet for the following week's Yoga class. Maybe that was a transition to walking alone after the course ended – Sofia thought to herself, trying to push away the feeling of dread.

The Swami proceeded to talk about Sahasrara chakra, commonly known as the crown chakra, located at the top of the head. He stated that in some traditions, Sahasrara is not even considered a chakra but a *padma* – a direct portal to the divine. As such, it has no *yin* and *yang* polarity, and holds not even a state of consciousness but a doorway to infinite states of consciousness. He indicated that this chakra is connected to universal consciousness, divinity, enlightenment and being one with the sacredness of the universe.

The Swami explained that expanding the consciousness beyond the limits of the universe and understanding its mysteries enables a state of deep inner wisdom and detachment from problems, putting things into perspective. Sahasrara allows us to contextualise the events of our personal life into the cosmic scheme of things. While it still allows for a complete day-to-day experience, this wider perspective brings a lightness, where problems are no longer felt as problems but contextualised within the bigger picture.

Ananda described that Sahasrara is the chakra that relates most directly to spirituality and accessing the individual soul and, through it, the universal spirit. It helps us connect to the universe from that broad, holistic perspective rather than a narrow individualistic one, bringing a sense of universal harmony, positivity, connectedness, bliss, and freedom from the limits of the personality.

When Sofia heard Ananda talk about the divine, or 'God', she noticed that she no longer felt resistance to that name. God no longer represented the all-mighty religious character she hated as an angry adolescent but the cosmic intelligence she had personally experienced, which underlaid everything in the universe. That thought brought back memories of herself as a child, communicating directly with God with the certainty that such intelligence existed. Yoga had helped her find her way back to the divine.

After the talk on Sahasrara, each student was given a pre-loaded debit card for essential expenses, food and accommodation. After that, Ananda told the group they could start trekking whenever they liked, and he defined the meeting point for the next class, one week from then.

People did indeed start trekking on their own or in small groups. Sofia organically started her journey with Merle, who had decided to walk barefoot. Like Anney, it had been months since the last time he had worn shoes. Sofia started by buying and analysing maps, planning which day to stay in which place and asking the locals for advice and recommendations. That took some effort, but it reassured her that she had a solid plan. Her usual way of finding safety was knowing what was next, creating the belief that she *needed* to plan ahead. However, planning cost her immense energy; it drained and frustrated her as it did not come naturally – not that she had ever questioned it, as she knew no other way. Merle, on the other hand, was not putting any effort into thinking even a single day ahead; if it were up to him, they would simply walk when they felt like walking and stop when they felt like stopping; that was how he liked to travel, which was a big mirror for Sofia. She felt puzzled and triggered by that because it left her to do all the planning, which was exhausting. After a few days of suffering, she realised that the present dynamic was unsustainable for her. To stop being resentful, she decided to stop planning – she was prepared to let everything crash and burn; either they would die in the mountain, or he would be forced to step up and take some responsibility. To her surprise, neither of those scenarios happened; instead, the absence of planning opened up the space for spontaneity and everything started unfolding perfectly for them. They would walk at their own pace, stop in places they found beautiful and enjoy the gifts that came their way. She witnessed first-hand how her planning was killing the magic, the freedom and the intuition, leading to circumstances that were not aligned. She reflected on her need for safety and the illusion that it comes from walking a commonly travelled path… When actually, in travelling that path, one misses out on going off the beaten track and finding hidden gems awaiting their discovery. Sitting on the top of a mountain after a long day's walk, Sofia took out her journal and wrote: *Not planning, or going with the flow – as new-age people like to call it – feels scary and uncertain. However, if I truly trust Spirit rather than just saying I do, should I not also trust that the Universe will guide me wherever I need to go and attract whatever I need to experience? I have gone through so many deaths and rebirths over the last few months, so many crumbling patterns and beliefs; this is just one more limiting belief I need to let go of.*

Also, I need to stop seeking the safety of other people's experiences and well-travelled paths. People's experiences are related to their path, not necessarily mine. My journey will naturally unfold distinctly because I am a different person. If we were born to be like everyone else, only one person would need to be created. Yet this seems to be one of humanity's ever-sought yet never achieved dreams: To be 'normal', or in other words, the same as everyone else. From now on, I will aim to embrace my uniqueness and carve my own path, rather than aiming for some robotic sameness. Changing her approach allowed Sofia to really start enjoying the ride.

The freedom from planning and control had lifted a weight off Sofia's shoulders that she had not even realised was there. She could just enjoy each moment, take in the breathtaking views, explore whatever little wonders she was drawn to along the way and inhale the mountain's pure, fresh air. Every few kilometres, they would pass through a little town where they could look around, eat their *dal bhat* – a traditional Nepalese meal made of vegetable curry, rice, lentils and pickles – or rest for the night. Villagers often found Merle funny when they saw him arrive barefoot; they would make conversation about how unusual it was and make up their own hilarious theories. They lived and hosted hikers in cute little solar-powered stone houses, which were freezing but welcoming. Sofia felt immensely grateful for them as it meant that people only had to carry the essentials in their backpacks. Nepal confronted her with a humble reality that contrasted with what she was used to. In Portugal, hotels would advertise their spas or premium services, whereas in Nepal, she would – at best – see them advertise *'clean rooms'*, which was apparently as much as one could aspire to. She was faced with constant reminders to not take *anything* for granted: that showers would have hot water, toilets would have flushing systems, power would be consistent, information would be available, food would be as ordered, or anything else.

It felt incredibly special for Sofia to share that journey with Merle, and vice-versa. To journey with someone who was also on the path, someone who realises that the journey is about being rather than doing. That highlighted how Western society believes that people need to be *doing* things for travelling to be worth it – or for living to be worth it, for that matter. To be visiting places, doing touristy things, seeing popular sites, etc. The concept that *being* was enough seemed theoretically and spiritually valid to Sofia but was also new and confusing, almost foreign to put into practice. Namely, what in the world does one do when just *being* is enough? It certainly felt like uncharted territory, so in their ample free time, she and Merle explored their inner worlds rather than the outer ones. They recurrently found themselves fighting demons, raising awareness, healing traumas, discovering strengths, connecting pieces of the puzzle, expanding love, shifting patterns, licking wounds, developing inner abilities, and understanding themselves, each other and the universe. Which was the type of journey that – Sofia believed – lives were worth journeying for.

Sofia had been menstruating since she first stepped foot on the Himalayas. She was surprised to realise that she felt no pain at all. Typically, Sofia would feel enormous pain in her right ovary because of the endometriosis, plus strong bleeding and extremely uncomfortable cramps in her womb. In fact, when she started trekking and realised that her bleeding had commenced, she was concerned that she might not be able to walk at all. Contrarily, whether it was because of all the Yoga practices, the realisations and integrations, or the holistic surgery in the grandmother plant journey, it seemed like something had healed or shifted in her. So far, she was not experiencing any pain. She made a note to herself to study psychosomatic illnesses and herbal medicine far more in-depth one day.

Sofia and Merle had reached the meeting point. The reencounters between the students who had arrived were very joyful. They enjoyed a wonderful evening together, and the following morning they had their Yoga class. Ananda talked about the imbalances of Sahasrara, which were mainly related to an unhealthy relationship with spirituality. He explained that, on the one hand, these included spiritual disconnection, cynicism around spirituality or religion, fear of death and apprehension about spiritual manifestations. On the other hand, they could manifest as spiritual pride, rigid belief systems and an obsession with spiritual matters.

The Swami elaborated that disruptions at the level of Sahasrara also relate to an existential disconnection from one's own body, soul or existence in general, living in an apathetic, joyless and lifeless state of detachment from the world. The isolation that this can result in, if extreme, can lead to an existential crisis, meaninglessness and lack of trust in a higher purpose. The person can also experience a lack of consciousness, wisdom and universal perspective, resulting in an attraction to materialistic things that do not matter from a spiritual point of view, taking things personally and believing them to be problematic, and having narrow perspectives on life.

Ananda also explained that Sahasrara connects people directly to their essence and who they really are. He described that when someone is disconnected from that, they look to others for reassurance and to fill their gaps, which creates social anxiety. As a result, they develop an external locus of control, meaning that their experiences in life are perceived to be primarily controlled by external forces, as they give their power away to others. Consequently, their self-esteem becomes dependent on others, who have a major influence on how they feel about themselves and in life. The solution to this vicious circle is for the person to discover and ground themselves in who they are. That creates genuine self-esteem, which in turn reduces social anxiety and makes for an internal locus of control. When they are fully connected to all aspects of their being, their external reality is consciously shaped by their inner qualities, values and features.

The Swami proceeded to tell the class where next week's meeting point would be and left them to continue on their journey.

Sofia stayed behind a bit longer after class to write some notes in her journal: *Sounds like the key to both social anxiety and low self-esteem is for us to realise who we are… Which begs a critical question: Who am I?* No answer came.

That night they all had dinner together. Elixir and Sofia were ecstatic when they saw each other; she jumped onto him and he grabbed her in the air; they could not stop smiling and embracing for a long time. In their embrace, she could feel his essence: so light, joyful and loving. He brightened up her day just by being in the room. There was nothing people could say to him that he could not put a positive spin on and no situation too gloomy that he could not find its beauty. He was fully accepting, uplifting and encouraging; it felt as if he never had any expectations of her, never judged her or shut her down. Sofia felt completely free around him. He naturally excelled at an important phenomenon that Tantrics call *transfiguration*, the ability to see the divine manifested in the other's human form. Elixir radiated unconditional love like the sun radiates heat: without expecting to receive anything back or even checking if someone is receiving it. He was uplifting, encouraging and inspiring, like a breath of fresh air; these were his gifts to the world. Sofia was thinking of how deeply she appreciated his essence. At that moment, she realised, *That's it, that is the essence of who he is and what he brings to the world!* That led her to mentally go through her closest friends and check what their essence felt like to her and what they brought. Anney brought rawness, spontaneity and connection to nature; Klaus brought innocence, empathy and generosity; Merle brought insight, open-mindedness and emotional depth… She was sure she could think of many other characteristics and people. Though what did she bring *herself*? Suddenly, her mind was blank. She was surprised at how easy it was for her to point out other people's gifts *versus* how hard it

208

was to see her own. She realised that she had leapt from her previous arrogant stance to an inferiority-based one, not recognising anything valuable about herself. She needed to find the middle way.

Sofia and Merle continued walking together; they constantly received signs that their paths were aligned, such as the two golden eagles flying directly above them in the Himalayan sky. Merle said that the eagle medicine was about Spirit, insight and seeing things from a higher perspective.

Gradually, the hike became more challenging… Sofia's feet hurt with occasional blisters; she could feel some light-headedness and lack of oxygen as the altitude increased, her body felt tired and her back was sore from carrying a backpack and sleeping in uncomfortable mattresses most nights. Yet she faced her pain with awareness and surrendered every step to the divine, channelling her sacrifice towards her intention: to open up the Sahasrara portal.

Something was shifting in Sofia. Beyond the land and the trees, she could feel the spirit of the mountain; in every bird that flew past, she sensed a supporting presence; in every gust of wind, the whisper of the mysteries. Along the way, they would sometimes see Tibetan flags, prayer wheels and monasteries, or at other times, wild horses and goats, which they would often playfully chase or photograph. "Involving technology is probably not a very spiritual thing to do!" Merle joked.

Sofia's auto-pilot response was to agree, but then she reconsidered: *Actually, why not? Everything is spiritual; everything is divine creation unfolding; nothing is devoid of spirit! We create altars and statues of deities to connect with what is sacred when actually, everything is already sacred; we only need those things because we have forgotten that fundamental truth. So, I'm all for bringing extra awareness to how we use technology or other elements often deemed 'not sacred' by some people in spirituality. But I don't want to feed that non-spirit duality. We don't need to find sacred things, only to realise the sacredness in everything. We don't need to pursue states of enlightenment, only to recognise the light in every state. We don't*

209

need to seek moments of equanimity, only to discover the equanimity in each moment. Everything we seek has been here all along.

Meeting the group again was, as usual, an exciting time of the week. Sofia had arrived at the place where they were gathering; it felt like a reencounter of her soul tribe, so joyful and familiar. Her soul rejoiced in seeing those brothers, sisters and non-binary siblings again. She wanted to take in all that warmth and connection to hold on to that in the times of loneliness and grief that would most likely follow their separation. She felt at home with those people, which was one of the feelings she treasured most in the universe. While she was aware that she should ideally feel at home within herself when she was by herself, it was not a feeling that was yet grounded in her.

When she returned to the room with Merle that night, they travelled their inner worlds and faced angels and demons again. Merle had felt abandoned when Sofia found her soul tribe, experiencing that as loss and rejection. He regressed into his inner child and dove into his abandonment trauma, feeling all the fear, sadness and grief that came with it. Sofia held his inner child through terror, despair and even panic attacks; she was adamant about not letting him go until he felt safe and loved. Her devotion opened up space for that sweet inner child who had long been wanting to come out but had previously felt unsafe. That little boy would sometimes break down in loneliness, lash out in anger, or sulk in jealousy, but he always had great courage to show his vulnerability. Sofia admired and adored him. The boy also trusted Sofia with his life and heart, and melted her own heart in the process. She would never stop holding him; that child would always be held and loved no matter the cost. Meanwhile, the adult part of Merle felt guilty for taking up space and being needy and demanding of Sofia. Yet for Sofia, those were trivial things compared to her love for that terrified boy, and she was prepared to pay that price with her very last bit of strength.

The following day, Sofia woke up exceedingly early to see the sunrise over the mountains at almost five thousand metres of altitude. The air was fresh and the silence was profound; she could feel the spirit of the land emanating peace, stillness, introspection and expansion. She also needed some space to recover from the intensity of the previous night. A random man sat next to her, who she had seen at dinner the night before. He had kind eyes and asked her *how she was*. He posed that question with so much care that Sofia recognised it as an expression of love as opposed to a greeting. Feeling that, she immediately broke down in tears, which she did not see coming. Feeling safe and held, she felt her own inner child coming out. She realised then that even though she had the deepest, most meaningful relationship with Merle, because he was often angry, triggered or upset at her, her inner child had never felt safe to expose herself to him. Moreover, Sofia recognised that she had been holding Merle's inner child through so much abandonment while her own inner child's abandonment remained unaddressed. So, her inner child felt heartbroken, vulnerable and in need of care and attention. Represented in that man who showed care for her was her dad; her inner child could feel all the times that she needed that care from him, all the times he had left her alone, desperate and without affection while he was away, all the times he did not see her pain and tears. Yet, when Sofia felt her inner child, she did not feel *only* the child's sadness and grief. She felt her innocence, open-heartedness and unconditional love. She had locked away those parts of herself to avoid getting hurt. She knew intuitively that only her inner child could unlock them. Sofia could tell that her inner child needed to be held, yet she sensed that seeking solace in the arms of a fleeting stranger would never offer the healing she sought. She wanted to hold her own inner child, love and protect her. To tell her that she would never leave her. To apologise for not having been there for her before. To promise that she would never be left alone again. After that, a memory arose of being a baby in the cradle and feeling like there were protective mystical dragons wheeling on top of her, cradling and comforting her. Surely, she must have imagined that. Or perhaps she was not entirely alone? In any case, Sofia suspected she had a long road ahead, to hold and integrate her inner child, and eventually forgive her father for something he would never be sorry for.

Later that morning, there was the Yoga class. Ananda introduced the theme of *Shambala*, a mystical kingdom made up of enlightened beings living in pristine lands by the values of Spirit. Some say that Shambala exists only in the astral realm, others claim that it exists in the physical, somewhere between the Himalayan mountains and the Gobi Desert, – amongst other theories – others claim that there are some periods when it exists in one and others in both. There are myths about the Earth descending into darkness and chaos one day and Shambala emerging to lead it into peace and light. There are others about Shambala continuously supporting the consciousness of the Earth energetically.

The Swami's mission for the class was for each student to establish a psychic connection to Shambala over the following month, to see what they could learn from their beings, and discover if and how they could support them. He said the group would be together during that time in a Tibetan Buddhist monastery slightly off-track from where they were. They were to observe silence throughout all that time; the monks would provide meals for them and Ananda would hold space for daily meditations with Shambala. To support that practice, they would be given a crystal to work with, meaning to meditate with it and receive its wisdom. They could keep the crystal at the end, infused with the energy of that practice, that place, and Shambala. Ananda laid out a group of crystals on the floor, asking each student to feel into which one called them the most. He urged them not to let the ego reach for the biggest and brightest. Each crystal held its own medicine and would draw the exact person who needed it. The students paused to admire their colours, sizes and shapes before picking them up, one by one. Sofia was one of the last to take a crystal. She was not only impressed that no one else had taken the one she felt drawn to, but also that the same seemed to happen to everyone else. Sofia's crystal was medium-sized, mostly transparent and of an asymmetrical, elongated, rectangular dipyramidal shape. On asking Ananda, she learned that it was Lemurian quartz. She felt excited about it, as she had heard of the mythical lost land of the Lemurians – a spiritually evolved society advanced in magic, people, wisdom and technology.

Sofia felt extremely resistant to being silent for a month. She felt like that was an enormous loss, especially so close to the end of the course. There was so much she could still share and learn from her classmates, with whom she was so eager to connect and enjoy many more moments together. She felt outraged about that being taken away from her. Nevertheless, she also understood that she was there to connect with God, not with others, and that her resistance was driven by egos of control and disconnection. She had to trust that there would be learnings from that experience; otherwise, the school would not have chosen it that way. *Embrace trust and relinquish control*, she said to herself.

The group walked together to the monastery where they would stay for the next month. It looked out onto the Himalayan mountain range from all sides and felt like the top of the Earth. It had various places to meditate, mindfully ornamented based on Tibetan themes. There were beautiful *yantras*, colourful prayer flags and an impressive row of golden prayer wheels with sacred symbols carved on them. Sofia was already familiar with the *yantras* and knew the concept of the flags (blowing prayers of peace, compassion, strength and wisdom into the world). However, the prayer wheels were new to her. One of the resident monks explained that they were used to accumulate wisdom and merit and purify negativities. In other words, to increase good *karma* and release bad *karma*. Sofia observed the monks as they spun the long row of golden cylinders clockwise; some would chant *om mani padme hum* thrice while doing so. It was said that the mantras and the turning of the wheels would help free humanity from suffering, for the good of all beings. Sofia turned the wheels many times that month.

Each week they had a new Yoga class, but there was little theory, as the focus was on experiential learning from Shambala. They practised the asanas and, as usual, learned a new one each week, which for Sahasrara chakra consisted mostly of inversions.

Sofia went into the Shambala meditations with an open mind and no expectations. She found it unusual that it was based on quite intense music, but Ananda explained that it was a particular song designed to put them in

213

resonance with Shambala. There was no guidance; the meditations were purely experiential. In her first meditation, as soon as Sofia started to concentrate, she felt herself being lifted. The more she rose, the more her denser layers were left behind and she entered increasingly subtle energies. At one stage, she felt as though she was only light. She stopped and dwelled in that light. In there, she started to notice that she was not alone; there were other beings in various places also meditating and emanating a beautiful bright light. When the music ended, she felt strongly resistant to coming back into her body. Eventually, however, she knew she had to return. When she did, everything seemed to be immersed in a subtle blue light; she had to open and close her eyes a few times to verify what she was seeing. While that was a fascinating phenomenon, she did not know what it meant, so she enjoyed it while it lasted and then gradually watched it disappear. Every day they would meet at that time. Given that powerful experience, Sofia was looking forward to connecting more with the mystical kingdom of Shambala. She found herself wondering *where* they were – she would love to be with those beings in the physical realm. Who knows, they could be just behind those mountains, she thought. Either way, she was glad she could at least meet them in the astral – assuming that was what was happening in the meditations. As usual, she also reserved space for the possibility that she was imagining all that and there were no other beings there except in her imagination.

As the days passed, not speaking a single word, doing her Yoga practice every morning, surrounded by scenic Himalayan landscape, and eating lovingly prepared nourishing vegetarian food, an interesting phenomenon started to happen to Sofia. She noticed her mind quietening. At first, there was less chatter, then there were fewer and fewer things to think about, and at some stage, there was absolute silence. She had never experienced anything like that; in fact, she used to joke because, in her best efforts, she could not meditate for more than literally five seconds without thoughts arising. With mental peace came emotional peace; she found herself in a state of equanimity, awareness and stillness. Verbal communication was

214

absent, yet she felt in energetic communion with nature and all its beings, elements and Spirit. That was not a lonely state but a deeply connected one.

Sofia's Shambala meditations got deeper and deeper. Every day she elevated her vibration, rose to a place of light and through her mind's eye found the other beings meditating. Sometimes she felt like they shared certain messages with her or that her questions would be answered. Sometimes she felt healing in her belly, head or back. She realised that they were not just meditating; they were also sending light out into the world. She started to become familiar with the beings there, who also began to recognise her. She also noticed that her resistance to coming back from that state was lessening, probably because her day-to-day resonance was becoming closer and closer to it. At some stage, there was little difference between her state in and out of meditation. Life had *become* a meditation. Then, even when she was not sitting down to meditate, she started to perceive that some of those beings were distributed along the monastery land, meditating and sending light into the world. As she progressed, she perceived more and more of them until they were many and constantly present. Sofia was not sure how to make logical sense of that. *Were those beings from Shambala? In which case, was it a specific group of beings from Shambala, or all of them? Were they actually on that land, yet most people could not see them because they were not in the same vibration? Were they present in other places of the world too? Was she crazy? Delusional? Oxygen deprived?* She had many questions and very few answers. In the end, not being allowed to speak, she decided it was not important either. While meditating with Shambala, she also started sending light to the world, as they did. When she did so, she felt as if she was nothing but a channel for that light. She ended the meditations feeling extraordinarily high, often seeing that mysterious blue light, which she also accepted without knowing what it was. *Perhaps the colour of a chakra?*

One day, as Sofia was walking through the balcony, she saw one of the male students from their Yoga group having a big emotional release – he was crouching, sobbing and holding his head in his hands. His girlfriend was further back, within eyesight, holding space for him energetically but respecting his distance. Those two were some of Sofia's favourite people in the world; she felt very empathetic and protective of him but held back from acting on her impulse to rescue him. *What was the right thing to do there?* Sofia wondered. If she tried to help, maybe she would hinder his process of emotional release or disempower his self-healing abilities. If she did not, he might become more distressed or feel unsupported. She connected with her intuition and decided to stay in a place of awareness instead of trying to *save* him. Merle, on the other hand, arrived with his incense and, after smudging the area, started playing his Shamanic shaker. The crying slowed down and peace was re-established. While that intervention felt harmonious, it was unclear if it led to permanent healing or instead halted his process, preventing him from going deeper. If Merle had not intervened, perhaps someone else would have, or no one would have and powerful self-healing might have happened, or more suffering would have been accumulated that could have provoked an imminent breakthrough. Either way – Sofia observed – there was no *right* or *wrong*, only reality unfolding and adapting. From that place of consciousness from where she was looking, she perceived the absolute perfection of all those options or any other ones. It became clear to her how each person was – mostly unconsciously, she thought – choosing a role in every moment and playing it. The Shaman, the healer, the spiritual seeker, the righteous warrior, the powerless victim, the helpless nine-to-five worker, the helpful friend, the good daughter, the stuck parent. She could see how people could have chosen any other role and it would have been equally valid. How the role was not necessarily needed, as reality was constantly rebalancing itself when the role dissipated, with different lessons learned. How different souls get drawn to specific lessons. How people's reality gets shaped by their roles, in which they get so involved that they forget their essence as Spirit. Their awareness gets micro-focused, the role gains importance, their ego-identification increases, and their emotions and actions start gravitating around it. Their roles interact with those of other people, leading them to play out *their* stories and roles too. All that was no more real or fake than any other story being played out. Yet, the ultimate reality was the place where they were creating reality *from*: the place of

216

Spirit, of consciousness, of pure awareness – the endless, the limitless, the *timeless*. Sofia witnessed how she was constantly choosing her reality and roles at any given moment; yet, through a single conscious decision, she could actually make any other choice. She realised how she continuously experienced only a small part of reality, limited by the roles she chose and the emotions and sensations in them, oblivious to the fact that her true self was the consciousness behind those feelings and actions, which is vast and boundless. Sofia closed her eyes for a moment and tapped into that underlying consciousness. It had always been there; it could never *not* be there. It permeated everything; nothing could exist outside its scope. It was her essence, where all the echoes inside her came from and pointed back to. Sofia realised that it was not that human beings carried *timeless echoes* inside them; they carried *echoes of the Timeless* itself! – of the infinite, the eternal, the divine. Like a beacon that would always guide their way Home. From that place, she could see how each moment in manifestation had such immensely profound depth and magic, and every expression was sacred. How everything balanced itself and peace was always possible because it dwelled in the place where she was looking *from*. When she connected to the fullness of that moment – or any other – she experienced profound and intense joy, humour, bliss, equanimity, ecstasy and interconnectedness. From that place of stillness, so many concepts that – from a human perspective – seemed paramount basically lost their relevance; they were inherent things that humans felt disconnected from and hence strived to acquire… *Emotional security*, for example – nothing is unsafe; our being is imperishable! *Power,* is embedded in us; we are literally constantly shaping reality. *Meaning,* is in the divine creation itself. *Sense,* is causal and karmically enforced. *Acceptance,* is what naturally exists when we have no expectations. *Harmony,* is ever-present in the big picture – just like water; agitated or still, liquid or solid, it just takes up different forms; the previous or future states do not matter; ultimately, it will flow and balance itself. The universe is simply energy moving, divine creation unfolding; things do not carry a mark of right or wrong – judgement is a mental creation. Things simply respond to action and consequence: If the temperature is below zero,

217

is that bad? If it freezes the lake and one can go ice skating, does it make it good? A virus comes and kills millions of people, is that bad? If it saves the Earth from overpopulation, does that make it good? A non-vegetarian person is murdered, is that bad? If seven thousand animal lives are spared because of their death, and one hundred and twenty-five million litres of water are saved, does that make it good? (Those were real-life estimates from José Rodrigues dos Santos' *The garden of animals with soul* book that Sofia had been reading). Perhaps different people would have different answers to those questions, or even the same person could change their response when they gained a different perspective – does that alone not prove that *good* and *bad* are, in fact, made-up relative terms? Security, meaning, power, sense, acceptance, harmony – like many others, these are *our own* creations. In reality, things just *are*! Each moment is perfect in itself and has everything needed, just as people always find themselves in the exact circumstances their holistic being calls for – even if they are not the ones their ego wants. Ego and suffering often lead people to feel like something is missing, as if they were not whole. Yet Sofia realised how – underneath that all-too-familiar layer of suffering – she had *always been whole*. She had spent a lifetime feeling a sense of lack, yet now she could see that nothing was *actually* lacking, except in her own awareness. The feelings of lack and suffering were a direct result of her not being consciously aware of or connected to the divine parts of herself, but instead being identified with her roles, just like the story of the lady and the ring. Sofia observed how free she felt when she was not playing any role. She intuitively knew that being fully connected to herself and being entirely present in each moment were fundamental keys to conscious living. She noticed how easily her mind took her away from that, either by going to the past or future, or by entering a role or story. *How infinite, deep and beautiful would each moment be if only she were able to be present?* Sofia had spontaneously entered a place of consciousness beyond emotions, where she could observe facts, feelings and behaviours; yet, all *she* experienced ('she' as consciousness, not 'she' as mind) was blissful presence. She knew intuitively that her elevated state would probably dissipate as her patterns of control, judgement and non-acceptance gradually resurfaced… However, going forward, she had a new tool: a point of reference, an idea of what life looks like through the lens of consciousness and equanimity. In other words, she knew what to *aim for*.

On their last day of silence, Sofia sat on the mountain to meditate. She held her Lemurian quartz crystal in her hands, as she had done many times that month. It seemed to transport her to a mystical place made of crystal, with a remarkably high vibration. She wondered if the crystal had played an important role in helping her raise her vibration closer to Shambala. She was also curious about other people's experiences during that time. Looking at the mountain, she closed her eyes, tuned into Shambala and emanated her energy as usual. She felt her energy expand into infinity, to the point where her individuality was no longer present; she *was* cosmic consciousness and felt the energy of the entire universe. Paradoxically, she was both everything that exists and nothing at all. That nothingness felt like home, as did the wholeness. They existed simultaneously; it was all one, all consciousness. That state of oneness was what Yogis referred to as *Samadhi*, another one of the eight limbs of Yoga. When Sofia finished her meditation, she humbly bowed down to the ground and expressed deep gratitude to Spirit, the land, the crystal, Yoga, Shambala and all the beings that had contributed to what she had experienced in the last month. As she was carrying that feeling of nothingness, Socrates' quote came to mind again: *One thing I know is that I know nothing. This is the source of my wisdom.* She reflected on the last part of it: *I know nothing. This is the source of my wisdom.* She wondered if his words pointed not to a lack of knowledge as the source of wisdom, but to the recognition of that *nothingness* she had just experienced as its true source. Yet another question she might never have the answer to.

Sofia observed the vast mountains one last time and felt into how small she was, how insignificant her problems were. Perceiving how one human life at one point in time is so small, compared to the entirety of the universe and all of time, led her to reflect on how unimportant individuality felt to her and how important things like sustainable living and conscious communities were. Like in an ant farm, there is a way in which one ant does not matter because it is only together that the ants create the space, avoid predators and bring in food to sustain the ant farm. Still, there is also a way in which it does matter because there could not be an ant farm without individual ants. Like ants, individual humans can contribute to raising the consciousness of societies and cultures, which can make a difference to the planet.

Sofia took out her journal and wrote what was coming through her: *There was an era when society needed single individuals to be great leaders, gurus or kings, but we have reached a new era. One where a multitude of individuals start to awaken all over the world and inspire each other with their light, essence and gifts. Where they learn from one another and grow together as a collective. The more people wake up, the more they heal the collective consciousness and evolve towards higher states of being. That aligns with the Age of Aquarius that astrology talks about. It also makes it vital for each person to wake up to their true nature, values and principles, as the flow has inverted: change has to come from the inside out.*

We can no longer wait for leaders to emerge; we must let our own leadership emerge. We can no longer wait for the light to arrive; we must shine it from within. We can no longer wait for love to come; we must be the ones emanating it. From that 'inside-out' perspective, it is no longer important for individuals to try to change the whole world; we have to change ourselves and embody our truth so that our flame ignites others, and together we start to remember who we are and what we are capable of. Only then will the world change.

I think of people all over the world, angry at the current system, which is not serving them. That would not contribute towards this 'inside-out' approach because it is about accusing or changing others rather than ourselves. Plus, changing unwilling others is rarely possible, especially with anger as fuel. On top of that, being angry at the world implies – necessarily – being angry, and anger is not a frequency that elevates us to a higher vibration. In that case, according to this inside-out theory, such anger is what we would be spreading, which does not lead to the world we aim to create. We cannot defend kindness by being unkind. We cannot rage on behalf of a nonviolent world. We cannot fight for peace. We cannot demand

220

freedom. These are antitheses. We are already peaceful. We are already free.
We are already love. Kindness is already within our reach. It is time to walk
the talk. Time to be who we truly are. Who knows, perhaps that will give
others permission, courage or inspiration to do the same so that everyone
lights up like stars in a beautiful sky.

Sofia smiled… That could very well be the answer to her question: *Why are we here?*

When their time at the monastery came to an end, it was difficult for Sofia to start speaking again. She felt there was so much loss in the loss of silence. She was afraid of losing her elevated state of consciousness. She did not feel a particular need to interact with people as she already felt connected and whole. Nevertheless, she rationalised that human interactions could still be pleasant and appreciated even if her craving for connection was absent. Perhaps she could experience friendship from a state of non-attachment. People gradually began to speak. They enjoyed their last week reaching the peak of the track, *Thorong La pass*, at 5416 metres of altitude, and then descending all the way to the bottom. *Jeep* cars brought them back to Pokhara, where they stayed at the lodge for their final Yoga class and the last full day of the one-year course.

As the last Yoga class came, somehow Sofia felt more prepared to finish the course. She had access to Spirit within herself, so she was less afraid of losing it as she ventured into the world. Ananda taught the last and allegedly most potent posture. After *asana* practice, they had a sharing circle, where they were invited to share their most precious takeaways from their one-year course. The students struggled to put such a deep journey into words. How could they describe what they had been through, the mystical journey that had opened up and how it had transformed them? How their whole universe had changed, how life made sense now, how much richer they were. How invaluable it was to have begun to awaken their heart, embody their spirit and live their truth. To shift patterns, transcend fears, heal wounds and discover their potential. How absolutely priceless it was to not feel lost and alone and to remember who they were and what they were there to do. They had become aware of the divine echoes that lived inside them. Most had glimpses of who they were, where they had come from, why they were there and where they were going. No words could ever do justice to that.

When it was Sofia's turn to share, she said, "The most significant element for me was *remembering*. I realised that, as human beings, we have forgotten the beginning: Where we've come from; how it all started. Our minds cannot recall… but our *essence* remembers. It manifests itself in the world: glorious, yet encapsulated in the twisted features we created for this reality, trying to replicate what our brain has forgotten yet is somehow still present. It is in everything; it permeates everything, underlies everything. It remembers that the Universe is one and that we are intimately connected with it all… Yet we can no longer *feel* it. So, we've created social networks to connect us to the entire world; we invented cell phones, the internet, the general press… We've developed rules and treaties because they remind us of the law and order that once naturally existed in our reality, although we can no longer perceive it. Magic and inexplicable things fascinate us because they remind us of the mysteries. We've created governments because they give us a sense of a higher power watching over us, where we are not alone. We feel good when we have attitudes of peace and love because they are our core values. When we move away from these values, having dishonest attitudes, anger or fear, we feel bad without understanding why. We don't wonder, for example, why no one feels good when they're afraid – we just accept it without question. We've created churches and schools of spirituality because we've forgotten that we have divinity within us. We've trivialised sex because our essence is trying to recreate alchemy – even if in poor, superficial ways. We've created social security systems because we remember compassion and solidarity. We are forgiving of children because they remind us of the simplicity and innocence of our soul without the ego. We are demanding of adults because the echoes in our subconscious sense the gap between our current harsh reality and the idyllic lifestyle we once had. We've created languages and dialects because they remind us of deeper forms of communication. Justice, because it reminds us of balance. Our appreciation for science is just admiration for the creativity of the Universe

– it gives us implicit proof that the human being could never have created something so perfect and complex, which comforts us, confirming that there is more than meets the eye. We know it! It runs through our veins and manifests itself in everything! We feel it, we experience it, we live it – we just don't realise it. We simply need to remember… So, thank you for showing me the way back to that remembrance; no gift in life could have been more precious."

Once all the students shared their feelings and insights, the class came to an end. Before they finished, each student was given a ticket back to Portugal, along with a shiny business card from the school. Sofia recognised the quote in the front, *Be prepared to change everything or nothing at all.* The card she had received from the stranger, which started her whole Yoga journey. Now she could *especially* relate to that quote. The Swami said to the students, "If you would like another person to have this one-year experience, you can donate a specific amount to the school, which will pay for their journey. In which case, you can use the technique we taught you to tune into the divine intelligence and trust that the Universe will guide you to the right person, and them to you. Once you have found your person, give them the business card and make your case in your own way, to inspire them to attend the one-weekend course, which will be on the next new moon. We will take it from there."

In her business mind, Sofia did not really see how that business model could work, as people could so easily take advantage of the system and not give back. She asked, "Won't the school have fewer and fewer students, as some people choose *not* to donate?"

Ananda smiled and replied, "I wouldn't know; it has never happened."

Prologue

Sofia had butterflies in her stomach as she was about to exit customs at Lisbon airport… Having just returned from the one-year Yoga journey, she could barely contain her excitement to see Paulo! As soon as the automatic doors opened, there he was, ready to receive her with open arms and ecstatic enthusiasm. It was as if no time had passed since they had last seen each other. They hugged tightly, exchanged loving words and sat down for a cup of tea. They had their whole future ahead of them, endless possibilities. After a long conversation, Paulo asked her, "Wow, so here we are; what do you think you will do next?"

Sofia sighed; her eyes wandered out the window in a pensive gaze. On the side of a tall building outside, there was a big commercial banner flashing about a new book that had been launched.

"I'm not sure," she replied, "perhaps I'll write a book."

Acknowledgements

Deep gratitude towards my unborn son Alex, who gave his life so that I could start my journey, to the people behind the characters in this book, without whom all these journeys and experiences could not have existed, and to all my teachers and guides, whether they came in the form of trained Swamis, Shamans, parents, family members, Nature, friends, strangers or other sentient beings. Lastly, many thanks to the dear friends who played a role in the creation of this book: Bryana for the editing and Eliška for the cover.

NAMASTE

I honour the place in you in which the entire Universe dwells.
I honour the place within you which is of Love, of Light, of Truth, and of
Peace.
When you are in that place in you, and I am in that place in me, we are
One.

May your echoes be loud and clear.
You are already Home.

www.ingramcontent.com/pod-product-compliance
Ingram Content Group UK Ltd.
Pitfield, Milton Keynes, MK11 3LW, UK
UKHW040300161125
465084UK00007B/72

9 781067 093013